THE HOME
PLUMBER

A practical guide to plumbing jobs
and emergencies

Edited by David Thomas

ORBIS · London

Acknowledgments

Advertising Arts pp 127 (top)–128; *Agaheat Appliances Ltd* p. 107 (left); *Arka Graphics* p 81 (bottom)–83; *Armitage Shanks* p 84 (bottom); *Balterley Bathrooms Ltd* p 84 (top); *Bath Studio* p 88; *Baxi Heating Ltd* p 98 (right); *Delta Capillary Products* pp 125, 137–39; *Dimplex Heating* pp 97, 122–23; *Doulton Sanitaryware Ltd* p 12; *Econa Parkamatic Ltd* p 93 (top); *Electricity Council* p 108 (centre); *Elizabeth Whiting Agency* p 72 (left); *Eugene Fleury* pp 76–77, 132; *Haigh Engineering Co Ltd* p 93 (bottom); *Hayward Art Group* pp 13, 14–25, 27–29, 31, 33–34, 36–37, 44, 49–51, 53, 55–58, 66–67, 69–71, 73–75, 79–80 (top), 85–87, 89 (bottom), 90 (bottom), 91–92, 94–96, 99–106, 121–122, 130–31, 134–35; *Houseman (Burnham) Ltd* pp 39, 43, 45–48; *Leisure Kitchen Products* p 90 (top); *Myson Group Marketing Ltd* p 107 (right); *Orbis Publishing Ltd* pp 26, 38, 42, 54, 119 (right)–20, 124; *Orbis/Dudley Reed* p 52; *Orbis/Langham Studios* pp 30, 32, 35, 133; *Orbis/Mike Trier* p 72 (right); *Orbis/John Rawlings Studio* p 88 (inset); *Orbis/Terry Trott* pp 59, 68, 78, 80 (bottom), 95 (top), 98 (left), 112–15, 126–27; *Orbis/Paul Williams* p 136; *Penney, David/Stuart, Ed* pp 40–41; *Potterton International Ltd* p 108 (bottom left); *Redring Electric* p 81 (top); *Studio Briggs* p 109 (bottom)–119; *Thorn Domestic Appliances Ltd* pp 108 (top), 109 (top); *TI Parkray Ltd* p 98 (top); *Trianco Redfyre Ltd* p 108 (bottom right); *Twyfords Bathrooms Ltd* p 89 (top); *Uni-Tubes Ltd* p 129; *Venner Artiss* pp 60–61.

First published in Great Britain as
The Home Plumbing Manual by
Orbis Publishing Limited,
London 1980
© Orbis Publishing Limited 1980
Reprinted as *The Home Plumber* 1982, 1983
Revised edition 1984

Printed in Portugal by Resopal
ISBN: 0-85613-713-8

THE HOME
PLUMBER

A practical guide to plumbing jobs
and emergencies

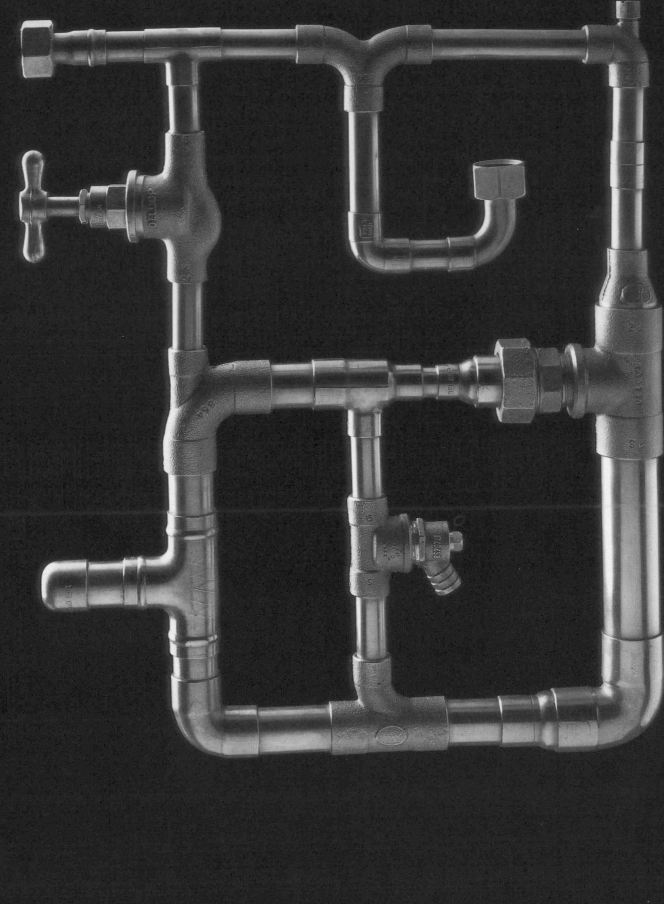

Contents

Introduction

Most people think of the plumbing system as a mysterious and hidden complex of pipes and joins that all function smoothly – until something goes wrong! Faults anywhere in the plumbing system must be located and repaired immediately. A leaky pipe can cause endless damage to your home and furniture but it is often difficult to persuade a plumber to come to the rescue straight away.

There is no reason why you should not tackle most plumbing jobs yourself if you have a few basic tools, some knowledge of how the system works and you also use the correct techniques. You can carry out all repairs and maintenance yourself and save a lot of money – without having to wait for an overworked plumber to come and do a hurried job. You can do your own installations as well as any professional and once you have gained confidence in your own abilities by doing some simple installations, you could even fit a back boiler and plumb in your central heating. Few people would think of trying to install central heating themselves, but it is perfectly possible providing the job is carefully planned and executed. You should be able to carry out many home improvements which you had thought beyond your reach simply because of the prohibitive labour costs involved on top of the cost of materials.

We start by showing you the range of basic tools you will need. They are a great investment and you do not have to buy them all at once. Then we explain how the whole system works, taking a standard house plan as a typical example in the diagrams. It is essential to know the intricacies of the hot and cold water systems, how water is piped into the home, how and where it goes once inside and how it is drained away after use. It is interesting and easy to learn and there are detailed diagrams which clarify the text.

Breakdowns can be prevented if a few simple tasks are performed now, and this section on precautionary plumbing shows you how you can guard against corrosion, how to cut down scale formation resulting from hard water, how to soften the water and how to protect the hot and cold water systems against cold weather. There are no burst pipes where the necessary precautions are taken.

Some repairs, however, are inevitable and maintenance is necessary from time to time, as there are many areas of the system in almost constant use which inevitably suffer wear and tear. Keeping the whole system in perfect working order cuts down the need for repairs and we explain exactly how this can be achieved. When repairs are necessary, we tell you the faults to look for and how to remedy them by the most effective yet easy to understand methods.

There are many installations you can do yourself. We show you how to install a bath, how to plumb in a washing machine or dishwasher, how to fit an outside tap, immersion heaters, sinks, basins, bidets, showers and waste disposal units. If you can follow the instructions and diagrams carefully you will be as good as a professional.

There is an extensive section on central heating as this is probably the most ambitious home improvement you can do yourself. If you invest in your own skills the value of your home will increase. We tell you how to fit a gas or solid fuel back boiler and how to calculate heat loss so you can determine the size of boiler you require. If you are going to install central heating you will have to decide what fuel to use; we tell you the pros and cons of solid fuel, gas, oil and electricity. Having chosen your fuel, we can then help you decide on the type of system to install and the type of appliance to fire it. A section on the control, installation and wiring of a small bore system confirms how inexpensive this type of work can be if you are prepared to tackle it yourself. We also give you an outline of some of the electric systems on the market to enable you to choose the type most suited to your requirements.

You must bear in mind when working on the domestic plumbing system that there are regulations governing the installations in your home. This is why you should always check when adding to the system that you are complying with those regulations laid down by your local water authority. These will vary from area to area. Although permission is not necessary if you are simply changing existing fittings, it is necessary if, for example, you are planning to install a shower or need to make a connection to the stack pipe.

Invest in your own skills – you cannot always rely on professionals and you cannot always afford to; you will also get a lot more satisfaction from tackling these plumbing jobs yourself.

The plumbing tool kit

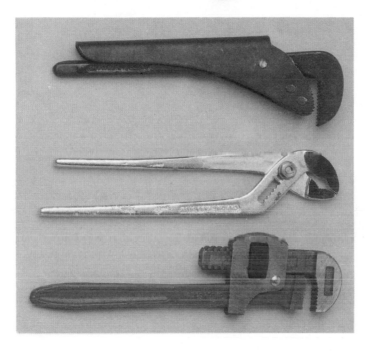

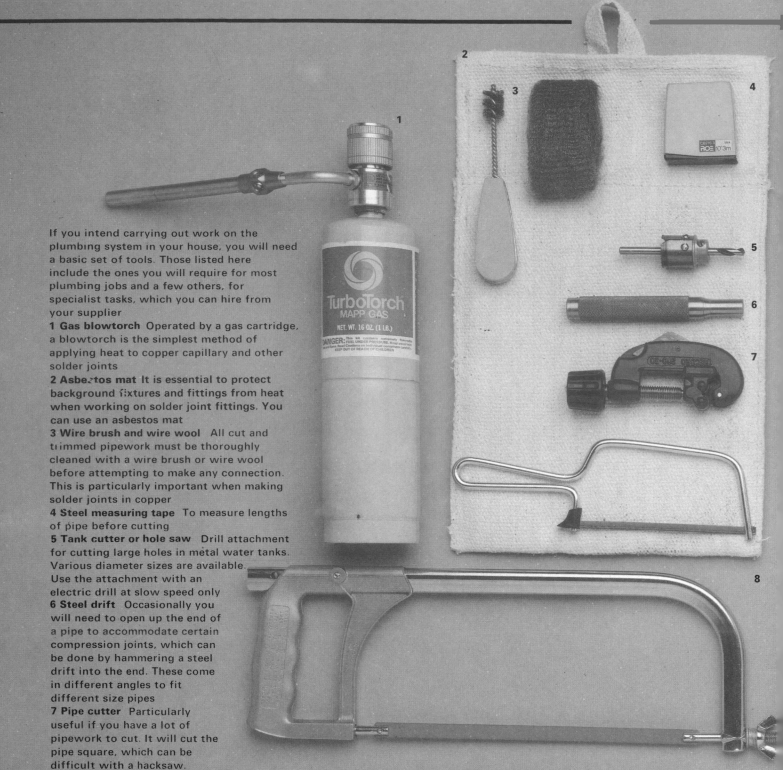

If you intend carrying out work on the plumbing system in your house, you will need a basic set of tools. Those listed here include the ones you will require for most plumbing jobs and a few others, for specialist tasks, which you can hire from your supplier

1 Gas blowtorch Operated by a gas cartridge, a blowtorch is the simplest method of applying heat to copper capillary and other solder joints

2 Asbestos mat It is essential to protect background fixtures and fittings from heat when working on solder joint fittings. You can use an asbestos mat

3 Wire brush and wire wool All cut and trimmed pipework must be thoroughly cleaned with a wire brush or wire wool before attempting to make any connection. This is particularly important when making solder joints in copper

4 Steel measuring tape To measure lengths of pipe before cutting

5 Tank cutter or hole saw Drill attachment for cutting large holes in metal water tanks. Various diameter sizes are available. Use the attachment with an electric drill at slow speed only

6 Steel drift Occasionally you will need to open up the end of a pipe to accommodate certain compression joints, which can be done by hammering a steel drift into the end. These come in different angles to fit different size pipes

7 Pipe cutter Particularly useful if you have a lot of pipework to cut. It will cut the pipe square, which can be difficult with a hacksaw. Clamp the cutter to the pipe and rotate it round the pipe, gradually increasing the pressure screw so the cutting wheel scores through the pipe to make a clean, accurate break. Remove the internal burr on the cut pipe by using the reaming part at the end of the tool

8 Hacksaw or junior hacksaw Both are useful for any type of metalwork and will cut all pipe used in domestic plumbing

9 Bending machine On pipes or tubes of 22mm (or ¾in) diameter and over, bends can be formed more easily with a bending machine; although expensive, it can be hired readily. It is designed to produce a curve without distorting the circular hole running though the bend. Be sure to use the right size former or guide around which you push the pipe for the bend you require. Hand benders are available for pipe up to 22mm (or ¾in) diameter

10 Bending spring To make bends in the small diameter metal pipes used in domestic plumbing. Make sure you use the right size spring for the tube being bent.

11 Files For trimming and smoothing flat and round surfaces in plumbing work use a flat file and a round rat's-tail file

12 Pipe wrench The coarse serrated teeth of a pipe wrench grip iron pipework firmly for turning. Never use a pipe wrench with copper pipe since the thin walls may collapse under the pressure. (Protect the surface of the pipe with cloth to prevent

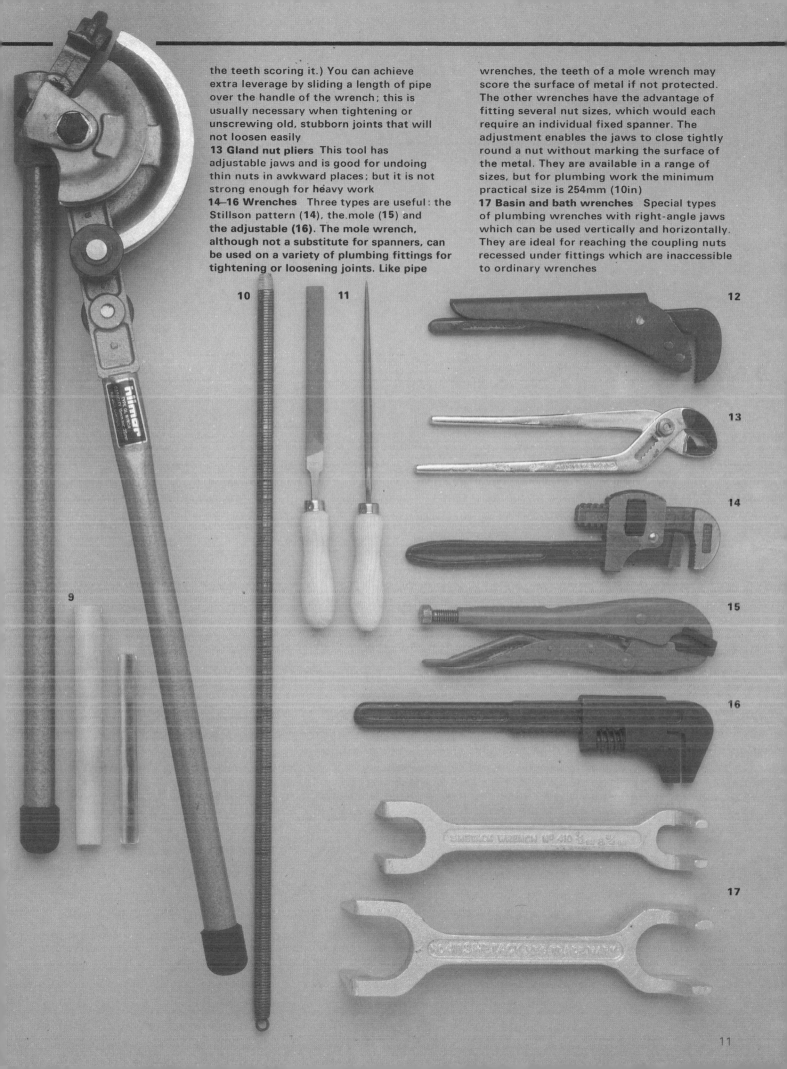

the teeth scoring it.) You can achieve extra leverage by sliding a length of pipe over the handle of the wrench; this is usually necessary when tightening or unscrewing old, stubborn joints that will not loosen easily

13 Gland nut pliers This tool has adjustable jaws and is good for undoing thin nuts in awkward places; but it is not strong enough for heavy work

14–16 Wrenches Three types are useful: the Stillson pattern (**14**), the mole (**15**) and the adjustable (**16**). The mole wrench, although not a substitute for spanners, can be used on a variety of plumbing fittings for tightening or loosening joints. Like pipe wrenches, the teeth of a mole wrench may score the surface of metal if not protected. The other wrenches have the advantage of fitting several nut sizes, which would each require an individual fixed spanner. The adjustment enables the jaws to close tightly round a nut without marking the surface of the metal. They are available in a range of sizes, but for plumbing work the minimum practical size is 254mm (10in)

17 Basin and bath wrenches Special types of plumbing wrenches with right-angle jaws which can be used vertically and horizontally. They are ideal for reaching the coupling nuts recessed under fittings which are inaccessible to ordinary wrenches

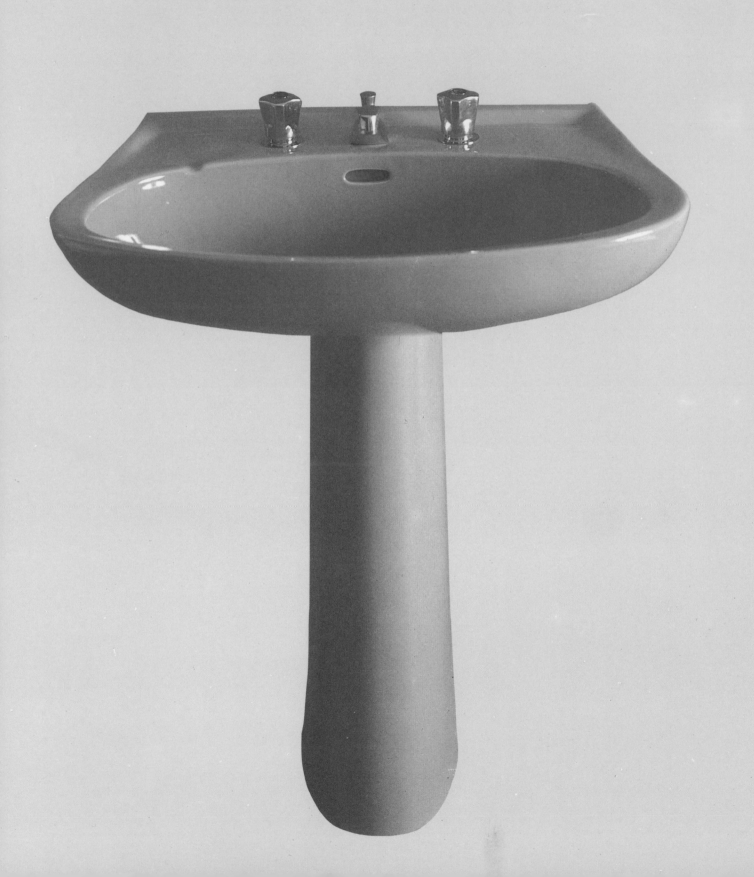

How it works

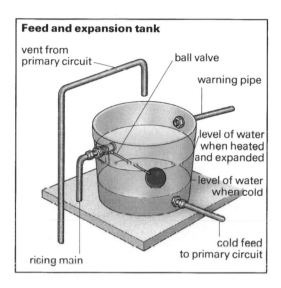

Feed and expansion tank

vent from
primary circuit

ball valve

warning pipe

level of water
when heated
and expanded

level of water
when cold

cold feed
to primary circuit

rising main

Cold water:
storage cistern and distribution pipes

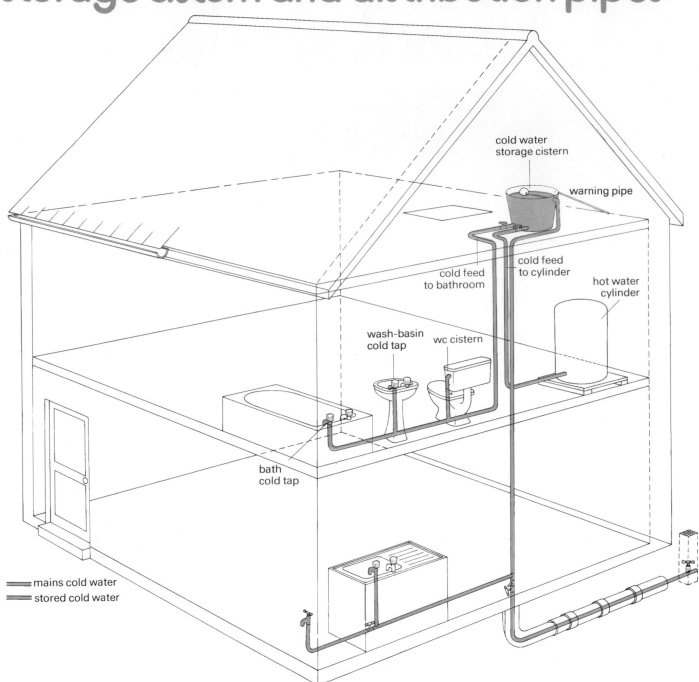

cold water
storage cistern

warning pipe

cold feed
to cylinder

cold feed
to bathroom

hot water
cylinder

wash-basin
cold tap

wc cistern

bath
cold tap

mains cold water
stored cold water

The water supply is pumped through the mains to your home – but the story doesn't end there. You must have a storage tank in order to keep an amount of water in reserve, and distribution pipes to feed it around the home.

The cold water storage cistern eases immediate demand on the mains during peak periods, such as first thing in the morning when large quantities of water are used for baths and WC flushing. The cistern will refill slowly, then more quickly as

demand on the mains drops. The storage cistern also provides a reserve of water against possible shut-down of the mains. When water is cut off for a few hours for mains repairs, you need only draw off in advance sufficient water for drinking and cooking; the cistern will keep the hot water system, bath taps and WC operating. It will also provide a supply of water under constant, relatively low pressure for a cylinder storage hot water system.

Although available in various capacities, most water authorities stipulate a maximum of 225 litre (50 gal) for storage cisterns. They are now usually

Above Our standard house plan shows the flow of cold water from the mains in blue and the stored cold water in green

made of plastic materials, although galvanized steel and asbestos cement types are still found. The cistern is normally situated in the loft and sometimes in the upper part of an airing cupboard. The loft is the best place, since it allows the maximum amount of fall from the cistern; water is supplied under greater pressure, ensuring a strong flow at the outlets. Since the full cistern will be heavy (the water in a 225 litre/50 gal cistern will weigh over 200kg/4cwt), it is usually placed over a dividing wall and if possible, as a frost precaution, against a flue in constant use.

The supply of water to the cistern from the rising main is controlled by a ball valve which shuts off the water when the cistern is full. A warning pipe extending outside the house and acting as an overflow is connected near the top of the cistern to indicate when the ball valve is faulty. This pipe must be of at least 22mm diameter and should be set at a slight fall to ensure a continuous flow of water.

There are also two distribution pipes, usually fitted near the bottom of the cistern: one serves the bathroom cold taps and the WC cistern, the other supplies the hot water storage cylinder. A vent pipe from the top of the hot water cylinder is positioned over the cistern. This allows air to escape when the cylinder is filling up. It should never enter the water as this would cause hot water to be siphoned into the cold cistern.

Replacing storage cistern

If you have a galvanized steel storage cistern that is badly corroded (rust patches around the tappings and on the inside walls) it will be cheaper and quicker in the long run to replace the cistern rather than to repair it, since the rust spots are likely to reappear in a few years.

The modern tendency is to install a cylindrical

replace the cistern, so plan your work for the least inconvenience.

Removing old cistern Cut off the water supply to the inlet pipe and turn on the bathroom taps to empty the cistern. Some water will be left in the bottom of the cistern below the distribution pipes and you will have to bale this out. Disconnect all fittings with an adjustable spanner and lower the cistern through the access hatch.

Fitting new cistern Do as much preparatory work as possible on the cistern before taking it up to the loft where space is likely to be restricted. The best way to cut the holes for the pipe connections is with a hand or electric drill and a hole saw attachment. The attachment, which has a circular cutter with a twist drill centre, should be the same diameter as that of the pipe connection thread which will pass through the wall of the cistern. Mark the centre of the hole to be made in the cistern, position the twist drill on the mark and drill a pilot hole; the circular cutter will then come into contact with the cistern wall and complete the hole.

Holes can be made in a plastic cistern by heating the end of the correct size metal pipe with a blowtorch and burning a hole of the exact diameter through the plastic wall with the hot end of the pipe.

First cut the hole for the water inlet pipe. If your cistern has a back plate to support the ball valve, the position of the hole will be dictated by the position of the ready-drilled hole in the plate. If the cistern does not have a back plate cut the hole about 40mm (or 1½in) from the rim.

Fit the stem of the ball valve into the hole using two large washers, one metal and one plastic, on each side of the cistern wall. The plastic washer should be next to the cistern with the metal one supporting it. Screw a nut onto the outside stem with an adjustable spanner. Now attach a com-

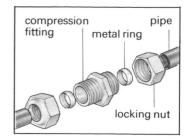

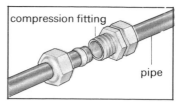

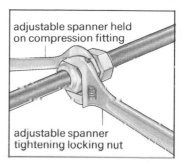

Above When fitting a compression joint, use one adjustable spanner on the locking nut and another to pull the other way on the compression fitting

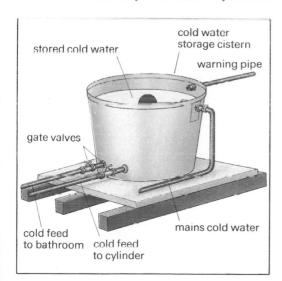

plastic cistern since this is light, easily fitted and will not corrode. It is also flexible enough to be squeezed through small trapdoors into lofts.

If your new cistern is smaller than the old one you will have to extend the pipework; make sure your extra pipe is of the same diameter. You will also need compression joints to connect the pipes: each joint has two locking nuts and two metal rings which fit over the ends of the pipes being joined. When the nuts are tightened the rings grip the pipes to give a watertight seal.

You will have to shut off the water supply to

pression tap connector to the protruding stem; the other end of the connector will be joined to the rising main inlet.

Make the hole for the overflow pipe opposite the ball valve and at least 19mm (¾in) below it. Cut the holes for the distribution pipes about 50mm (2in) from the base of the cistern to prevent grit and debris being drawn into the plumbing system. Using metal and plastic washers as before, fit compression joint tank connectors to the holes and attach nuts outside.

When all the connections have been made take

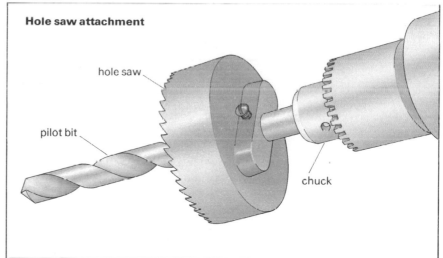

Above left A typical polythene storage cistern in position – on a platform for extra pressure – with distribution pipes connected
Above This saw hole attachment can be fitted to either an electric or hand drill to cut holes for the pipe connections when installing a new metal cold water storage cistern

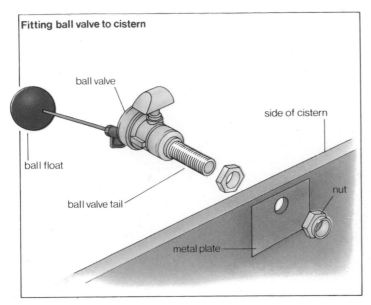

Fitting ball valve to cistern

ball valve
ball float
ball valve tail
side of cistern
nut
metal plate

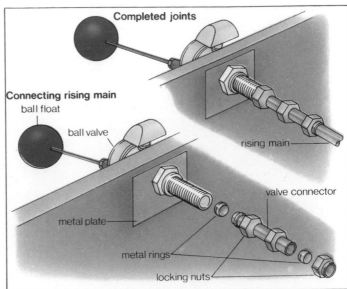

Completed joints

Connecting rising main
ball float
ball valve
rising main
valve connector
metal plate
metal rings
locking nuts

the cistern up into the loft. Stand it on a firm, level platform – stout planks or a piece of chipboard nailed to the joists – so its entire base is supported. Connect all the pipework squarely to the cistern walls to avoid straining the plastic when the nuts are tightened. Turn on the water and watch for any leaks as the cistern fills. If leaks do occur shut off the water supply, drain the cistern and tighten any loose joints. Never try to tighten joints with water in the cistern as you may split the plastic and cause a flood.

When the cistern is nearly full the ball valve must be set so the water level is at least 25mm (1in) below the warning pipe. Carefully bend the float arm to the correct angle (on some valves you merely adjust an alignment screw). To check the valve is working properly draw off a small amount of water and watch that the cistern refills to the correct level.

Repairing steel storage cistern

If you have a galvanized steel storage cistern that is showing signs of corrosion on the inside, you can recondition it.

Cut off the water supply and drain the cistern as already described. Dry the cistern thoroughly and remove every trace of rust with abrasive paper or a wire brush (always wear protective spectacles when using the latter). Fill any deep pit marks in the metal with an epoxy resin filler and, when set, apply

two coats of a taste and odour-free bituminous paint, leaving it to dry between coats. Make sure the paint is completely dry before refilling the cistern. This treatment will protect the cistern from rust for at least two years and can be repeated when necessary.

You can treat a new galvanized steel cistern with bituminous paint to protect it from corrosion, but first rub down the interior with abrasive paper to provide a key for the paint.

Above left Make sure when you are fitting a new valve stem to the cold water storage cistern that the plastic washer sits inside the metal one
Above The compression tap connector is joined to the protruding stem. Join the rising main to the unattached end of the connector
Below left When repairing a galvanized cistern, clean off all rust with a wire brush
Below centre Make good all pit marks with an epoxy resin filler
Below Give the tank a protective covering with a coat of taste and odour-free bituminous paint

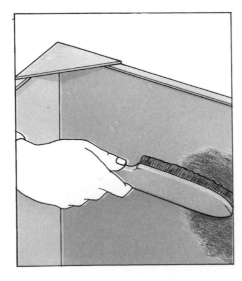

To replace cistern
adjustable spanners
electric or hand drill
saw hole drill attachment
compression joints
extra matching pipework
　(if extending pipes)
metal and plastic washers
stout planks or chipboard (for platform)

To repair steel cistern
abrasive paper or wire brush
protective spectacles
epoxy resin filler
bituminous paint (taste and odour-free)

equipment

Cold water:
from mains to storage cistern

hinged lid

15mm service pipe

communication pipe from main

protective drain-pipe

water authority stopcock

An unlimited supply of water 'on tap' is assumed by most of us to be a basic service and, apart from exceptional circumstances such as a drought, we barely give a thought to its source and distribution.

Cast iron mains, buried deep below the surface, take water from the area authority's reservoirs through the consumer area. A communication pipe links the main to the boundary of each property and it is at this point that the responsibility of the householder for his own water supply begins.

Main supply
Outside each house – possibly set into the footpath – is a hinged metal plate. This covers a purpose-made pit, 1m (3ft) or more deep, which houses the main stopcock connecting the water authority's communication pipe to the service pipe. This stopcock, unlike those inside the house, may have a specially shaped shank that can be turned only with one of the authority's turn-keys.

Pipe/tubing dimensions Before metrication, water supply pipes were designated by their internal diameters. The sizes most commonly used in domestic plumbing were $\frac{1}{2}$, $\frac{3}{4}$ and 1in. Since then thin-walled tubing, such as copper and stainless steel, has been designated by its external diameter. The equivalent sizes of tubing are 15, 22 and 28mm respectively. Thick-walled tubing, such as lead or iron, is still designated by its internal diameter (12, 19 and 25mm/$\frac{1}{2}$, $\frac{3}{4}$ and 1in sizes).

Copper is now the material most commonly used in plumbing and, except where otherwise stated, pipe sizes relate to thin-walled copper or stainless steel tubing.

Service pipe Properties built in Britain before 1939 will probably have a lead or iron service pipe. In a more recent house, however, this pipe is likely to be of 15mm copper tubing, though a pipe of larger diameter may be used in areas where water pressure is low.

The service pipe should slope slightly upwards to the house to allow air bubbles to escape. But it is extremely important, as a precaution against frost, that it should be at least 750mm (30in) below the surface of the soil throughout its length. You should remember this if, at any time, you want to

Domestic water comes from a main buried deep beneath the highway, through a communication pipe, and is connected just inside your boundary with a stopcock, which is reached via a hinged lid at ground level and should only be turned on and off with a special water board key. A service pipe takes the water (protected from risk of subsidence by being threaded through old or cracked drain-pipes) under your garden and foundations through to the kitchen

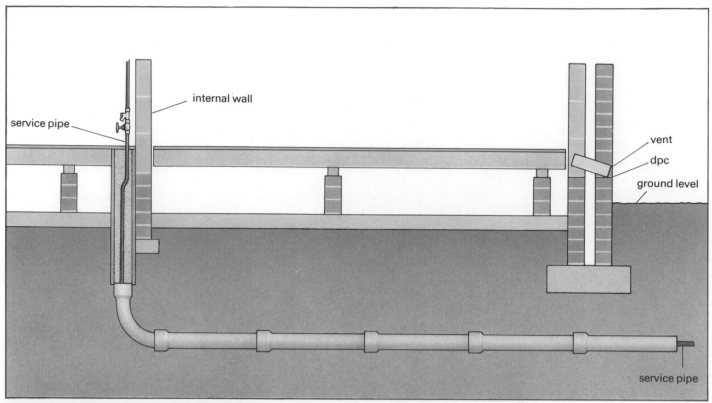

internal wall

service pipe

vent

dpc

ground level

service pipe

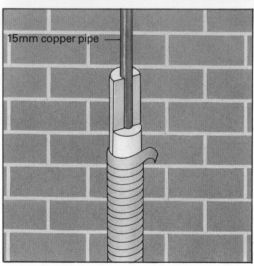

15mm copper pipe

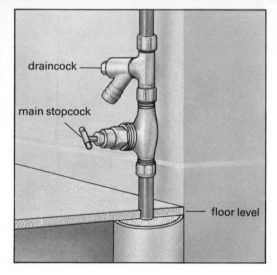

draincock

main stopcock

floor level

landscape the front garden. A sunken garden, constructed over the service pipe, could reduce the depth of soil insulation below the required minimum, which might be disastrous during a period of severe and prolonged frost.

Protection Where the service pipe passes under the foundations of the walls of the house it should be threaded through lengths of drain-pipe to protect it from possible damage resulting from settlement.

In most cases the service pipe enters the house through the solid floor of a kitchen. If the kitchen has a hollow, boarded floor special precautions must be taken against the risk of frost damage. There is little point in protecting the pipe throughout its journey to the house, only to expose it to icy draughts that may whistle through the underfloor space.

The best means of protection is to thread the pipe, at the time of installation, through the centre of a 152mm (6in) drain-pipe and to fill the space between the service pipe and the walls of the drain-

pipe with vermiculite chips. An existing pipe can be protected – without having to dismantle it – by snapping over it two sections of expanded polystyrene pipe-lagging and binding these with several thickness of glass fibre pipe wrap.

Internal supply
The main stopcock is fitted into the service pipe just above ground floor level and immediately above it is the draincock. These two fittings enable the water supply to the house to be cut off and the internal system to be drained whenever required.

Stopcock This is probably the most important piece of plumbing equipment in the home. The first step in virtually any plumbing emergency – burst pipe, leaking cold water storage cistern or leaking boiler – should be to turn off this stopcock to cut off the water supply.

Make sure every member of the household knows where it is and how to operate it. Turn it on and off two or three times at least twice a year to ensure it

Above Diagram showing where the service pipe or rising main (as it is often called) sometimes enters the house through a boarded floor – which means special precautions should be taken to protect it from icy underground draughts. After leaving the protection of the old drain-pipes beneath the house the service pipe should be threaded through stone pipe packed with vermiculite chips
Far left Alternatively you should lag it by snapping round it two sections of expanded polystyrene lagging and binding them with glass fibre wrap
Left The internal water supply can be cut off in any emergency by closing the main stopcock – usually found under the kitchen sink. The draincock immediately above makes it easy to empty the internal water system

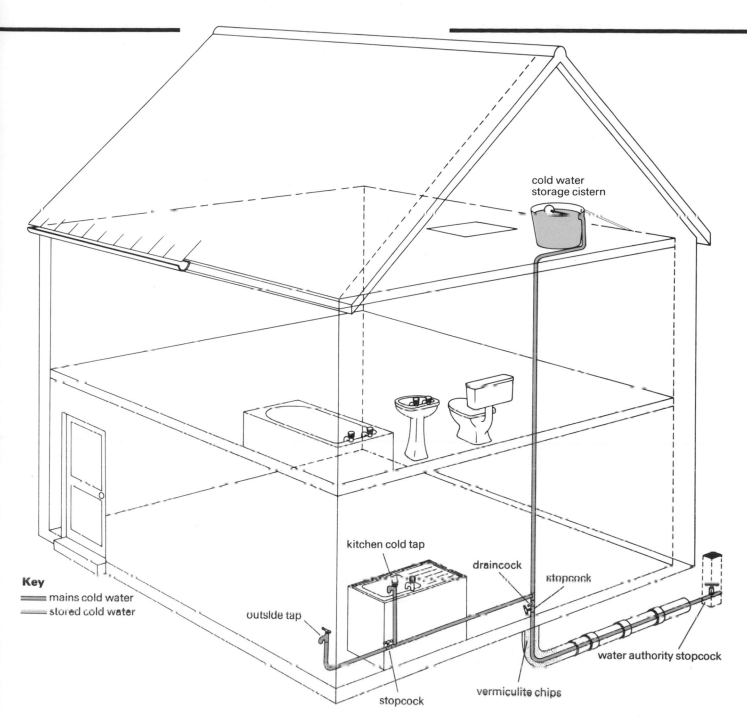

cold water
storage cistern

kitchen cold tap

draincock

stopcock

outside tap

water authority stopcock

Key
— mains cold water
— stored cold water

stopcock

vermiculite chips

will move easily. A neglected stopcock can jam and therefore prove troublesome in an emergency.

Main connections There will be at least one branch 'teed off' from the service pipe – often referred to as the rising main – about 600mm (24in) above floor level. This is the 15mm supply pipe to the cold tap over the kitchen sink. Since this tap supplies water for drinking and cooking it is important it is connected direct to the main.

In some places the cold water supply to the bathroom and WC flushing cisterns is also taken direct from the main. Hot water supply may be provided by a multi-point instantaneous water heater and the need for a main cold water storage cistern eliminated altogether.

Most water authorities, however, allow only the cold tap over the kitchen sink – and perhaps a garden water supply – to be connected directly to the main. Bathroom cold water services are supplied from a storage cistern usually situated in the roof space.

Roof space The rising main travels to the roof space by the most direct route, preferably against an internal wall. However with cavity wall infilling and efficient thermal insulation this is less important than it used to be.

The roof space through which the rising main passes to connect to the ball valve serving the main cold water storage cistern is vulnerable to frost. This is particularly so where the ceilings have been lagged to conserve warmth in the rooms below. The bedrooms will be warmer, but the roof space will be that much colder. If the floor of your roof is insulated, you should remove the covering from the area directly under the storage tank to allow warm air to rise from the rooms below to the tank.

The rising main in the roof area should be as short as possible, thoroughly lagged and kept well away from the eaves. Particularly where the cold water storage cistern is made of modern plastic material, the rising main should be securely fixed to the roof timbers to reduce noise from vibration.

The equipment we describe is shown in colour – kitchen sink, outside tap and stopcock, bath, wash-basin, WC, cold water storage tank, rising main, internal stopcock, draincock, service pipe and water board stopcock. Mains cold water is shown in blue, stored cold water in green, domestic hot water in red and central heating water in purple

Hot water:
simple cylinder systems

Running hot water used to be regarded as a luxury in many homes. Today we would probably consider life unbearable without it—and even the Government accepts this fact by making grants available to help install this facility in older properties. Whether you use electricity, gas, oil or solid fuel as a means of heating, there is a system available to suit your needs—and your pocket. But do make sure you decide first what your own requirements are, since this will ultimately affect what system you choose as the most suitable for your home.

There are a number of ways to provide a 'whole house' hot water supply, but one of the most popular is undoubtedly the simple, direct cylinder storage hot water system. Simple cylinder systems are heated either by electricity or by solid fuel, gas or oil-fired boilers, sometimes supplemented by an electric immersion heater for use during the summer months.

Copper cylinders are the most common, with capacities from 115–160 litre (25–35gal). The cylinder is supplied with water from the cold water storage cistern by means of a 22 or 28mm (¾ or 1in) distribution pipe, which enters the cylinder near its base.

A 22mm (¾in) vent pipe rises from the dome of the cylinder to terminate open-ended over the cold water storage cistern. This vent pipe branches off to supply the hot water taps in the bathroom and over the kitchen sink.

The cylinder is connected to the boiler by 28mm

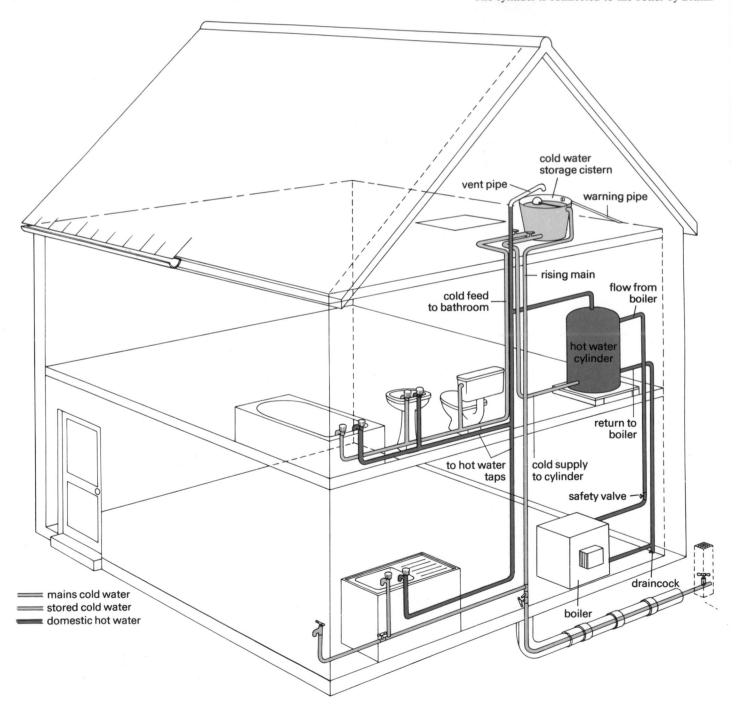

mains cold water
stored cold water
domestic hot water

(1in) pipes. The flow and return pipes of the boiler connect to the cylinder's upper and lower tappings respectively. If the cylinder is to be heated by an immersion heater only, the cylinder flow and return tappings are blanked off.

A boss, or fitting, is usually provided in the dome of the cylinder to enable a vertical immersion heater to be inserted. Alternatively there may be one or more bosses in the cylinder walls for shorter horizontal immersion heaters. A vertical immersion heater should extend to within 75mm (3in) of the base of the cylinder as only the water above the level of the heating element will be heated.

How the system works
When the boiler is first lit the water in it heats up, expands and becomes lighter. It is pushed up the flow pipe into the upper part of the cylinder by the colder, heavier water flowing down the return pipe from the lower part of the cylinder to the boiler.

This circulation continues for as long as the boiler fire is alight. Hot water is stored in the upper part of the cylinder ready to be drawn off from the taps and gradually spreads downwards until the cylinder is filled with hot water. The hot water draw-off points are taken from above the dome of the cylinder so if the water supply to the house is cut off the cylinder will still be full of water after the hot taps have stopped running.

Provision must be made, therefore, for the cylinder to be drained when necessary. Where the system has a boiler, a draincock with a hose connector is fitted on the return pipe close to the boiler. If the cylinder is heated by an immersion heater only, a draincock is fitted on the cold water distribution pipe to the cylinder, close to its connection to the cylinder. A spring-loaded safety valve is usually fitted close to the boiler on either the flow or return pipe to eliminate any risk of a dangerous buildup of pressure within the system.

Many homes built in Britain before 1939 have a rectangular hot water storage tank instead of a cylinder. These tanks are fitted with a circular hand hole with a bolt-down cover to give access for cleaning. If you have a tank of this kind remember it cannot be drained from the hot taps. Never attempt to unscrew the bolts and remove the cover without first emptying the tank by the draincock provided.

Packaged plumbing systems
Demands for the provision of hot water on tap in older homes and the conversion of large old houses into self-contained flats have resulted in the development of packaged plumbing systems in which the cold water storage cistern and the hot water storage cylinder form one unit.

Early forms of packaged plumbing consist of a 115 litre (25gal) capacity cylinder underneath a relatively low capacity circular copper storage cistern. These cisterns are large enough to supply the hot water system, but not the bathroom cold taps or the WC cistern, which have to be connected directly to the rising main. These units can only be

Below Comparison between modern and old direct cylinder systems
Below right Essential features of an early packaged plumbing unit; the oval shape makes the unit easy to fit in confined spaces

Modern system

- vent pipe
- warning pipe
- cold water storage cistern
- gate valves
- rising main
- cold feed to bathroom
- hot water cylinder
- hottest water at top ready for use
- to hot water taps
- draincock if using immersion heater only
- cold supply to cylinder
- safety valve
- boiler
- draincock

Old system

- cold feed to bathroom
- vent pipe
- warning pipe
- rising main
- cold water storage tank
- to hot water taps
- hot water storage tank
- hand hole cover
- flow pipe continued as standpipe within tank
- boiler
- draincock

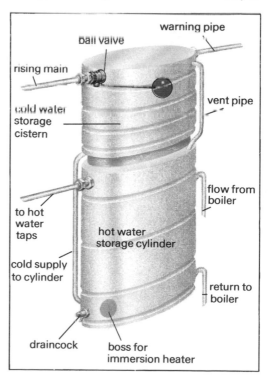

- ball valve
- warning pipe
- rising main
- cold water storage cistern
- vent pipe
- to hot water taps
- flow from boiler
- cold supply to cylinder
- hot water storage cylinder
- return to boiler
- draincock
- boss for immersion heater

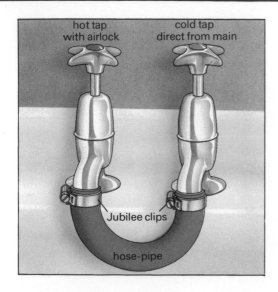

fitted where this arrangement is permitted by the local water authority.

More recently larger packaged units have been developed with hot water cylinders of up to 160 litre (35gal) capacity and cold water storage cisterns with the standard capacity of 225 litre (50gal). These may be regarded as 'whole house' packaged plumbing systems. They need only be connected to a cold water supply and provided with a heat source to supply all hot and cold water demands.

Airlocks

A poor or intermittent flow of water from a hot tap, sometimes accompanied by hissing, spitting or bubbling, indicates an airlock is obstructing the supply pipe. Airlocks can usually be cleared by connecting one end of a length of hose-pipe to the tap giving trouble and the other end to the cold tap over the kitchen sink which is usually supplied direct from the rising main. When both taps are turned full on the mains pressure should blow the air bubble out of the system.

Airlocks recur when the cold water supply pipe to the hot water storage cylinder is too small. If this pipe is only 15mm ($\frac{1}{2}$in) in diameter it will be unable to replenish water drawn off from the 22mm ($\frac{3}{4}$in) pipe to the hot tap over the bath. The water level in the system's vent pipe – normally the same level as that in the cold water storage cistern – will fall, allowing air to enter a horizontal length of pipe. If a gate valve is fitted into the cold water supply pipe to the cylinder, it must be the correct size – at least 22mm ($\frac{3}{4}$in) – and must be kept fully open.

Other possible causes of persistent airlocks are too small a cold water storage cistern (it should be the standard 225 litre/50gal) or a partially jammed or sluggish ball valve serving the cistern.

Scale and corrosion

Direct cylinder hot water storage systems are prone to scale formation and corrosion.

Scale formation When hard water – and most water supplied in central, southern and eastern England is hard – is heated to 71°C (160°F) and above, calcium bicarbonate dissolved in the water is changed to insoluble calcium carbonate. This is deposited in solid form as scale or fur on immersion heaters and the inside of boilers.

When scale forms inside a boiler it insulates the water from the heat of the fire and the water in the

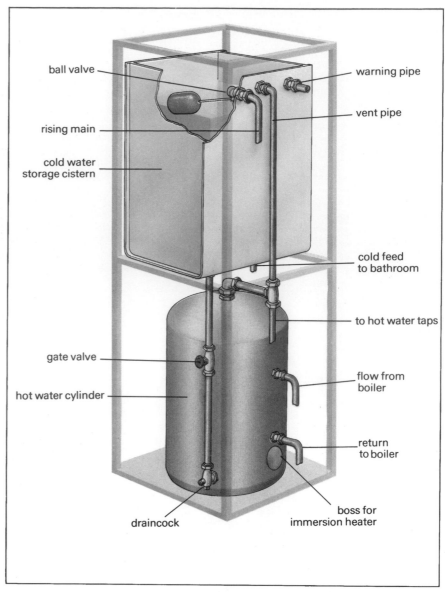

cylinder takes longer to heat. As the scale accumulates hot water is forced through ever narrowing channels, resulting in gurgling, hissing and banging. Scale also insulates the metal of the boiler from the cooling effect of the circulating water – the metal becomes thinner and eventually a leak develops.

Corrosion A flow of rusty red water from the hot tap is a sure indication corrosion exists somewhere in your water supply system. It may be in the cold water storage cistern, so empty the cistern and treat the inside with taste and odour-free bituminous paint. However, if the cistern is free from rust, corrosion must be taking place within the boiler and you should take early action to avoid a leaking boiler.

Remedy There are many products available which remove boiler scale but it is better to prevent it forming in the first place by using chemical additives in the cold water storage cistern.

A corroded boiler must be replaced or the metal will wear through and a leak will occur. To protect a new boiler use a chemical scale inhibitor which also helps avoid corrosion.

Chemical additives, however, do need continual renewal and a more positive, permanent remedy is to install an indirect hot water system.

Above A whole house packaged plumbing system which will cope with all hot and cold water demands
Above left Clearing an airlock in the supply pipe to a hot tap

Storing hot water is one area of plumbing that might well be a mystery to many householders. But it is important to understand the basic principles of the systems available and how they operate, particularly if you want to use hot water as a form of heating in the home.

Hot water: indirect cylinder systems

If you decide to install central heating an indirect storage hot water system is essential. But even if this is not among your immediate plans, an indirect system is a good investment if you live in an area where water is hard or corrosive, since this system is more resistant to scale formation and corrosion.

The system has two circuits. A primary circuit is heated by the boiler, flows to a closed coil, or calorifier, in the hot water cylinder and returns to the boiler to be reheated. The secondary circuit flows from the outer part of the hot water cylinder, where it is heated indirectly by the hot water passing through the calorifier, to the taps.

The water in the primary circuit is never drawn off and any losses from evaporation are made up from a small, usually 23 litre (5gal) tank – this is why indirect systems are relatively free of the problems of scale and corrosion. When the water in the primary circuit is first heated, dissolved air – a prerequisite of corrosion – is driven off. At the same time calcium bicarbonate dissolved in the water is converted into a small amount of calcium carbonate which is deposited on the inside of the boiler. Since any given volume of water contains only a certain quantity of scale-forming chemicals, no more scale will form in the boiler. Deposits that may form in the outer part of the storage cylinder will be minimal as the stored water will rarely reach the temperature at which scale forms.

An indirect system does not, however, mean absolute freedom from corrosion since air will dissolve in the water in the tank supplying the primary circuit and may also enter the circuit via cracks too small to allow water to escape.

The tank supplying the primary circuit also copes with the expansion of heated water, so the ball valve in the tank should be adjusted to provide for only 25 or 50mm (1 or 2in) of water when the primary circuit is cold. Hot water will flow back into the tank, rising to a level above the ball float.

The cold supply should connect to the primary circuit at its coldest point, normally close to the boiler on the return pipe from the cylinder. The cold supply used to be connected to the vent pipe of the primary circuit at high level, but water in the feed and expansion tank tended to overheat, leading to heat loss and condensation problems in the roof – and sometimes even to the plastic ball float melting in the heat. So this practice was discontinued.

Indirect systems and central heating
If you plan to combine your hot water system with central heating, the two must connect at the primary circuit. The flow pipe to a small, gravity-activated, central heating circuit is usually taken at high level from the boiler to cylinder flow pipe. It is then dropped to the radiators it will supply; the return pipe is taken to the return pipe from cylinder to boiler. A larger, pumped, central heating system will probably be connected to flow and return tappings on the opposite side of the boiler to those serving the hot water cylinder.

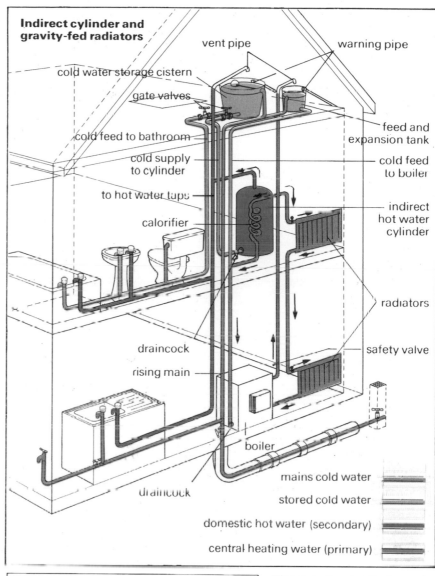

Indirect cylinder and gravity-fed radiators

vent pipe
warning pipe
cold water storage cistern
gate valves
cold feed to bathroom
cold supply to cylinder
to hot water taps
calorifier
draincock
rising main
draincock
boiler
feed and expansion tank
cold feed to boiler
indirect hot water cylinder
radiators
safety valve

mains cold water
stored cold water
domestic hot water (secondary)
central heating water (primary)

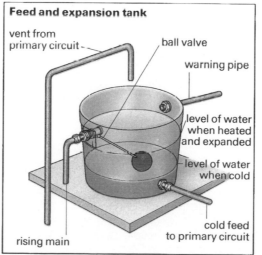

Feed and expansion tank

vent from primary circuit
ball valve
warning pipe
level of water when heated and expanded
level of water when cold
cold feed to primary circuit
rising main

Above Indirect cylinder system with two gravity-fed radiators
Left Ball valve in tank supplying primary circuit should be adjusted to prevent water overflowing when it expands on heating

Indirect cylinder and pumped central heating

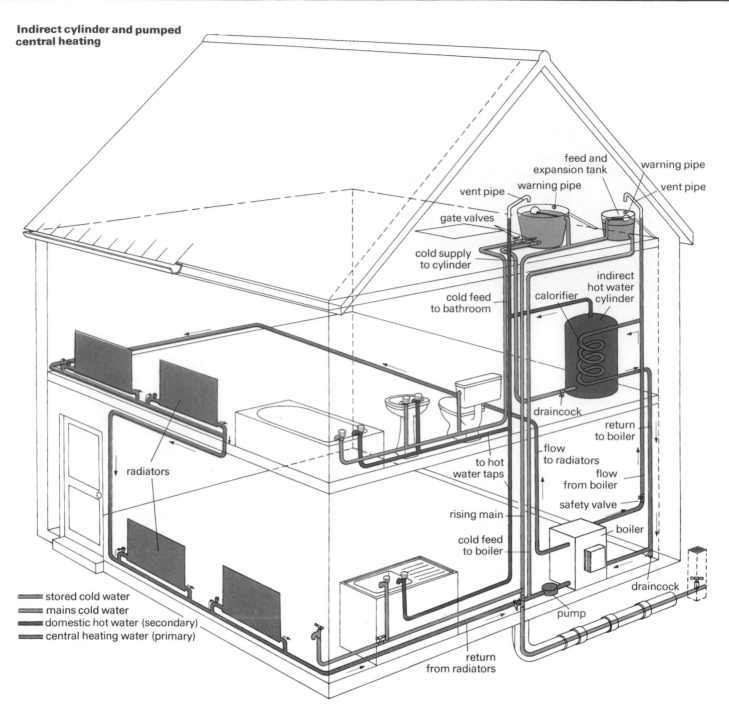

feed and expansion tank

warning pipe

warning pipe

vent pipe

vent pipe

gate valves

cold supply to cylinder

indirect hot water cylinder

cold feed to bathroom

calorifier

cold feed to bathroom

draincock

return to boiler

flow to radiators

to hot water taps

flow from boiler

radiators

safety valve

rising main

boiler

cold feed to boiler

draincock

pump

stored cold water
mains cold water
domestic hot water (secondary)
central heating water (primary)

return from radiators

Above Indirect cylinder system with pumped central heating
Right With self-priming cylinder, water flows through secondary cylinder and up vertical pipe into primary cylinder. When system is full, air trapped in primary cylinder prevents return of primary water to secondary cylinder. When water is heated, air in primary cylinder is displaced back to secondary cylinder, thus maintaining airlock between systems

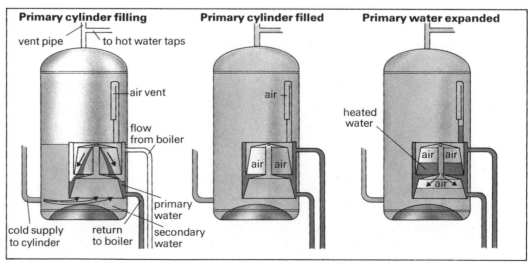

Primary cylinder filling

vent pipe

to hot water taps

air vent

flow from boiler

primary water

cold supply to cylinder

return to boiler

secondary water

Primary cylinder filled

air

air | air

Primary water expanded

heated water

air | air

air

Indirect packaged unit

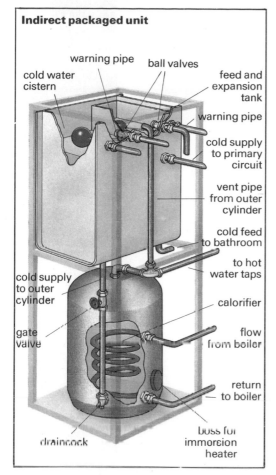

- cold water cistern
- warning pipe
- ball valves
- feed and expansion tank
- warning pipe
- cold supply to primary circuit
- vent pipe from outer cylinder
- cold feed to bathroom
- to hot water taps
- cold supply to outer cylinder
- calorifier
- gate valve
- flow from boiler
- return to boiler
- draincock
- boss for immersion heater

Self-priming indirect cylinder and pumped central heating

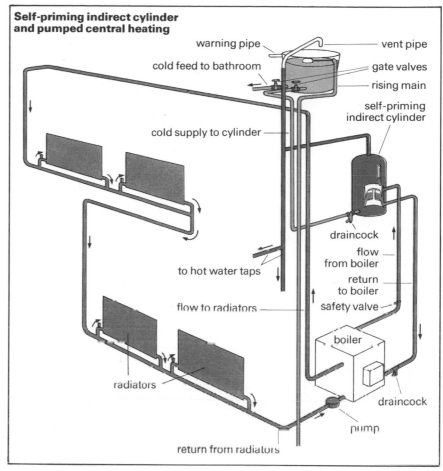

- warning pipe
- cold feed to bathroom
- vent pipe
- gate valves
- rising main
- self-priming indirect cylinder
- cold supply to cylinder
- to hot water taps
- flow to radiators
- radiators
- draincock
- flow from boiler
- return to boiler
- safety valve
- boiler
- draincock
- pump
- return from radiators

Above Self-priming indirect cylinder used with small central heating unit
Above right Conventional indirect packaged plumbing unit with small feed and expansion tank within cold water cistern
Right Packaged plumbing unit with self-priming indirect cylinder

Self-priming packaged unit

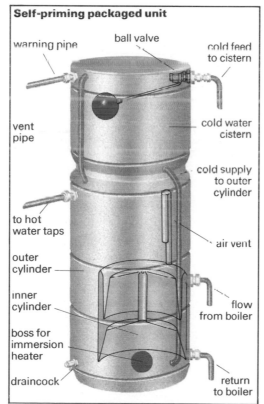

- warning pipe
- ball valve
- cold feed to cistern
- vent pipe
- cold water cistern
- cold supply to outer cylinder
- to hot water taps
- air vent
- outer cylinder
- inner cylinder
- flow from boiler
- boss for immersion heater
- draincock
- return to boiler

Warning If the central heating system has copper circulating pipes and thin-walled pressed steel radiators, use a reliable corrosion inhibitor in the feed and expansion tank to prevent any possible electrolytic corrosion.

Self-priming cylinders

Supplied direct from the cold water storage cistern, self-priming indirect cylinders do not need a separate feed and expansion tank and can, therefore, provide a simple and relatively cheap means of converting a hot water system from direct to indirect operation.

When a hot water system incorporating a self-priming cylinder is first filled with water, this overflows into the primary circuit through an inner cylinder which also serves as a heat exchanger. Once the circuit is full a large air bubble forms in the inner cylinder to prevent the return of the primary water. The inner cylinder also provides for the increased volume of the primary water as it expands upon heating.

The water in the primary circuit must never be allowed to boil as this would displace the air bubble in the inner cylinder and allow the primary and domestic hot water to mix.

When buying a self-priming cylinder make sure the particular model is large enough to cope with the expansion of the primary – and any central heating – circuit.

Packaged plumbing

There are packaged plumbing indirect systems as well as direct ones. Some of these combination units have a self-priming cylinder while other conventional units have an ordinary indirect cylinder and a small 14 litre (3gal) feed and expansion tank within the cold water storage cistern.

Hot water: gas and electric systems

As long as hot water is available at the turn of a tap most of us are happy. But have you thought whether your heating system is really suitable for your needs? Your heater may be providing water that you don't use and therefore is wasting money. Gas and electric heaters offer a choice to give you the hot water you want.

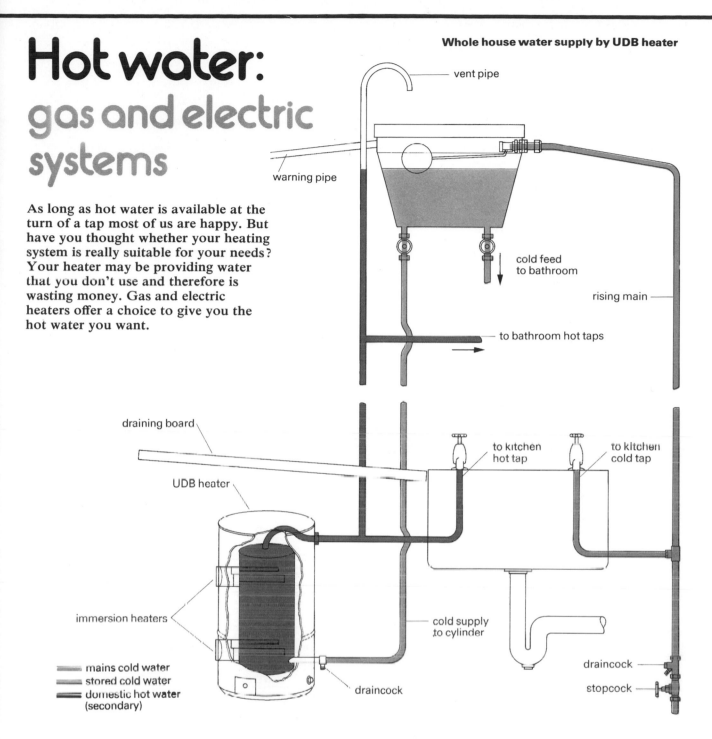

Whole house water supply by UDB heater

vent pipe

warning pipe

cold feed to bathroom

rising main

to bathroom hot taps

draining board

UDB heater

immersion heaters

to kitchen hot tap

to kitchen cold tap

cold supply to cylinder

draincock

stopcock

cold supply to cylinder

draincock

mains cold water
stored cold water
domestic hot water (secondary)

There are two main types of gas or electric heaters storage cylinder and instantaneous – to provide running hot water in the home. Your choice will depend on how much hot water you use: if you require a constant supply in large quantities, a storage cylinder heater is probably the best, although large multi-point instantaneous gas heaters can also be used. If you need small quantities of hot water for relatively short periods at a time, instantaneous heaters are the answer since they will provide an adequate supply.

Storage water heaters

Available to run off either gas or day (or off-peak) electricity, storage heaters will give an ample supply of hot water. These are available to provide the whole house with hot water or to supply one particular area.

UDB heaters

If you intend to use one or more electric immersion heaters as the sole heat source for a simple, direct cylinder hot water system, it is best to install an Under Draining Board water heater instead of a conventional cylinder.

UDB heaters are specially designed to heat water economically by electricity. They have a 115 litre (25gal) capacity, are very heavily insulated and, as the name suggests, fit under the draining board of the kitchen sink, close to the hot water draw-off point in most frequent use.

They usually have two horizontal immersion heaters, one about a third of the distance from the top of the cylinder and the other near the base. The upper heater is switched on all the time to provide an immediate source of hot water for hand basins and sinks. The lower heater should be switched on about an hour before larger volumes of water are

Off-peak water heater

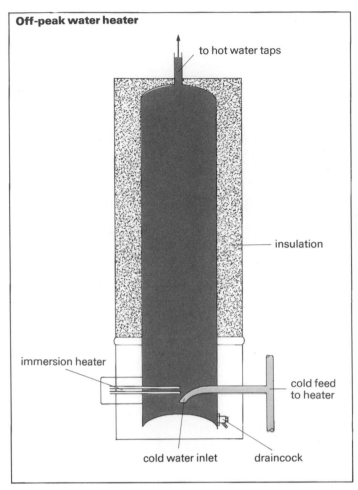

to hot water taps

insulation

immersion heater

cold feed to heater

cold water inlet

draincock

Open outlet heater

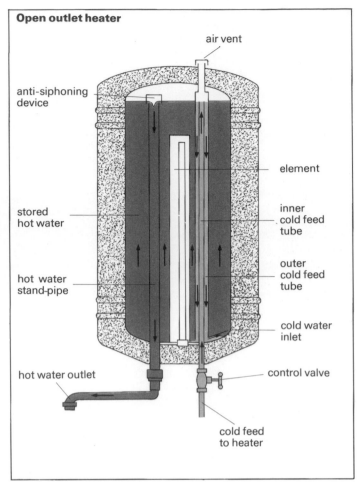

air vent

anti-siphoning device

stored hot water

hot water stand-pipe

element

inner cold feed tube

outer cold feed tube

cold water inlet

hot water outlet

control valve

cold feed to heater

Instantaneous gas water heater

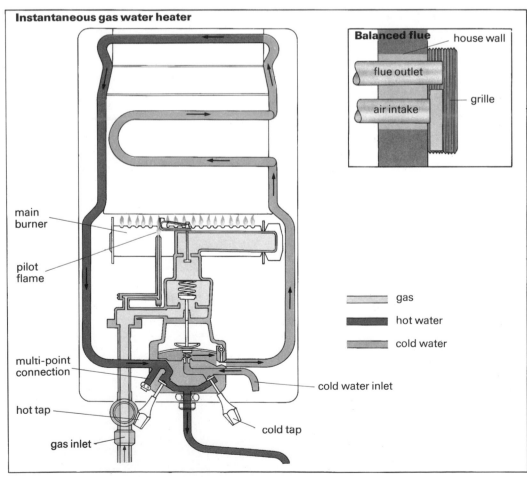

Balanced flue

house wall

flue outlet

air intake

grille

main burner

pilot flame

multi-point connection

cold water inlet

hot tap

gas inlet

cold tap

gas

hot water

cold water

required, such as for baths or household washing.

UDB heaters must be supplied from the main cold water storage cistern and must have a vent pipe, as with other cylinder hot water systems.

Off-peak heaters

These are a development of the UDB heater, designed to take advantage of the cheaper electricity rates available during the night. Storage heaters of this kind are tall, slim, heavily insulated cylinders with a 225 litre (50gal) capacity – estimated as sufficient to meet the daily demand of the average family. The immersion heater, situated near the base, switches on at night and off in the morning, leaving the cylinder full of hot water.

The shape of these heaters encourages the separation of hot water stored in the upper part of the cylinder from cold water flowing in near the base to replace the water drawn off. The cold water inlet usually has a special spreader which distributes water evenly over the base to prevent it mixing with hot water at a higher level.

Open outlet heaters

Designed for use with gas or electricity, open outlet heaters are usually of 5 or 10 litre (1 or 2gal) capacity and are installed immediately above the area they serve. This type of heater may, if the local water authority permits, be connected direct to the rising main (in which case a cold water storage cistern would be unnecessary) or be supplied from the cold water cistern.

When hot water is required, a control valve on the inlet side of the appliance is opened. Cold water flows into the base and hot water overflows down a stand-pipe, through an open outlet and into the sink. The stand-pipe lip is fitted with an anti-siphoning device which, when water has been drawn off, ensures the level within the heater is about 12mm ($\frac{1}{2}$in) below the lip to allow for the increased volume of heated water.

Instantaneous water heaters

The great advantage of this type of heater is that you heat only the water you are going to use immediately; there is no reserve of stored water which, however thoroughly the cylinder is lagged, slowly loses its heat.

There are drawbacks to this method of water heating: the rate of hot water delivery is lower than that of a storage system and, in hard water areas, there is a tendency for scale to form. Also these heaters do not raise water to one particular temperature: they raise it through a range of temperatures as it passes through the heater. In cold weather you may find the temperature of the water at the outlet too low or the rate of flow markedly reduced.

Like the open outlet type, instantaneous heaters may be connected direct to the rising main. Incoming cold water flows through a system of small bore copper tubing within the appliance and is heated either by a gas flame or by a powerful electric element as it flows.

Multi-point gas heaters

Large multi-point instantaneous gas heaters can provide the whole house with hot water. The development of the balanced flue means gas appliances can be used, with complete safety, in any room having an outside wall. A balanced flue gas appliance has its combustion chamber sealed

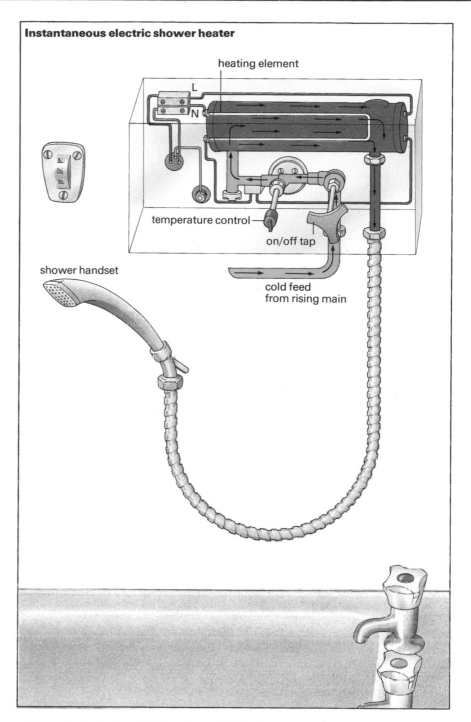

Instantaneous electric shower heater

heating element

L

N

temperature control

on/off tap

shower handset

cold feed from rising main

off from the room in which it is situated. The air intake and flue outlet are positioned close together on the outside wall; however strongly the wind may be blowing against the flue outlet, it will be blowing equally strongly against the fresh air inlet and the appliance will continue to operate.

The use of the balanced flue is not, of course, limited to instantaneous water heaters. Gas space heaters and gas boilers for use with central heating systems may also have balanced flues.

Electric heaters

A hot water supply for the whole house cannot be provided with electric instantaneous heaters, but this type is particularly valuable for use with showers where there would not otherwise be enough pressure for the shower to operate efficiently, and for providing hot water in outside WCs not connected to the main sources of hot water.

Single stack above-ground drainage

Building regulations introduced in Britain in the mid-1960s required all main drainage stacks to be confined within the fabric of the building as a frost precaution. This provided drainage installers with a strong incentive to keep the number of pipes to a minimum and encouraged the use of the single stack system; but there was opposition to its adoption, since it is possible for waste seals to be sucked out by the force of waste matter passing from more than one fitting at the same time, allowing drain gases to enter the house. There is also the possibility of a blockage at the foot of the stack, resulting in sewage backing up into the kitchen sink. These problems should not arise, however, if the system is properly designed and installed.

Layout and design
Compact planning of rooms with sanitary fittings is essential for a successful single stack plumbing design. In a two-storey house the bathroom should be immediately above the kitchen and, in multi-storey blocks of flats, kitchens and bathrooms should be one above the other throughout the building.

Preventing loss of seal Branch waste pipes from baths, showers, basins, bidets and sinks should be kept short and have minimal falls to the main stack. Pay particular attention to the waste pipe from any wash-basin, since this pipe will be of small diameter – about 30mm (or 1¼in), and is very likely to run full when the basin is emptied. This can result in the seal being sucked or siphoned out. To prevent siphonage this pipe should be no longer than 1.68m (or 66in). If this is impossible, take a 15mm (or ½in) diameter vent pipe from immediately behind the trap to join the main stack at least 1m (or 3ft) above the highest connection to it.

As a further precaution, it is essential all waste fittings have a deep seal trap of 75mm (or 3in) instead of the shallow seal traps commonly used with a two-pipe drainage system.

Avoiding contamination To prevent the outlets from baths, sinks and basins being fouled by discharges from the WC, the branch pipes from these fittings should be connected to the main drainage stack either well above or well below the point where the stack is joined to the pipe from the WC. This is usually not a problem with sink and basin waste pipes, but there may be difficulties in the case of pipes from baths, showers or bidets. You can deal with this by offsetting the waste pipe and taking it through the bathroom floor to discharge into the stack well below the WC pipe connection. An easier solution is to use a patent collar boss, a fitting which allows bath, basin and shower wastes to discharge into the stack at the same level as the pipe from the WC but with no risk of blockage or contamination.

The main stack Soil pipes used in older two pipe drainage systems are often only 75mm (or 3in) or 87mm (or 3½in) in internal diameter; in one-pipe systems the main stack must have an internal diameter of at least 100mm (or 4in). It should

connect to the underground drain by an easy bend to prevent blockages or foaming back of detergent filled water.

Ground floor wastes
Where single stack drainage is installed, ground floor sanitary appliances may be connected to the main stack. Alternatively, their wastes may be disposed of in the same way as in a two pipe drainage system: WC wastes are taken directly to the underground drain by a short branch drain; bath, sink and basin wastes are taken to discharge over a yard gully. This system has the advantage of eliminating the risk of blockage at the foot of the stack which, while unlikely in a properly designed single stack system, is not entirely non-existent. Where ground floor appliances are connected to the stack, the first sign of such a blockage is sewage flowing back into the bath or kitchen sink.

If branch waste pipes discharge over a yard gully, make sure the discharge takes place above the level of the water in the gully but below the grid. This stops the grid becoming foul from waste discharges, prevents the risk of flooding if the grid becomes choked with fallen leaves and ensures the full force of the discharge is available to cleanse and flush the gully. Providing a back or side inlet gully will serve this purpose best. There are also gully grids manufactured with slots through which waste pipes can be passed and which are useful where a new waste pipe is to be taken to an existing gully.

Making connections
Modern single-stack drainage systems are almost universally constructed of PVC tubing. Small diameter branch waste pipes are joined by solvent welding; ring seal jointing (which allows for thermal expansion and contraction) is used to join sections of large diameter main stack pipe. These processes can be carried out by the home handyman, but if you intend making a connection to the drainage system of your house – for a new shower or wash-basin for example – you must obtain the approval of your local authority. The building inspector will give you advice on how to carry out the work so you do not create a health risk or impair the functioning of the system.

Above In the single stack drainage system, developed in the 1960s, all appliances discharge into one main pipe which connects to the underground drain; there is no separation of soil and waste discharges as in older systems. The narrower pipes on the houses above are rainwater downpipes and not connected to the internal drainage system

Right How the single stack system works. To prevent all risk of outlets from waste appliances being contaminated by discharges from the WC, you can fit a collar boss to the main stack (**Inset A**); alternatively you can offset the waste pipe and connect it to the main stack well below the point at which the stack meets the WC soil pipe (**Inset B**); ground floor sinks can be connected to the main stack or be taken to discharge over a yard gully (**Inset C**)

Single stack system

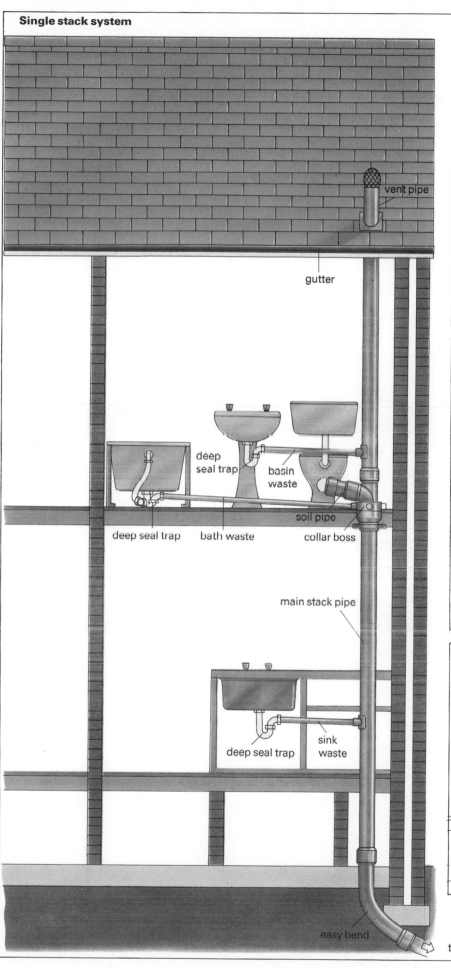

vent pipe

gutter

deep seal trap

basin waste

deep seal trap

bath waste

soil pipe

collar boss

main stack pipe

deep seal trap

sink waste

easy bend

to main sewer

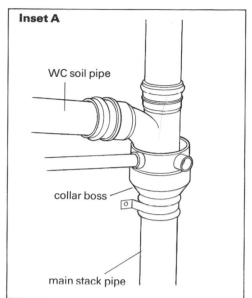

Inset A

WC soil pipe

collar boss

main stack pipe

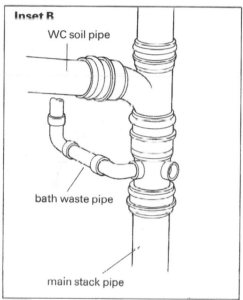

Inset B

WC soil pipe

bath waste pipe

main stack pipe

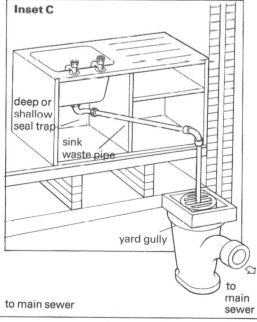

Inset C

deep or shallow seal trap

sink waste pipe

yard gully

to main sewer

Two pipe above-ground drainage

The two pipe system of above-ground drainage was developed in the 19th century when, for health reasons, it was felt that soil pipes disposing of waste from WCs and slop-sinks should be kept separate from waste pipes from sinks, basins, bidets and baths. This system was used until the 1960s, which means the rear elevation of many homes in Britain is marred by two iron pipes, at least one of which rises to above the level of the eaves. Buildings of more than two storeys, in which there are a number of soil and waste fittings, might well have more than two pipes on the external elevation.

Soil pipes
If soil appliances such as WCs are situated on the ground floor, they are connected by a short branch to the main underground drain at the nearest inspection chamber or manhole. The outlets from upper floor soil appliances are connected by a short branch soil pipe to a main soil pipe (usually made of heavy cast iron) running vertically down an external wall and joined at its base to the underground drain. This extends above the level of the eaves and acts as a vent pipe to allow sewer gases to escape. A cage is fitted on the upper end to protect it from rubbish and birds' nests.

Waste pipes
Sinks, basins, bidets and baths are not directly connected to the underground drain. The outlet pipes from ground-floor appliances discharge over the grid of a yard gully joined by a branch drain to the nearest inspection chamber.

Arrangements for the disposal of wastes from upper floors depend on the local drainage by-laws in force at the time the system was installed. Sometimes the wastes discharge over a rainwater hopper head set into the upper end of a rainwater downpipe,

Above An old fashioned drainage system, with at least two iron pipes running down the outside wall
1 The two pipe system where waste and soil appliances discharge into separate pipes
Inset Hooper head set in a rainwater downpipe

Following page
2 The range of traps: plastic 'P' (**a**) plastic 'S' (**b**) plastic 'P' bottle (**c**) plastic 'S' bottle (**d**) metal 'P' (**e**) metal 'S' (**f**)
3 The depth of seal on 'P', 'S' and 'P' bottle traps

which in turn discharges over a yard gully. This is **1**
not very satisfactory since rainwater hopper heads
are not self-cleansing and soapy water decomposing
on their internal surfaces can be a source of unpleasant smells. Draughts up the rainwater downpipe can carry even more unpleasant smells from
the yard gully. To prevent this, the drainage by-
laws of some local authorities require upstairs
wastes to flow into a main waste pipe, discharging
over a yard gully but, like the main soil pipe, taken
upwards to terminate open-ended above the level of
the eaves.

Waste traps

Bends in pipes at the outlets of sanitary fittings are
filled with water which provides a seal to prevent
gases from the drain or waste pipes passing back
through the fittings. These are known as traps and
in the case of yard gullies and WCs are an integral
part of the appliance. Separate traps, made of
brass, gunmetal or PVC, must be fitted immediately
below the waste outlet of all other appliances.
Where outlets from more than one appliance are
connected to the same branch soil or waste pipe, the
traps of these appliances must be ventilated to
prevent the water seal being sucked out by the force
of waste matter passing through. The vent pipes
either end above the level of the eaves or are taken
back to join the main soil or waste pipe at least 1m
(or 3ft) above the highest connection to it.

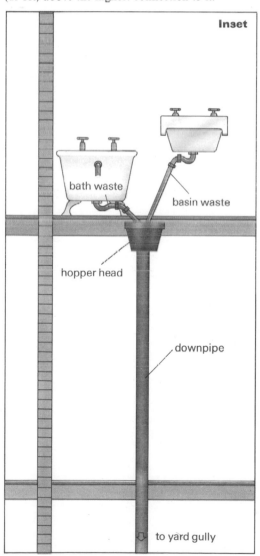

Inset

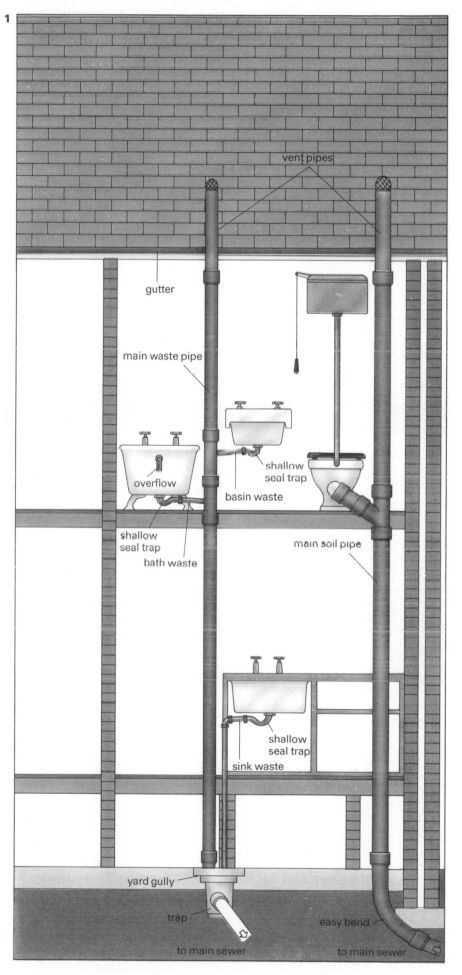

2 Types of trap

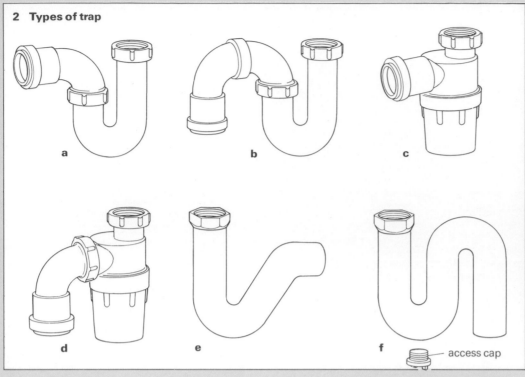

a

b

c

d

e

f — access cap

3

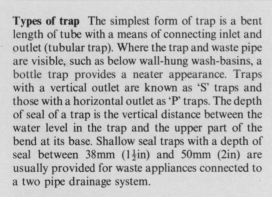

'P' trap

'S' trap

'P' bottle trap

depth of seal

4 Using force cup to clear blockage. **5a** To clear blocked 'U' trap, remove drain plug with rod. **5b** Push wire into trap. **5c** Probe round bend with curtain wire. **5d** Replace drain plug **6a** To clear bottle trap, unscrew bottom. **6b** Push curtain wire into pipe to remove blockage

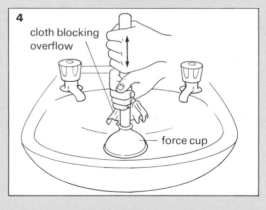

4

cloth blocking overflow

force cup

Types of trap The simplest form of trap is a bent length of tube with a means of connecting inlet and outlet (tubular trap). Where the trap and waste pipe are visible, such as below wall-hung wash-basins, a bottle trap provides a neater appearance. Traps with a vertical outlet are known as 'S' traps and those with a horizontal outlet as 'P' traps. The depth of seal of a trap is the vertical distance between the water level in the trap and the upper part of the bend at its base. Shallow seal traps with a depth of seal between 38mm (1½in) and 50mm (2in) are usually provided for waste appliances connected to a two pipe drainage system.

Clearing blockages

Since traps retard the flow of waste water they are the most common site of blockage in the outlet of any soil or waste appliance. If water fails to flow away when you remove the outlet plug from a sink, wash-basin or bath, try clearing the blockage by plunging. For this you will need a force cup or sink waste plunger which you can obtain from any hardware store. Place the cup over the waste outlet of the appliance. Hold a dampened cloth firmly against the overflow outlet to prevent the force of the plunger being dissipated up the outlet and plunge down sharply three or four times. This should move the blockage and allow waste water to run away.

If plunging fails to clear the trap, it is likely a solid object is lodged in it. All traps are provided with some means of access to enable you to remove

such objects. The entire lower part of a bottle trap can be unscrewed and other traps have a screwed-in access cap at or near their base. Remember to place a large bucket under the waste pipe before unscrewing a cap or removing the lower part of a bottle trap. To clear the blockage, probe into the trap with a piece of flexible wire, such as expanding curtain wire.

A very slow discharge from the appliance indicates a partial blockage, usually caused by a build-up of grease. To deal with this, pour a proprietary chemical drain cleaner into the waste outlet.

Warning Chemical cleaners are usually based on caustic soda; so they should be kept away from children and used with extreme care, strictly according to the manufacturer's instructions.

5a

5b

5c

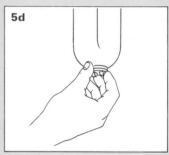

5d

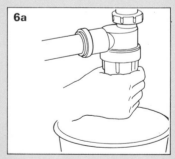

6a

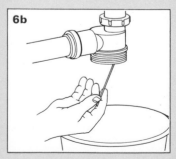

6b

Underground drainage

There are two principal systems for disposing of wastes after they have been discharged from above-ground pipes; your home will have one of them. Here we describe the construction and layout of the two systems, where blockages are likely to occur and how to detect and clear them.

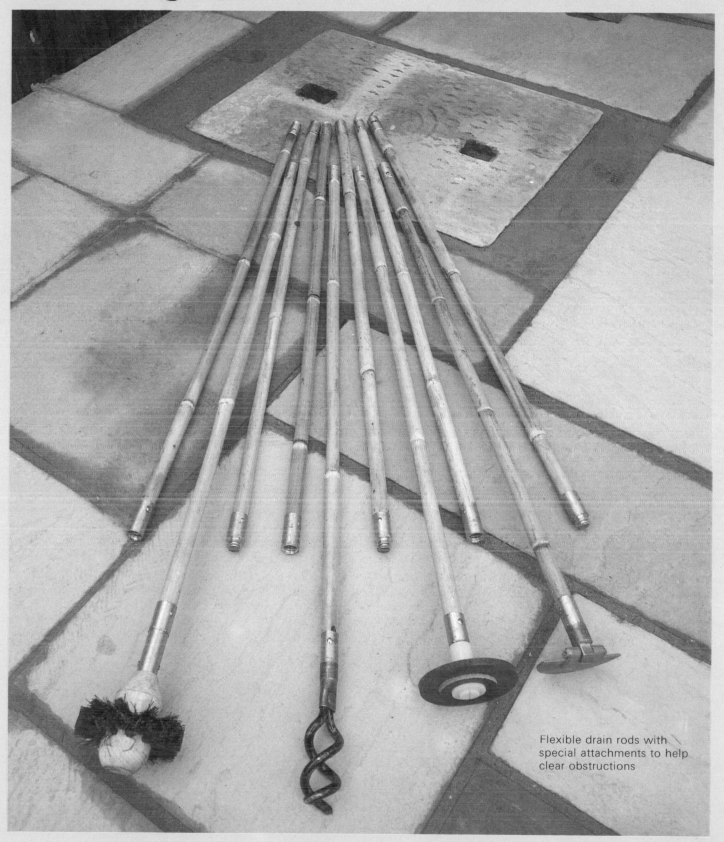

Flexible drain rods with special attachments to help clear obstructions

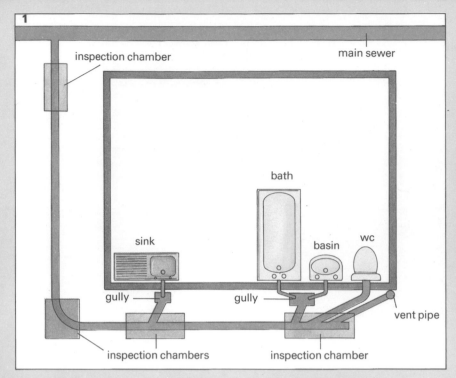

1

inspection chamber

main sewer

bath

sink

basin

wc

gully

gully

vent pipe

inspection chambers

inspection chamber

Domestic underground drainage systems, which take the wastes from pipes above ground to the public sewer, are laid out according to certain general principles. For example, drains must be laid in straight lines and sloping downwards so they are self-cleansing. They should be adequately ventilated and protected from damage which might arise from subsoil settlement. There must also be an inspection chamber or similar means of access at junctions of branch drains and changes of direction in the system to enable blockages to be cleared.

Older systems

Many older houses have systems constructed of glazed stoneware pipe 610mm (2ft) long with an internal diameter of 100mm (or 4in), laid on a 150mm (or 6in) deep concrete bed to give protection against settlement. Pipes are joined either with neat cement or a strong cement/sand mix and are laid at a gradient of 1 in 40 – or 75mm in 3m (3in in 10ft). Inspection chambers are made of brick, usually rendered internally with cement and sand. Drains pass through these chambers in stoneware half-channels with a concrete ledge or benching built up on each side.

There is an intercepting or disconnecting trap in the final inspection chamber before connection to

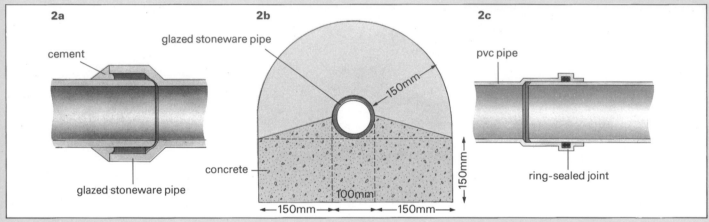

2a

cement

glazed stoneware pipe

2b

glazed stoneware pipe

150mm

concrete

100mm

150mm

150mm

150mm

2c

pvc pipe

ring-sealed joint

3

fresh air inlet

manhole cover

rodding eye

rodding arm

stoneware stopper

drainpipe

stoneware half-channel

to main sewer

intercepting trap

the public sewer. This is designed to prevent sewer gases, and possibly rats, entering the house drains. To allow fresh air along the drains to carry gases out through the above-ground soil and vent pipes, a low level ventilator or fresh air inlet is usually connected to the final inspection chamber. It ends above ground in a metal box with a hinged mica flap resting against a grille inlet.

Modern systems

Modern houses have systems constructed from 100mm (or 4in) pipes, but these are more likely to be made of PVC or pitch fibre than glazed stoneware; ring-sealed joints are used to connect them. Drains of this kind will move or give slightly to accommodate any ground settlement and do not need to be laid on a concrete bed. Smoother internal surfaces and a reduction in the number of joints means gradients shallower than in older systems can be safely used. Falls of 1 in 60 – or 75mm in 4.5m (3in in 15ft) – and 1 in 70 – or 75mm in 5.25m (3in in 17ft 6in) – are common.

Inspection chambers may still be made of brick, but they are not rendered internally since cement rendering is likely to flake off and cause a blockage. Any rendering necessary is applied to the outside of the chamber before earth is filled in. Some pre-

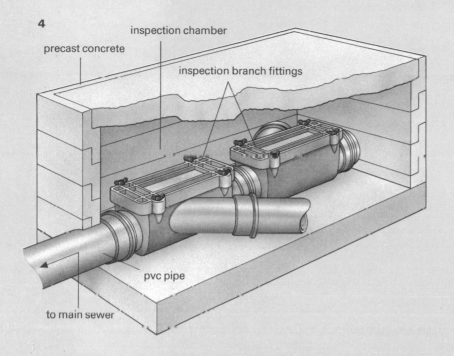

4

precast concrete

inspection chamber

inspection branch fittings

pvc pipe

to main sewer

Clearing blockages Before you can clear a blocked drain, you need to know where the blockage is. Raise the covers of the inspection chambers. If the chamber nearest to the house is flooded but the one nearest to the boundary is clear, the blockage must be situated between these two points. You can remove the blockage by a process known as rodding, for which you need a set of flexible drain rods. Screw two or three rods together, lower one end into the flooded manhole or chamber and feel for the entrance to the drain. When you have found it, push the rods towards the blockage, screwing more on as needed. Twist in a clockwise direction to help the rods move along the pipe. You must never twist them anti-clockwise or the rods will unscrew and you could end up with several lengths left in the drain. When you reach the blockage, give one or two sharp prods which will usually clear it. There are special tools available which you can screw onto the ends of rods to help clear difficult obstructions.

If all the inspection chambers are flooded and your drainage system has an intercepting trap, it is likely the trap is the site of the blockage. To clear it, screw two drain rods together and a 100mm (or 4in) rubber disc or drain plunger onto the end. Lower the plunger into the chamber, feel for the half-channel at the base and move the plunger along it

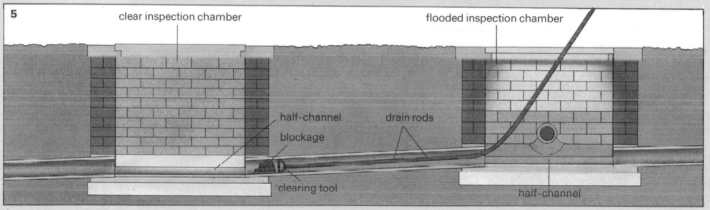

5

clear inspection chamber

flooded inspection chamber

half-channel

blockage

drain rods

clearing tool

half-channel

1 A typical domestic underground drainage system
2a Section through the joint of stoneware pipes
2b Foundations for a stoneware pipe
2c Section through the joint of PVC pipes
3 An early inspection chamber with intercepting trap and fresh air inlet
4 A precast concrete inspection chamber
5 Clearing a blocked drain: lower drain rods into the flooded chamber and push them into the drain until you reach the blockage. A few sharp prods should clear the system

fabricated chambers are made of concrete sections or plastic reinforced by glass fibre.

The intercepting trap has been abolished as it is the commonest area of blockage in older systems. There is no need for it where there is a properly designed and ventilated sewer which should contain neither offensive smells nor rats. There is no fresh air inlet which, being situated at ground level, is likely to be subjected to accidental damage and is a common source of drain smells. In modern systems where drains are connected without interception directly to the sewer, all domestic drains and the sewer are adequately ventilated by their above-ground drainage stacks.

Drain blockages

Trace the course of your drainage system so you will be able to take appropriate action when a blockage occurs and inspection chambers are flooded. Make sure the covers of the chambers can be easily raised and note where branch drains enter and if there is an intercepting trap in the final chamber. Learn to recognize the signs of blockage, such as a flooding gully and sewage leaking from the cover of an inspection chamber. Another indication is when you flush your WC and water rises to the flushing rim and subsides very slowly.

until it reaches the point at which the half-channel descends into the intercepting trap. Plunge down sharply three or four times to remove the blockage.

After clearing a blocked drain remember to run the household taps to flush water through the drain and to wash down the sides and benching of the chambers with hot water and washing soda.

Rodding eye stopper blockage The length of drain from the intercepting trap to the public sewer is the responsibility of the householder, even though it may lie wholly or partly under the public highway. Intercepting traps are provided with a device known as a rodding eye, connected to a rodding arm and sealed with a stoneware stopper, through which this section of the drain can be rodded. Sometimes, as a result of back pressure from the sewer, the stopper falls out into the trap to cause a partial blockage. Regularly check the stopper is in place. If its loss and a subsequent blockage remain undetected, the level of sewage rises in the inspection chamber until it reaches the rodding arm and then flows down this arm to the sewer; meanwhile the sewage in the base of the chamber decomposes and becomes more and more foul. Discovery of the blockage usually follows investigation of a complaint about an offensive smell near the front gate.

Keeping out of trouble

Guarding against corrosion

Some plumbing fittings are subject to corrosion. When this occurs, they are weakened and eventually leaks develop. There are several ways of preventing this happening in your system.

Modern galvanized steel water storage cisterns frequently show signs of rust within a few months of being installed. Older plumbing systems, which were constructed entirely of lead or galvanized steel, could generally be expected to last, without this kind of deterioration, for 50 years or more. In modern systems the use of copper, which itself virtually never corrodes, has greatly increased the risk of corrosion to any galvanized iron or steel fittings incorporated in the system.

The process which gives rise to this corrosion is known as electrolytic action. This is the same principle on which the simple electric battery cell is based; where rods of zinc and copper are in electrical contact with each other and are immersed in a weak acid solution which is able to conduct an electric current (an electrolyte), electricity will pass between the rods, bubbles of oxygen will be produced and the zinc rod will slowly dissolve away. A plumbing system in which copper water supply and distribution pipes are connected to a galvanized steel cold water storage cistern or hot water storage tank, may reproduce these conditions; the copper tubing and the zinc coating of the galvanized steel are in direct contact and the water in the cistern or tank, if very mildly acidic, will act as an electrolyte. This results in rapid failure of the protective galvanized coating, allowing aerated water to penetrate to the vulnerable steel underneath; eventually rust will form.

A particular form of electrolytic corrosion may result in damage to brass plumbing fittings, such as compression joints and stop valves. Brass is an alloy of copper and zinc; electrolytic action may result in the zinc in the fittings dissolving away to leave them unchanged in appearance but totally without structural strength. Where these fittings in your plumbing system are showing signs of leakage, it would be worth checking with a local plumber if the type of water in your area is likely to create a situation favourable to electrolytic corrosion. If so, you should replace brass fittings with those made of a special alloy classed as 'dezincification resistant'. The fittings are marked with a special symbol – CR. Although these fittings are more expensive, you should use them where this problem of corrosion exists.

Warning Corrosion as a result of electrolytic action is also likely to occur in pipework if a new length of copper tubing is fitted into an existing galvanized steel hot or cold water system. Always use stainless steel tubing instead – this is not liable to the same risk.

Protecting cisterns and tanks
There are steps you can take to prevent corrosion in galvanized steel cisterns and tanks. For example, when you are installing a new cistern or tank, it is important to make sure you remove every trace of metal dust or shaving resulting from drilling holes

for tappings. The least fragment remaining will become a focus for corrosion.

One way of protecting a cold water storage cistern is to ensure the metal of the cistern does not come into direct contact with the water it contains. This can be done by painting the internal surfaces with two coats of a taste and odour-free bituminous paint using an old 50mm paint brush. Before applying this treatment to a new tank, cut holes for the pipe connections; when you are painting, pay particular attention to the areas in the immediate vicinity of these holes.

Warning Galvanized steel hot water storage tanks, which can still be found in many older homes, cannot be protected by this paint treatment.

Cathodic protection A sacrificial magnesium anode which dissolves instead of the zinc coating will

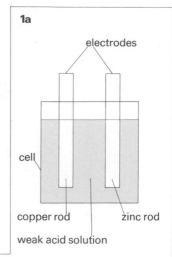

1a

electrodes

cell

copper rod   zinc rod

weak acid solution

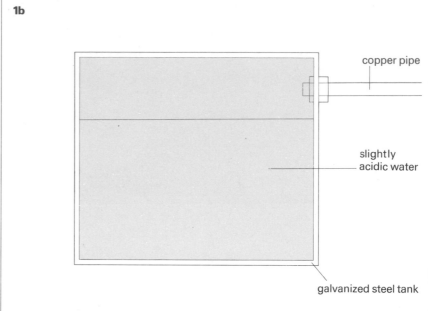

1b

copper pipe

slightly acidic water

galvanized steel tank

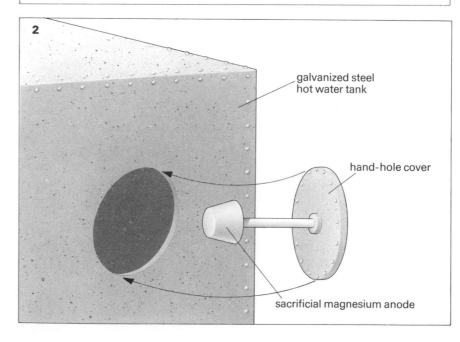

2

galvanized steel hot water tank

hand-hole cover

sacrificial magnesium anode

1a & b The process which causes corrosion in plumbing systems with copper and galvanized iron or steel fittings is principally the same as the process which takes place in a battery cell
2 Fit a sacrificial magnesium anode into a galvanized steel hot water tank to prevent corrosion
3 When venting a radiator check for the presence of hydrogen – which indicates internal corrosion – by holding a lighted taper to the escaping air
To remove magnetite sludge from a central heating system, drain the system (**4a**) and introduce a special solvent into the feed and expansion tank (**4b**)

protect both galvanized steel cold water storage cisterns and hot water tanks. The procedure for a hot water tank involves fitting the anode to the hand-hole cover of the tank. Turn off the water supply and drain the system from the draincock beside the boiler; unscrew the bolts retaining the hand-hole cover and remove it. Drill a hole in the centre of the cover, use abrasive paper to rub down the area of metal around the hole and screw in the anode before replacing the cover.

Protecting central heating systems

A form of electrolytic corrosion can take place in a central heating system where copper tubing is used in conjunction with pressed steel radiators. Some air – a prerequisite of corrosion – will always be present in the system; it dissolves into the surface of the water in the feed and expansion tank and may also enter through minute leaks too small to permit water to escape.

Electrolytic corrosion within a central heating system results in the formation of black iron oxide sludge (magnetite) and hydrogen gas. This leads to impeded water flow and radiators will need continual venting to release airlocks to keep up the required heat level. The iron oxide sludge is drawn towards the magnetic field of the circulating pump and its abrasive qualities contribute towards early pump failure. Also the metal of the radiators, from which the magnetite and hydrogen are produced, becomes thinner until leaks eventually develop in the radiators.

Removing airlocks by venting the radiator is a simple process. A key supplied for this purpose is inserted in the radiator when the water is warm and turned anti-clockwise to open the vent valve. Hold a container underneath the key since some water may escape when the valve is opened. Air will come out of the radiator – when it stops doing so and water begins to flow you should tighten the valve. If a radiator in your heating system needs to be continually vented, it is worth testing for internal corrosion while you are carrying out this operation. Apply a lighted taper to the gas escaping from the radiator; hydrogen gas burns with a blue flame and indicates the presence of corrosion.

Protection treatment A chemical corrosion-proofer can be introduced into the feed and expansion tank to protect the system against corrosion. It is best to do this when the system is first installed, but it can be carried out with an existing system; it will not, however, undo damage already done. Before introducing a corrosion-proofer into an existing system you should get rid of any magnetite sludge with a special solvent. Like the corrosion-proofer, this is introduced into the feed and expansion tank and you should drain the system first. Disconnect the fuel supply to the boiler and switch off the ignition system several hours before draining to give the water time to cool. Tie up the ball float arm of the feed and expansion tank and fit a hose to the draincock near the boiler, running the hose to a drain outside. Undo the draincock, empty the system and, when you have closed the draincock, free the ball float arm in the feed and expansion tank. Allow the system to refill, introducing the solvent at the same time. Follow the manufacturer's instructions for the length of time you should allow for the solvent to complete its work before carrying out treatment with the corrosion-proofer.

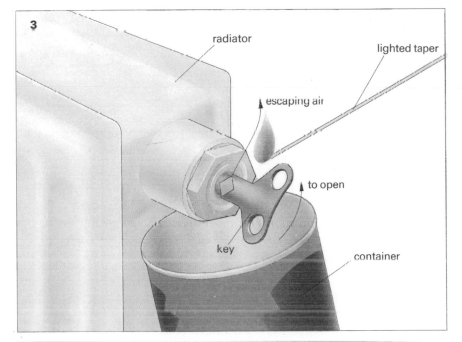

3

radiator

lighted taper

escaping air

to open

key

container

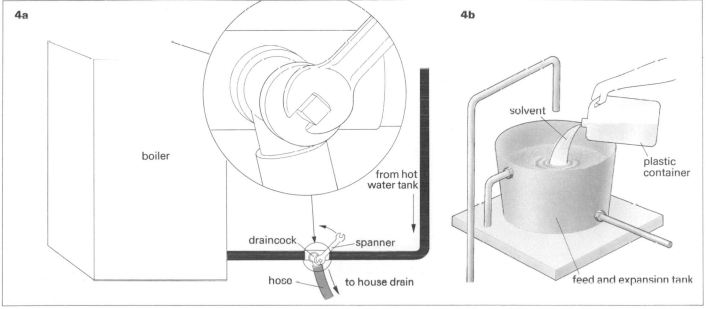

4a

boiler

from hot water tank

draincock   spanner

hose   to house drain

4b

solvent

plastic container

feed and expansion tank

Protection from hard water

Scale formation is all too common in hard water areas and its effect on the plumbing system can be as dramatic as the damage shown in the photograph opposite. Protective measures should therefore be given serious consideration, such as the nstallation of a Permutit automatic domestic water softener, one example of which is shown in the illustration below.

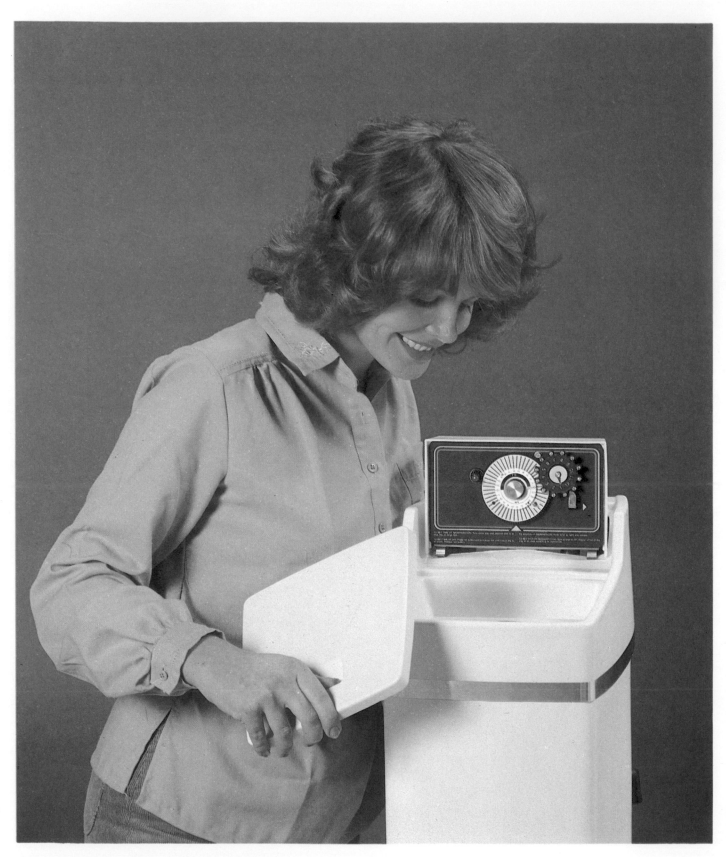

A hot water cylinder choked
by scale formation; it became
ineffective after only five
years' service

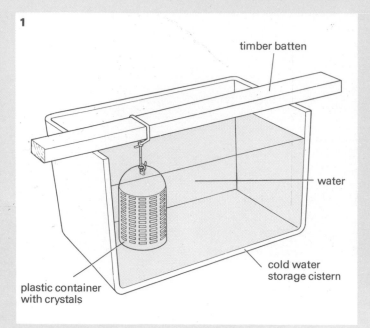

1

timber batten

water

cold water
storage cistern

plastic container
with crystals

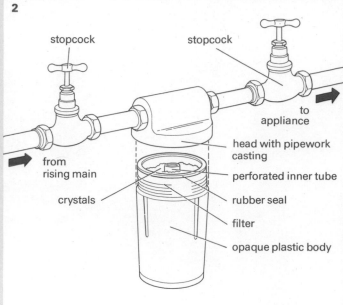

2

stopcock

stopcock

to
appliance

from
rising main

head with pipework
casting

perforated inner tube

crystals

rubber seal

filter

opaque plastic body

You can tell whether you have hard or soft water by the effect it has on soap. Soft water dissolves soap readily, producing a rich lather; hard water tends to produce a sticky, insoluble curd that matts woollens, produces poor lather from shampoo and leaves a dirty tide mark round baths and wash basins. Another obvious sign is the amount of scale in a kettle; if the kettle regularly 'furs up', there is a need to protect your plumbing system from the action of hard water scale.

Hardness is caused by dissolved bicarbonates, sulphates and chlorides of calcium and magnesium, which are present in the geological structure of much of Britain in the form of chalk and limestone. The natural water table dissolves these mineral salts in varying proportions, so the hardness varies from area to area depending on the source of supply. Water hardness can be expressed in various ways. The most common measurement is parts per million of carbonate hardness in water; for example water of 200ppm contains 200g of carbonate hardness per cubic metre of water. It is generally accepted that water containing between 100 and 200 ppm is 'medium hard' and above that it is 'hard' to 'very hard'.

Excluding the South West and a few small districts, the whole area south of a line drawn from the Wash to the Bristol Channel has hard water. Above this line, the East Midland counties and the North East are predominantly hard water areas.

How hard water affects plumbing
When water is heated to temperatures in the region of 71°C (160°F), the dissolved bicarbonates of calcium and magnesium are changed into in-soluble carbonates which are deposited as scale on immersion heaters and the internal surfaces of boilers, hot water cylinders and pipework.

Because scale is a poor conductor of heat, it insulates the water in the boiler from the heat source and, as scale accumulates, more fuel is needed to heat the same volume of water, pipes become blocked and circulation is impeded. Each time the water is heated more scale builds up, insulating the metal of the heater from the cooling effect of the water and leading to burnt out immer-sion heaters and leaking boilers.

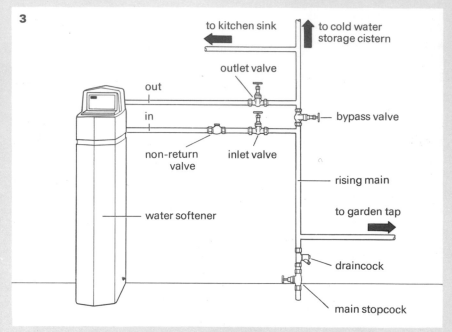

3

to kitchen sink

to cold water
storage cistern

outlet valve

out

in

bypass valve

non-return
valve

inlet valve

rising main

to garden tap

water softener

draincock

main stopcock

There are two ways of dealing with the problem. You can reduce or prevent the formation of scale by various means, without softening the water, or you can use a water softener.

Reducing scale
You can reduce the formation of scale by various mechanical means or by using a chemical scale inhibitor. Since scale forms at temperatures around 71°C (160°F), you can help prevent it by keeping the thermostat of your electric immersion heater set at 60°C (140°F). If you have a gas or oil-fired boiler, you should be able to keep the temperature of that at 60°C (140°F) too, but a solid fuel appliance may be less controllable. If you have a direct hot water system, you can convert it to an indirect system, which is less susceptible to scale on radiator circuits.

Chemical scale inhibitor Scale formation can be reduced or prevented in many cases, by introducing into the water supply minute quantities of a proprietary non-toxic chemical. It stabilizes the -

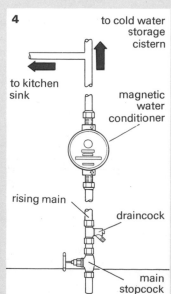

4

to cold water
storage
cistern

to kitchen
sink

magnetic
water
conditioner

rising main

draincock

main
stopcock

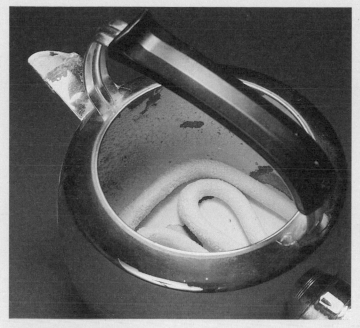

1 A container of scale inhibiting crystals suspended in the cold water storage cistern will stabilize bicarbonates in the water supply so they do not produce insoluble scale when the water is heated
2 Hot water supply appliances fed directly from the rising main, such as an instantaneous water heater, can be protected against scale formation by plumbing a special dispenser, containing crystals, into the rising main
3 An automatic water softener, again plumbed into the rising main, will give complete protection to the central heating and hot water systems
4 A magnetic water conditioner will prevent scale forming in the system as long as water is in motion.

Above You can easily check whether you have hard water by noting the scale formation in a kettle. If it 'furs up' regularly, your water is hard and you should protect the plumbing system
Above right Joints and bends in pipework are very susceptible to heavy scaling, if the scale is allowed to build up, it will impede circulation

bicarbonates in the water supply to prevent an insoluble scale when heated. But it does not soften the water and the effect on soap will be unchanged.

The chemical crystals come in an open-work plastic container which you suspend in the water of the cold water storage cistern. They dissolve very slowly in the water and are effective for six months, when the container should be refilled. There is a special grade of crystals for a combination tank since the water in the cold water feed tank becomes warm because of its proximity to the hot water storage cylinder.

Some scale inhibitors have a dual role. In naturally soft water areas the crystals can protect the system against corrosion caused by the acidic nature of the water. Other crystals can be used to protect hot water supply appliances fed directly from the rising main. In this case a special dispenser is plumbed into the supply pipe leading to the appliance. Fit it on the outlet side of the stopcock in the cold water pipe but as far away as possible from the hot water storage vessel. It can be fitted to a horizontal or vertical pipe. In both cases you need to leave clearance to allow for refilling with new crystals. If you fit a stopcock each side of the container, you will not need to turn off the water at the mains when you renew the crystals. Use the same type of metal for the connections between the stopcocks, scale reducer and storage vessel.

Magnetic water conditioner This conditioner, recently developed for domestic use, precipitates the hardness salts in the water into microscopic crystals by passing the incoming mains water supply through a magnetic field.

The self-powered permanent magnet prevents the normal conglomerates of interlinked crystals forming insoluble scale as long as the water is in motion. The magnetic unit does not affect water pressure and, as long as the individual hardness salts are held in suspension by water flowing, existing scale will dissolve.

The small compact magnetic unit is easily plumbed into the rising main as it enters the house. It can be mounted vertically or horizontally as long as it is easily accessible. Since there is an integral strainer which requires occasional cleaning, it is advisable to fit a stopcock on each side of the unit.

If continuous water flow is required while any servicing work is being carried out, a bypass with its own stopcock may be introduced round the unit.

Softening water
The installation of an automatic (mains) water softener will convert even the hardest water supply to total softness and give complete protection to the hot water and central heating systems.

A mains water softener operates on the principle of 'base exchange' or, as it is commonly called, 'ion exchange'. A container, plumbed into the rising main, holds a specially manufactured synthetic resin through which incoming hard water flows. The resin is not a chemical and no chemicals are used in the softening process. The resin absorbs the unwanted calcium and magnesium ions and releases sodium ions in their place.

After a period of use, the resin becomes saturated. When this happens the softener automatically washes, rinses and flushes the hardness salts from the resin with a salt solution, leaving the resin 'regenerated' so the softening process may continue. All you have to do is put fresh supplies of common salt in granular form into the appliance at frequent intervals to keep the salt topped up.

When buying a mains water softener, make sure you get the size suited to the needs of your household; the supplier will be able to advise you on this. It is possible to install a water softener yourself, but since installation may vary slightly from one model to another it is important to follow the manufacturer's instructions.

The total removal of the hardness salts from water means soap no longer produces sticky insoluble curds. This gives rise to other benefits not possible with the alternative methods of scale prevention. Not only will softened water slowly dissolve existing scale deposits, but it will also make savings on soaps, shampoos and similar items as well as prevent washing machines clogging and dishwashers breaking down.

Recent medical evidence does suggest that the risk of heart attacks is increased in soft water areas. For this reason, therefore, you would be advised not to soften the drinking water supplied through the kitchen-sink cold tap.

Softening water

Most people in Britain take the quality of their water for granted; but the water which comes out of the taps is often far from perfect. Depending on the location it is soft, moderately soft, slightly hard, moderately hard, hard or very hard – and it is these classifications which affect the home to a much greater extent than is often realized.

Types of water

Pure water does not exist in nature. The nearest approach to purity is rainwater, although even this picks up gases, dirt, soot and other impurities as it falls through the air. When it reaches the ground it collects even more impurities, depending on the type of soil and rock with which it comes in contact.

Surface water Scotland, parts of Northern England, Wales and the West Country have a high rainfall and a rocky terrain giving rise to surface water, which tends to pick up organic matter in the form of such things as decaying vegetation and animal matter. This water is relatively soft.

Ground water The rest of Britain, including parts of the North, East Anglia, most of the Midlands, the South and South East, has a sedimentary geological structure; so water drains down to a water table. This ground water dissolves calcium and magnesium, iron, silica and other mineral salts from the porous chalk and limestone through which it flows. This water, with its high dissolved mineral content, is relatively hard.

Hard and soft water

The classifications of water are part of a system of measurement from which you can tell to a greater or lesser extent the degree of calcium and magnesium carbonate hardness in water. This is expressed in parts per million of carbonate hardness or degrees of hardness, as indicated in the following table.

Classification	Degree	PPM
soft	0–3	0–50
moderately soft	3–7	50–100
slightly hard	7–11	100–150
moderately hard	11–14	150–200
hard	14–21	200–300
very hard	over 21	over 300

The effects of hard water can be quite dramatic and it is in the kitchen and bathroom that hard water can be seen to be most damaging – furring up kettles, scumming and discolouring baths and wash-basins, blocking shower roses, leaving stainless steel surfaces greasy and spotty, clogging washing machines and hindering the operation of dishwashers.

But plumbing is probably the greatest sufferer, since scale deposits accumulate on immersion heaters and other heat transfer surfaces; more fuel is therefore needed to heat the same quantity of water. Tests have shown 15 percent more fuel is used when scale is 1.5mm ($\frac{1}{16}$in) thick, 20 percent with 3mm ($\frac{1}{8}$in) scale, 39 percent with 6mm ($\frac{1}{4}$in) scale and 70 percent with 13mm ($\frac{1}{2}$in) scale. This is not only a waste of energy while the scale is forming, but also expensive when it comes to replacement, especially when a breakdown due to scale deposits

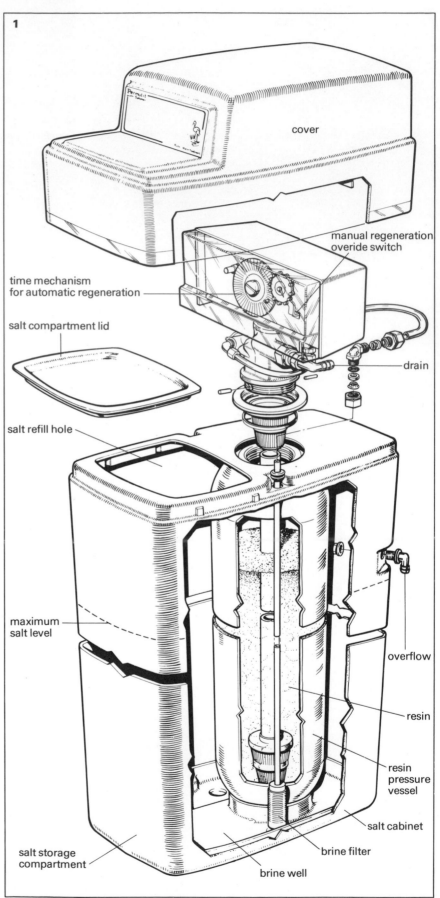

1

cover

manual regeneration overide switch

time mechanism for automatic regeneration

salt compartment lid

drain

salt refill hole

maximum salt level

overflow

resin

resin pressure vessel

salt cabinet

salt storage compartment

brine filter

brine well

can occur within four years in an area of 28 degrees (400ppm) hardness.

It is generally accepted hard water problems become most apparent in areas of over 16 degrees (229ppm) hardness. Most of the heavily populated areas of Southern England are affected; London, for example, has 20 degrees (286ppm) hardness. If you want to check on the hardness in your area, the local water authority will be able to give you the information.

Living in a soft water area is, therefore, of considerable advantage. There is none of the scaling of hot water pipes or tanks which can lead to water pressure problems or inefficient heating systems and soft water will mean lower housekeeping bills, especially those related to soap powder.

Corrosion Naturally soft water can be slightly acidic in some areas and this aggressive characteristic can set up a corrosive action in plumbing systems. The problem can be overcome by adding a proprietary non-toxic corrosion inhibitor to the water system, as described earlier. In any event, the advantages of living in a soft water area far outweigh any of the minor disadvantages. It should be noted hard water is rarely aggressive and water softening does not cause acidity to develop.

Scaling This can be cured in the same way as corrosion; scale inhibitors can be introduced into the water system, as explained earlier. But they

will not, of course, soften water. The installation of a water softening appliance will not only prevent all the problems of hard water already outlined, but will also slowly remove existing scale deposits.

Water softeners

The water softener has existed in various forms since the early 1900s, but it was not until quite recently that automatic machines became available. Modern automatic domestic softeners are designed to blend into most kitchen or bathroom settings and are manufactured in a range of sizes to meet the varying requirements of the house and family.

If installing a softener outside Britain, it will be necessary to check with the relevant local authority since different factors affect water in different parts of the world and the mineral content will vary.

As with most appliances, the bigger the unit the greater the capacity it has for producing softened water. The choice will, therefore, depend on the size of the home and family in relation to the hardness of the water; it is important you ask the manufacturer or your local supplier for advice on exactly the right model to suit your needs, bearing in mind the area in which you live.

It has been estimated the benefits and savings on household purchases related to a water softener can cover the initial cost of the appliance within five or six years.

1 Exploded view of a water softener, showing the relevant parts, including the resin vessel and salt compartment
2 A typical water softener installation adjoining the kitchen sink, showing the plumbing and wiring connections. Here a tap for unsoftened cold water has been fitted to the sink, although this is optional. If the stand pipe discharges directly into a gully, no 'P' trap is required. Only occasionally will you need to fit a pressure reducer

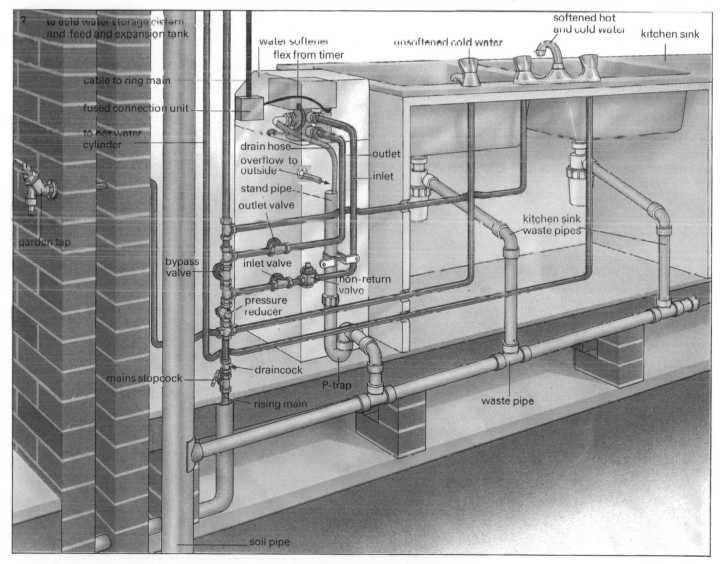

Installing a water softener

Since a water softener is plumbed into the rising main, the positioning of the appliance could be in one of any number of areas in the home. But bear in mind there must be access to an electrical power circuit and a suitable drain outlet. The plumbing in of the average appliance is no more complicated than for a washing machine and is a job which can be tackled by the competent DIY worker, provided the manufacturer's instructions are followed.

Before deciding on the siting of an appliance, remember if you prefer to drink hard water you must leave the kitchen cold tap supplied from the rising main below the water softener – or install a separate tap in this position. If you do keep the kitchen cold tap on hard water supply, you will not prevent the problem of fur in the kettle. Outside taps should remain on the hard water supply.

Plumbing in a softener

Once the water softener has been sited near the rising main and a suitable drain outlet, you will have to alter the existing pipework above the main stopcock. To make any servicing or moving of the appliance easier, you should fit a bypass. Two compression tees and a bypass valve are fitted into the rising main and an inlet and outlet valve suitably positioned in the new pipework so you can isolate the softener from the water supply.

Depending on local regulations, you may also have to fit a non-return/air brake valve assembly between the inlet valve and the appliance. In some areas subject to high water pressure it may be advisable to fit a pressure reducing valve between the main stopcock and the inlet valve to the water softener. This will not only safeguard the appliance, but will also prevent water pressure problems in dishwashers and washing machines.

Waste outlets A water softener has a waste outlet which can be run into any open gully or stack pipe. A standard 32mm (or 1¼in) plastic pipe system is adequate and the fitting arrangement is similar to that required for a washing machine. The hose normally supplied with the appliance for this purpose is cut to length and clipped onto the drain spigot before being inserted into the waste pipe. A second length of hose connected to the overflow spigot must be passed through an outside wall as a warning pipe.

Final connection After checking the new pipework is free from swarf and debris, make the final plumbing connections to the softener and fill it with granular salt to the recommended level.

Wiring up a softener

Most water softeners operate from a 220/240v supply and can be connected through a normal socket outlet. Most manufacturers, however, recommend the appliance is wired to a fused connection unit to prevent you accidentally switching it off. The supply should be fused at 3 amps.

The electrical supply is needed to operate the softener's time clock, on which the regeneration sequence is programmed. This sequence will vary depending on the size of the house and family and the hardness of the water. The programming of the softener is a fairly simple operation described in the manufacturer's instructions.

Operation cycle of a typical domestic water softener: **3a** Service. **3b** Backwash.
3c Brine. **3d** Slow rinse. **3e** Fast rinse.
3f Brine refill

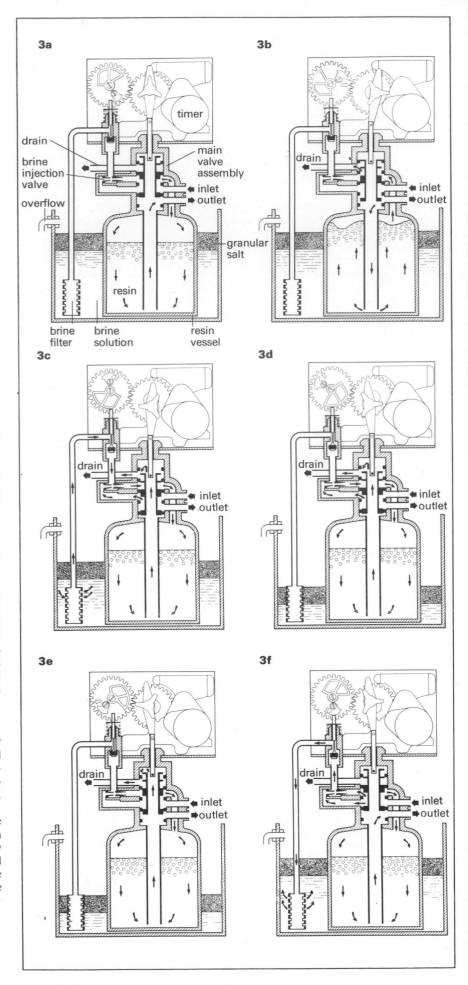

Frost and the hot water system

A well designed hot water cylinder storage system provides any home with its best insurance against the risk of frost damage. No matter how effectively a cylinder is lagged, some warmth will always be conducted along the pipework and rise up into the roof space, giving a measure of protection to the cold water storage cistern. This again emphasizes the importance of having the cold water storage cistern sited directly above the hot water cylinder – and not insulating the area immediately below the cistern.

A packaged plumbing system, in which the storage cistern and hot water cylinder are combined in one unit, gives virtually total protection to the cistern and the pipes in the immediate vicinity as long as the water in the cylinder is hot.

Boiler explosion

One of the great fears, particularly where water is heated by means of a boiler, is still that of a boiler explosion – and people often worry a great deal more about their hot water system during cold spells than they do about the cold water supply pipes. However, if you can understand the cause of boiler explosions and take simple and straightforward precautions to avoid them, you need never have a moment's anxiety over this happening.

A cylinder hot water system is, in effect, a large 'U' shape tube with the boiler at its base and the vent pipe and open storage cistern providing the two open ends. Provided the pipe run between the boiler and the vent pipe – or the boiler and the cold water storage cistern – is not obstructed, there can be no dangerous build-up of pressure. A spring-loaded safety valve, positioned on either the flow or return pipe in the immediate vicinity of the boiler, provides a final line of defence.

Boiler explosions usually take place when a house is reoccupied after having been empty during a prolonged spell of severe weather. The existence of the normal protective measure – lagging – will not add warmth to the plumbing system; all it can do is slow down the rate of heat loss. While the house is occupied, this is all that is needed; the fabric of the house is warm and water is constantly being drawn off and replaced. When the house is empty, however, the fabric chills off and water stagnates in the supply and distribution pipes. If a spell of cold weather intervenes, a severe freeze-up is inevitable. Plugs of ice will form in the upper part of the vent pipe and in the cold water supply pipe from the cistern to the cylinder. Ice may even form in the boiler itself and in the pipes between the boiler and the cylinder.

The real danger comes if, under these circumstances, the boiler fire is lit. Water in the boiler will heat up, but it will not be able to circulate or

1 The 'U' shape of a cylinder hot water system prevents a dangerous build-up of pressure, provided the pipe run between the boiler and the vent pipe, or between the boiler and the cold water storage cistern, is not obstructed.

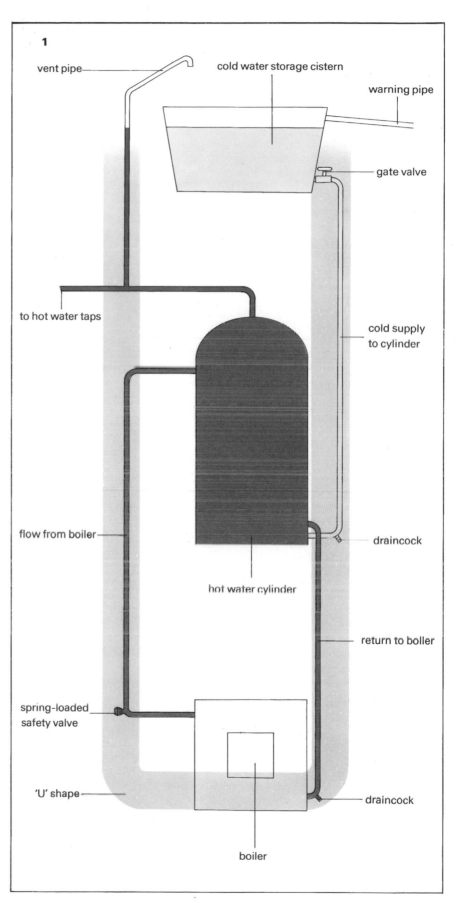

vent pipe
cold water storage cistern
warning pipe
gate valve
to hot water taps
cold supply to cylinder
flow from boiler
draincock
hot water cylinder
return to boiler
spring-loaded safety valve
'U' shape
draincock
boiler

2

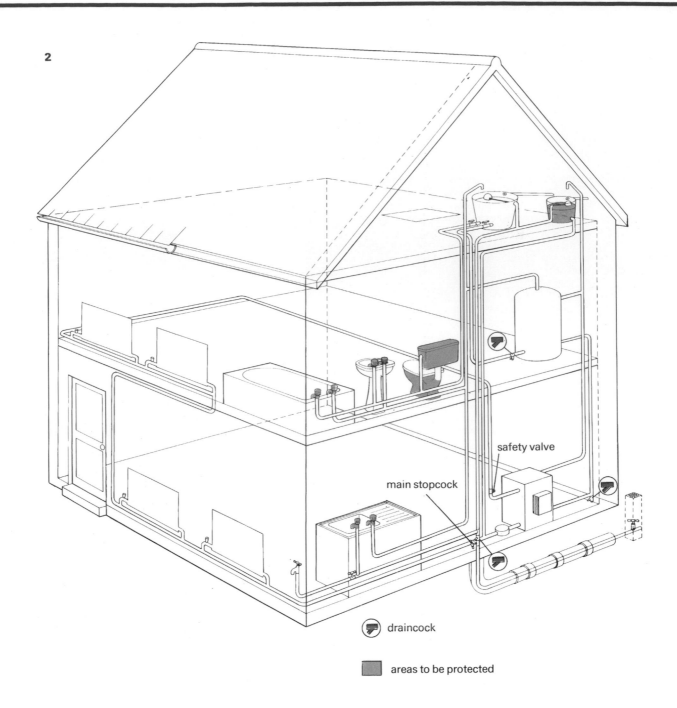

safety valve

main stopcock

draincock

areas to be protected

expand. Internal pressure will build up until, ultimately, something gives and releases it. In an instant the superheated water in the boiler will turn into steam, with many thousand times the volume of the water from which it was formed, and the boiler will explode like a bomb – with equally devastating results.

Cylinder implosion
Boiler explosions are, happily, an extremely rare occurrence. Cylinder implosion – or collapse – is rather more common in frosty weather; this is particularly likely to occur when the boiler is allowed to go out at night. Small plugs of ice form in the upper part of the vent pipe and in the upper part of the cold water supply pipe to the cylinder. The warm water in the cylinder and boiler cools and

contracts, producing a partial vacuum. Cylinders are not constructed to withstand external pressure and, when this occurs, the storage cylinder will collapse like a paper bag under the weight of atmospheric pressure.

The way to avoid either cylinder collapse or boiler explosion is to keep the boiler fire alight and the house warm during cold weather, although this may be difficult if you have to go away for any length of time.

Useful precautions
If you have a reliable automatic central heating system, the best precaution is to leave it turned on at a low setting or under the control of a 'frost-stat'. Keep internal doors open to allow warm air to circulate through the house and partially remove

2 Our standard house plumbing layout shows the points at which you should drain the hot and cold water systems if, during cold weather, the house is to be unoccupied for any length of time. Also shown are the points at which you can take steps to guard against frost damage: turn off the main stopcock; turn on all taps until water stops running; add anti-freeze to the feed and expansion tank; flush the WC to empty the cistern and add salt to the WC pan

the flap to the loft space to permit some warmth to penetrate to this area as well.

You may not be able to control your central heating system in this way; but both it and the primary circuit of your indirect hot water system can be protected by the addition of a proprietary anti-freeze solution. Don't, however, be tempted to use the same anti-freeze you put in your car radiator, since it is quite unsuitable for central heating systems. There is a corrosion inhibitor available which, when introduced into the system, will afford protection against up to $-1\frac{1}{2}$°C (29°F). Below that temperature any ice which forms will tend to be soft and mushy – and therefore unlikely to cause damage. Anti-freeze solutions, suitable for domestic central heating systems, are available which give protection against even more severe conditions.

The only other really safe precaution is to drain the domestic hot and cold water systems. Turn off the main stopcock (located where the mains water enters the house) and empty the system by opening the draincock immediately above it if there is one. Remember to attach a length of hose and run it to the sink or outside, otherwise you will flood the room. Open all the taps as well until water stops running. The hot water storage cylinder and – with a direct hot water system – the boiler will still be filled with water. With a direct system this can be drained by connecting one end of a length of hose to the draincock beside the boiler and taking the other end to the sink (if nearby) or outside. Open

the draincock and wait while the boiler empties. If you have an indirect hot water system – or a direct system heated only by an immersion heater – the appropriate draincock will be located by the cylinder, probably at the base of the cold water supply pipe which feeds it.

Warning Always remember to switch off the immersion heater before you drain the system.

There is one final precaution you can take: before you leave the house, flush the WC cistern to empty it – and throw a handful of salt into the pan. When you return home, remember the system is empty – and make sure you refill it before lighting the boiler fire. To reduce the risk of air locks forming as you do this, connect one end of a length of hose to the cold tap over the kitchen sink and the other end to the boiler draincock. Open up the tap and the draincock and the system will fill upwards, driving air before it.

3 A spring-loaded safety valve will give extra protection to your hot water system. If pressure builds up, the safety valve opens and relieves pressure in the pipes. Before fitting a safety valve, bind it with PTFE thread sealing tape
4 Wiring a frost-stat into an automatic central heating system. For a programmer with separate hot water and central heating settings, you will need a double pole frost-stat as shown in the diagram. The programmer selector should be set to 'Off' when the frost-stat is to be used

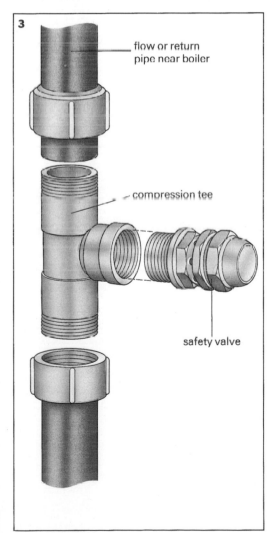

3

flow or return pipe near boiler

compression tee

safety valve

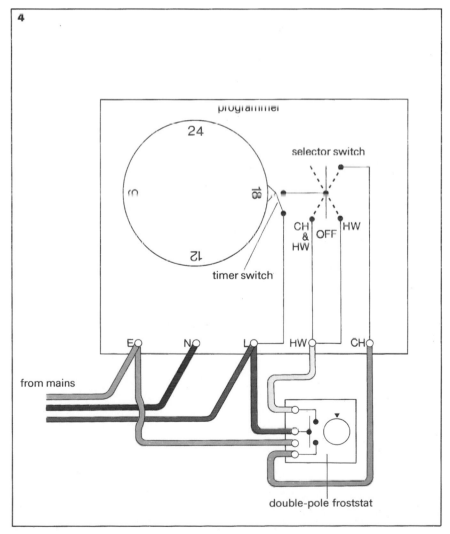

4

programmer

24

selector switch

18

CH & HW | OFF | HW

timer switch

E NO L HW CH

from mains

double-pole froststat

Cold weather protection

If the plumbing system in your home is not adequately protected, severe weather can cause water to freeze in the pipes, producing blockages and burst pipes. You can deal with these yourself, but it is better to prevent any damage by checking your anti-frost defences every autumn.

Protecting plumbing

Frost protection is built into the structure of a well-designed, modern home and the important design points are explained below.

Service pipe This pipe conveys water from the water authority's communication pipe to the house and should be covered by at least 750mm (or 30in) of earth throughout its length. If it enters the house by a hollow, boarded floor, it should be thoroughly protected from draughts. The pipe should be taken up into the roof space – to supply the cold water storage cistern – against an internal wall.

Storage cistern The cold water storage cistern is best situated against a flue which is in constant use.

To prevent icy draughts blowing up the warning pipe leading from the cistern, you can fit a hinged copper flap over the outlet; there is, however, a risk that this will jam in the open or closed position. A better method is to extend the pipe within the cistern and bend it over so its outlet is about 38mm (1½in) below the surface of the water. There are gadgets, such as the frostguard, which make it easy to extend internally the warning pipe from a storage or flushing cistern.

The boiler, hot water storage cylinder and cold water storage cistern are best installed in a vertical column so the vulnerable cold water cistern receives the benefit of the rising warm air.

All lengths of water pipe within the roof space should be kept short and well away from the eaves.

Lagging Efficient lagging of storage tanks and pipes reduces the rate at which water loses its warmth and protects pipes exposed to cold air; but it cannot make up for a bad plumbing design and it will not add heat to the system.

Pipes to lag are those against external walls, under the ground floor and in the roof space. Don't omit the vent pipe of the hot water system since the water in this pipe is not as hot as that in the rest of the system and, if it freezes, it can create a vacuum which could damage the cylinder.

There are several types of pipe lagging available and it is best to use inorganic materials. These include wrap-round glass fibre; moulded polystyrene (which comes in rigid sections which fit round the pipe) and flexible moulded foam plastic (which you split open to fit round the pipe). Polystyrene is rather awkward to use, but is good for underground pipes since it does not absorb water. The moulded types of lagging come in a variety of sizes to fit different pipes, so make sure you buy the appropriate size.

Whichever type you use, make sure you lag behind pipes against external walls to protect them from the cold wall. Cover the tails of ball valves and all but the handles of stopcocks and gate valves; if you are using rigid lagging sections, you will need some of the wrap-round type for these areas.

Bind wrap-round insulation round the pipe like a bandage, overlapping it to prevent gaps, and secure it with string or adhesive tape. Where a pipe joins a cistern, make a full turn and tie it to hold the end in place. When joining two lengths overlap them and tie securely.

Secure moulded sections with plastic adhesive tape, starting at the cistern. Where the sections join along a length of pipe, seal the joint with tape. Open up flexible moulding along one side, slip it round the pipe and seal the opening with adhesive tape, taking particular care at any elbows. If you lag the pipes before fitting them, there is of course no need to slit the lagging; you can slide the pipe length through it. Where pipes go through a wall, make sure the insulation goes right up to the wall.

You also need to protect the cold water cistern. The easiest way to cover a square cistern is to use expanded polystyrene slabs. For a circular cistern use glass fibre tank wrap. If you have insulating material between the floor joists in the loft, make sure the area immediately below the tank is left uncovered so warm air is allowed to reach the tank.

Dealing with frozen pipes

If, in spite of your precautions, a freeze-up does occur, it is essential to deal with it immediately. If there is any delay the plug of ice will spread along the pipe and increase the risk of damage.

You can gauge the position of the freeze-up from the situation of the plumbing fittings which have stopped working. If, for instance, water is not flowing into the main cold water storage cistern but is running from the cold tap over the kitchen sink, the plug of ice must be in the rising main between the branch to the kitchen sink and the cistern.

Strip off the lagging from the affected pipe and apply heat – either with cloths soaked in hot water and wrung dry or a filled hot water bottle. If a pipe is inaccessible, direct a jet of warm air towards it from a hair dryer or the outlet of a vacuum cleaner. Fortunately modern copper tubing conducts very well and a small plug of ice can often be melted by applying heat to the pipe about a metre from the actual location of the ice.

Burst pipe If the freeze-up results in a burst pipe the first indication will probably be water dripping through a ceiling, since pipes in the loft are most likely to burst; wherever the leak, immediate action is vital. Turn off the main stopcock and open up every tap in the house. This will drain the cistern and pipes and reduce the damage. When the system is completely drained, find the position of the leak.

Damaged copper piping If you have copper piping, you will probably find a compression or soldered capillary joint will have been forced open by the expansion of ice. All you need to do in this case is fit a new joint. Copper piping does sometimes split under pressure. If that happens, you will have to cut out the defective length and insert a new length. An easy way of doing this is to insert a repair coupling.

Cut out the damaged section of pipe with a fine tooth hacksaw, leaving a gap of not more than 89mm (3½in) between the pipe ends. Remove the burr from the tube ends with a small file. One end of the coupling has a tube stop, the other is free to

Right Efficient lagging will protect pipes against freezing conditions

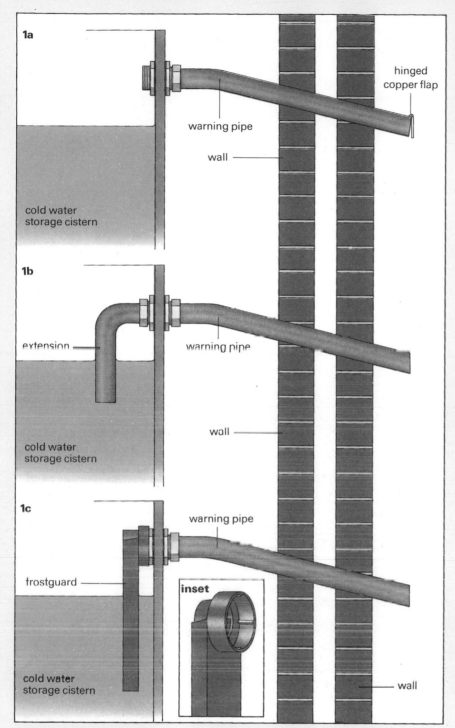

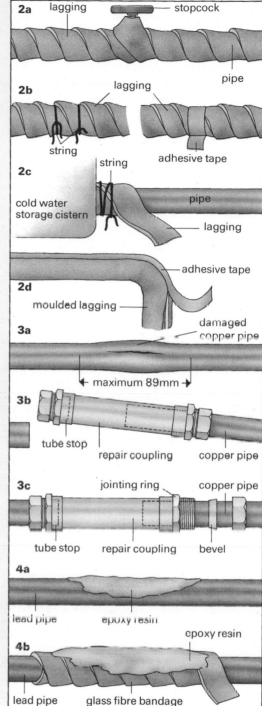

1a-c Ways of protecting cold water cistern from severe external conditions. 2a Lagging pipe but leaving handle of stopcock clear; 2b Secure lagging with tape or string; 2c Where pipe meets cistern, make full turn and bind lagging firmly; 2d Cut moulded lagging along one side, place round pipe and seal join with tape. 3a-c Removing damaged section of copper pipe and fitting repair coupling. 4a-b Making temporary repair to lead pipe with epoxy resin and bandage

slide along the pipe. Slacken the nuts of the coupling, spring one end of the pipe out just enough to allow you to slide the repair coupling over it. Line it up with the other pipe end and push the coupling on to it until the tube stop is reached. Unscrew the nuts and slide them and the copper jointing rings along the pipe. Apply jointing compound or gloss paint into the bevels of the fitting and around the leading edge of the jointing rings. Tighten the nuts with a spanner so the tube is lightly gripped; make another turn, or a turn and a quarter, making sure you do not overtighten.

Burst lead pipe The orthodox and approved method of repairing a burst lead pipe is to cut out the affected length and replace it with a new length of pipe; this job is best left to an expert.

You can, however, make a temporary repair with

one of the epoxy resin repair kits available. Dry the affected length of pipe thoroughly and knock the edges of the split together with a hammer. Rub down with abrasive paper. Make up the resin filler according to the manufacturer's instructions and apply it round the pipe to cover the split and the surrounding area. While the filler is still plastic, bind round it with a glass fibre bandage and 'butter' a further layer of resin filler over the bandage. When thoroughly set, rub down with abrasive paper to make an unobtrusive joint. You will be able to use the pipe again within a few hours.

Repairs and maintenance

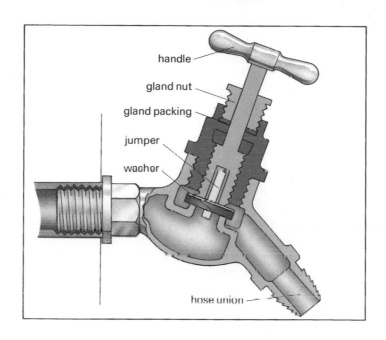

handle

gland nut

gland packing

jumper

washer

hose union

The WC suite

Whichever type of WC you are dealing with, you can carry out installation and repair work yourself. As well as ensuring efficient operation, you may have to mend leaking joints or replace damaged pans.

WC suites can be designated by the basic kinds of flushing action into two main types: wash-down and syphonic. The former, where the bowl is cleansed after use by the weight and momentum of a 9 litre (2gal) flush delivered from a high or low level, is more commonly in use in British homes. Where efficient, discreet and silent operation is more important than initial cost, it is likely a siphonic WC suite will have been installed. This depends upon siphonic action where falling water creates a partial vacuum so atmospheric pressure pushes more water through the system. This gives a larger water area and permits the use of a close coupled suite in which the flush pipe is not visible and where the flushing cistern and pan are combined in one unit.

Wash-down When this type of suite is working correctly, flushing water should flow with equal force round each side of the pan with the two streams meeting at the front; there should be no whirlpool effect as the pan empties. If flushing fails to cleanse the pan effectively, there are a number of faults you should look out for. Check the cistern is filling to its full capacity, a point about 13mm ($\frac{1}{2}$in) below the level of the overflow pipe usually indicated by a mark on the inside wall of the cistern. Also, for a low level cistern, see if the diameter and length of the flush pipe are those recommended by the manufacturer and if it connects squarely to the flushing inlet of the WC pan.

Another case of ineffective flushing is blockage of the flushing inlet and the flushing rim of the pan by jointing material, hard water scale, flaking, rust or other debris. Also check with a spirit level to make sure the pan is set dead level and see if the outlet of the pan connects squarely to the socket of the branch drain or soil pipe. If not, you will have to remove the pan and reposition it (see below).

Siphonic There are two types of siphonic suite:

single trap and double trap, the former being the simplest. It has an outlet which is at first restricted and then enlarged. When flushed the overflow from the pan fills the restricted section of the outlet completely and, passing on to the wider section, carries air with it to produce the partial vacuum on which siphonic action depends.

Double trap siphonic suites have a pressure-reducing device connecting the space between the two traps with a channel through which flushing water passes. The flow of water over this device draws air from the space between the two traps to produce an instant partial vacuum. When the system is working properly you can see the water level in the pan fall before the flushing water reaches the pan. If it is not working properly, the most likely cause is blockage of the pressure-reducing device by scale or other debris and you will have to remove the cistern to get access to the pressure-reducing device and clear the obstruction.

Warning Remember to tie up the ball valve arm and empty the cistern before starting any work.

Pipe joint problems

It is now common practice to use a flexible joint to connect both upstairs and downstairs WCs to the branch drain or soil pipe. The joint may be made with a plastic push-on drain connector or by filling the space between the pan outlet and the soil or drain-pipe socket with a non-setting mastic filler. In older systems downstairs WC pans are connected to the branch drain with a joint made either of cement or two parts cement to one part sand. If this kind of joint were used for the outlet of a WC in a compartment with a timber floor, it would tend to crack and fail due to the movement of the floor-boards; upstairs WCs are therefore connected with a putty joint to the socket of the branch soil pipe. The putty may harden and crack over time, result-

1a Low level wash-down WC suite
1b If the flush pipe or flushing rim becomes blocked, the WC will not operate efficiently
1c Use a spirit level to check the pan is level
2a Single trap close-coupled siphonic WC suite
2b Double trap close-coupled siphonic WC suite
3a Standard push-on drain connector
3b Offset connector where the top pipe is set slightly to one side of the lower pipe
3c Conversion bend; the top pipe is at an angle of about 100 degrees to the lower one
4a You can bring a pan forward by using an extension piece between the conversion bend and the flexible connector
4b Where there is a shortage of space, fit a modern, slimline cistern

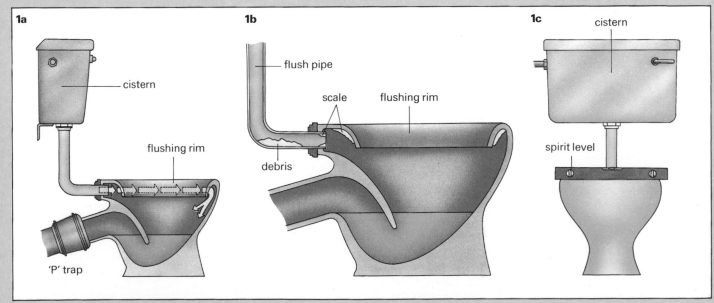

1a cistern / flushing rim / 'P' trap
1b flush pipe / scale / flushing rim / debris
1c cistern / spirit level

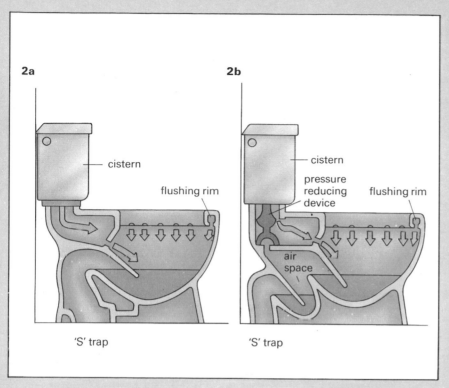

2a

cistern

flushing rim

'S' trap

2b

cistern

pressure reducing device

flushing rim

air space

'S' trap

ing in a leak between the pan outlet and the soil pipe socket; you should deal with this as soon as you notice it.

Generally it is possible to stop the leak without removing the pan. Rake out the existing jointing material and bind waterproof building tape two or three times round the pan outlet, caulking it down hard into the soil pipe socket. Fill the space between the outlet and the socket with a non-setting mastic filler – making sure there are no unfilled areas – and bind waterproof tape twice around the joint. Alternatively you can disconnect the flush pipe, unscrew the pan from the floor, pull it forward and, after raking out the jointing material, replace the existing joint with a push-on drain connector.

Conversions and improvements

You may have to repair your WC system or modernize it for more efficient operation. In doing so you may run into difficulties, but these can be overcome if you take the right action.

Changing level The pan of a low level suite should be 50–75mm (2–3in) further from the wall behind it than the pan of a high level one. If you are converting a high level suite to low level operation, you may find you have fitted the new cistern with its short flush pipe in such a way that the projection of

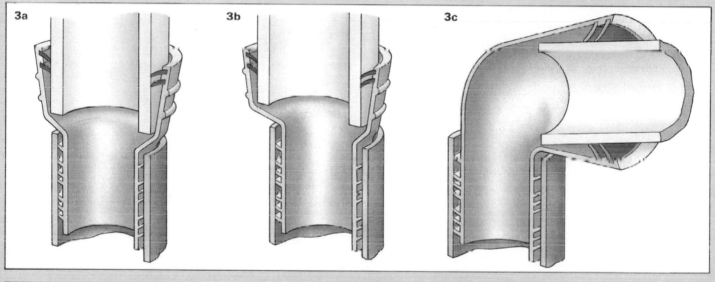

3a

3b

3c

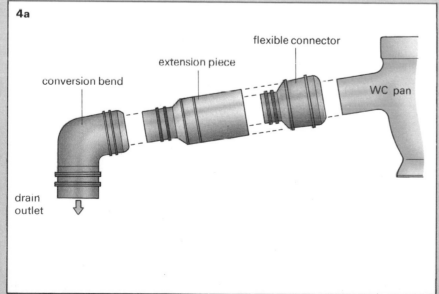

4a

conversion bend

extension piece

flexible connector

WC pan

drain outlet

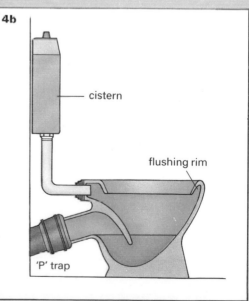

4b

cistern

flushing rim

'P' trap

the cistern makes it impossible to raise the WC seat. To correct this you can bring the pan forward about 50mm (or 2in) using elongated connectors to join it to the drain. This may cause space problems in small bathrooms or WC compartments; as an alternative and simpler solution you can fit a modern slimline flushing cistern or flush panel instead of a conventional low level cistern.

Removing and replacing pans If your toilet pan is cracked or has a crazed surface, you will have to replace it since there is no safe or effective way of renovating it; you should carry this out as soon as the problem becomes apparent. Removing a WC pan in order to replace it where there is a mastic or putty-jointed outlet can be a simple task: undo and remove the fixing screws, disconnect the flush pipe and pull the pan forward. In older systems, however, downstairs WC pans are set into a bed of cement and sand and, if this has been done with yours, you will need a cold chisel and club hammer to prise the pan from the floor.

When you are removing a pan with a cement-jointed outlet, you will have to disconnect the flush pipe, unscrew and remove the fixing screws and break the pan outlet just behind the trap. Pull the pan forward, leaving the jagged remains of the pan outlet protruding from the drain socket. Stuff a wad of newspaper into the drain to prevent pieces of outlet and cement falling in and causing a blockage. Carefully break away the remains of the pan outlet with a cold chisel and hammer, keeping the blade of the chisel pointing towards the centre of the pipe. Aim to break the outlet down to the shoulder of the socket at one point and the rest of the outlet should come out fairly easily. Remove the jointing material in the same way. Try not to damage the drain socket; if you accidentally do so, you can use push-on drain connectors directly into the drain. Carefully remove the wad of newspaper with the cement and pieces of stoneware it has trapped, so none of the debris falls into the drain.

Before installing a new pan, remove all cement from the floor to give a level surface. Don't set the new pan in a bed of cement; fix it down with brass screws, drilling and plugging the floor beforehand if necessary. You should slip lead washers over the screws before inserting them to avoid damaging the ceramic surface of the pan and should use a mastic joint or push-on connector to join the outlet of the new pan to the branch drain or soil pipe. If you find the pan is not set level, unscrew it slightly, lift it up and place pieces of scrap wood or linoleum underneath it.

Warning If you have to leave the pan unconnected for any length of time, cover the drain socket with a board held in place by a heavy weight to prevent rats from the sewer entering the home.

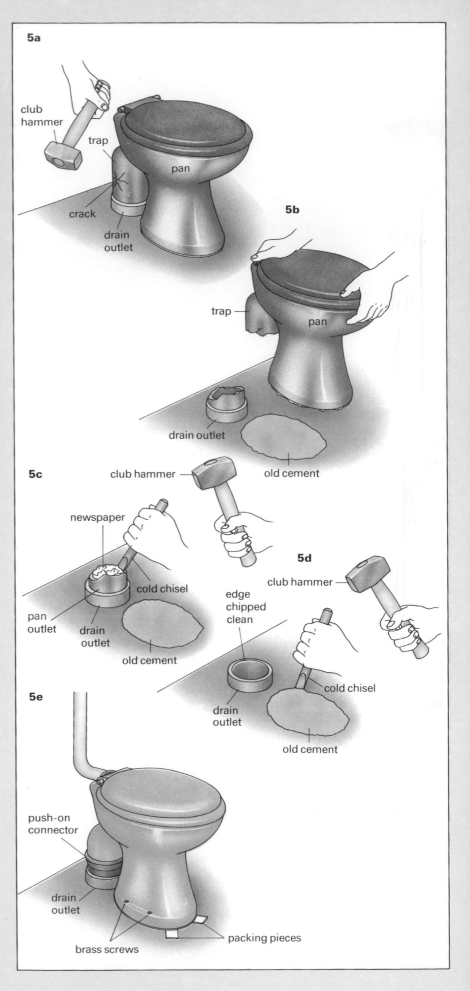

5a To remove a pan with a cement-jointed outlet, break the outlet just below the trap. **5b** Lift the pan clear. **5c** Chip away the edges of the outlet. **5d** Remove the old bedding cement. **5e** If necessary, use packing beneath the new pan

A basic item of plumbing equipment, the tap is constantly used by all the family and must periodically be serviced or adjusted. So the sooner you learn to do this for yourself the better. One of the commonest faults is washer failure, identified by a dripping tap.

Repairing taps and washers

The types of tap most common in the home
Right Shrouded-head tap
Far right Supatap
Below right Bib tap
Below Washer failure is causing this pillar tap to leak and drip water – a fault that can be easily put right

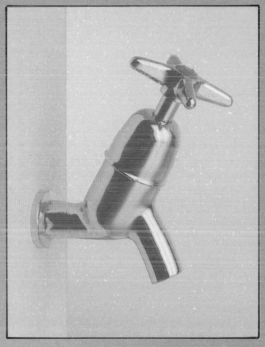

Plastic taps

Although all the taps included here are made of metal, plastic types are now available. These have some important advantages over metal ones. They remain cold to the touch even when controlling very hot water. They also have a non-rising spindle and an 'O' ring seal, which can be replaced if it wears. If you are connecting this type of tap to copper pipe, take care not to overtighten the female brass connection coupling or you may damage the plastic fitting.

Pillar taps

To rewasher the conventional pillar tap (see 1), you must cut off the water supply to the tap. If the fault is in the cold water tap over the kitchen sink (which should be supplied direct from the mains) you will need to turn off the main stopcock. Other taps may have a stopcock or gate valve on the distribution pipe serving them; if so, turn off this valve. If there is no such valve, tie up the arm of the ball valve serving the main cold water storage cistern and open all bathroom taps and the kitchen hot tap to drain the cistern and distribution pipes.

Unscrew the protective cover of the tap (see 2a). You should be able to do this by hand, but if not you can use a pipe wrench (see below), although you must pad the jaws to avoid damaging the chromium plating on the tap.

Insert an adjustable spanner (see below) under the base of the cover (see 2b), unscrew the headgear nut and remove the headgear. The jumper (or valve) of the cold water tap over the kitchen sink will usually be resting on the valve seating in the body of the tap (see 2c). Remove it, unscrew the small retaining nut (see 2d) and replace the washer. If the nut proves difficult to unscrew you can replace the jumper and washer complete.

Some taps may have the jumper pegged into the headgear. Although it will turn, it may not be easy to remove. You may have to unscrew the retaining nut with the help of a little penetrating oil. If the retaining nut will not move, insert the blade of a screwdriver between the plate of the jumper and the base of the headgear and break the pegging. Replace the jumper and washer complete, but burr the stem of the jumper with a coarse file to ensure a tight fit. Reassemble the tap and turn on water.

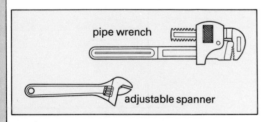

pipe wrench

adjustable spanner

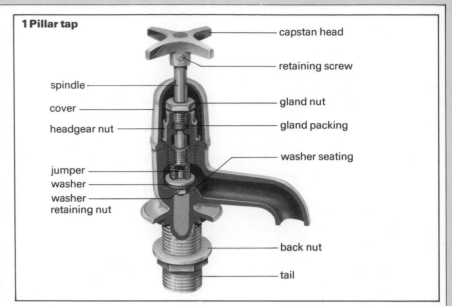

1 Pillar tap

capstan head
retaining screw
spindle
cover
gland nut
headgear nut
gland packing
washer seating
jumper
washer
washer retaining nut
back nut
tail

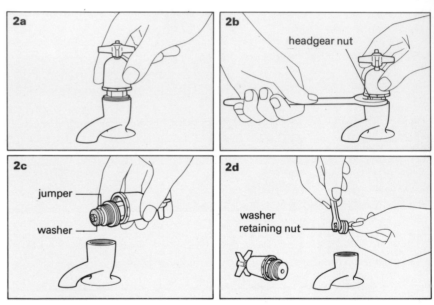

2a

2b
headgear nut

2c
jumper
washer

2d
washer retaining nut

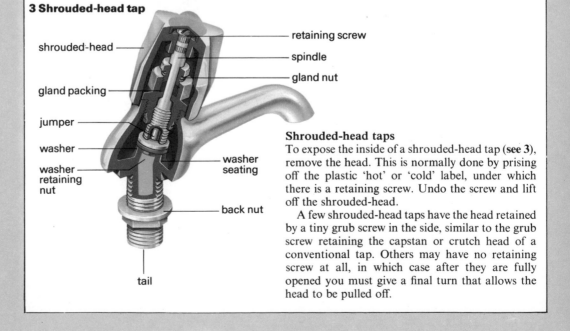

3 Shrouded-head tap

shrouded-head
retaining screw
spindle
gland nut
gland packing
jumper
washer
washer retaining nut
washer seating
back nut
tail

Shrouded-head taps

To expose the inside of a shrouded-head tap (see 3), remove the head. This is normally done by prising off the plastic 'hot' or 'cold' label, under which there is a retaining screw. Undo the screw and lift off the shrouded-head.

A few shrouded-head taps have the head retained by a tiny grub screw in the side, similar to the grub screw retaining the capstan or crutch head of a conventional tap. Others may have no retaining screw at all, in which case after they are fully opened you must give a final turn that allows the head to be pulled off.

Supataps

Rewashering a Supatap is a quick job that avoids cutting off the water supply. Open the tap slightly and with a spanner unscrew and release the retaining nut at the top of the nozzle (see **4a**). Start turning the tap; there will be an increasing flow of water, but this will cease as the check valve falls into position. The nozzle will then come off in your hand (see **4b**).

Tap the nozzle on a hard surface (not one that will chip) to loosen the anti-splash device in which the washer and jumper are fixed. Turn the nozzle upside down and the anti-splash will drop out. (see **4c**). Remove the washer and jumper by inserting a blade between the plate and the anti-splash (see **4d**) and insert a new set. Replace the anti-splash in the nozzle (see **4e**) and reassemble the tap, remembering the nozzle screws back on with a left-hand thread (see **4f**).

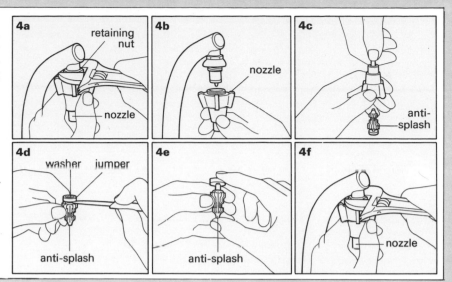

4a retaining nut

4b nozzle

4c anti-splash

4d washer jumper anti-splash

4e anti-splash

4f nozzle

Continued dripping

Occasionally a tap will continue to drip even after being fitted with a new washer. This indicates the valve seating has been scratched and scored by grit in the water supply and no longer gives a watertight connection.

There are reseating tools available, but the simplest way to deal with this problem when it affects a conventional tap is to use a new nylon washer and seating kit (see **5**). The nylon seating is placed squarely on the brass seating of the tap. Put the new washer and jumper in the headgear of the tap and screw them down hard into the tap body, forcing the nylon valve seating into position. This method cannot be used on Supataps, but the manufacturers of these taps make and supply a reseating tool for the purpose.

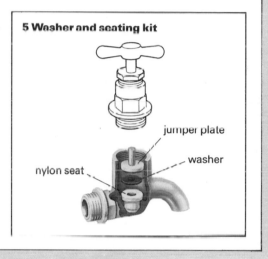

5 Washer and seating kit

jumper plate

washer

nylon seat

6 Removing tap head

retaining screw

wood blocks

7 Shrouded-head tap with 'O' ring

retaining screw
shrouded-head
'O' ring seal
head nut
'O' ring seal
washer stem
washer

tail

back nut

Gland failure

Another common fault in taps, gland failure, is indicated by water escaping up the spindle when the tap is turned on. The tap can also be turned on and off very easily, with just a spin of the fingers, which often causes water hammer (the effect of shock waves in the pipes produced by the sudden cessation of flowing water). Causes of gland failure may be back pressure resulting from the connection of a hose or detergent-charged water running down the spindle and washing grease from the gland packing.

To adjust or renew the gland of a conventional tap, remove the capstan or crutch head by unscrew-ing and removing the tiny retaining grub screw. If taking off the head proves difficult, open up the tap and unscrew and raise the protective cover as high as possible. Insert two pieces of wood (at back and front) between the base of the raised cover and the body of the tap. Then close the tap down again and the upward pressure of the cover will force off the head or handle (see **6**).

The gland-adjusting nut is the first nut through which the spindle of the tap passes. To tighten, turn in a clockwise direction. Eventually all the allowance for adjustment will be taken up and the gland packing will have to be renewed. To do this, unscrew and remove the gland packing nut. Existing gland packing material can be removed with the point of a penknife. Repack with strands of wool steeped in vaseline, press down hard and reassemble the tap.

Some modern taps have a rubber 'O' ring seal instead of a conventional gland (see **7**). These are less likely to give trouble, but if they do simply renew the ring.

Fitting new taps

Before you renew a tap the existing one has to be taken out and this can be the most difficult part of the job. The back nut, which secures the tap underneath, is likely to be inaccessible and may well be firmly fixed by scale and corrosion.

Cut off the water supply to the tap and then unscrew the 'cap and lining' nut that connects the tail of the tap to the water supply pipe. With a basin or sink it may be necessary to disconnect the waste pipe, take the appliance off its mounting and turn it upside down on the floor in order to get a better purchase on the back nut. A cranked 'basin spanner' will help do this.

Removal of old bath taps can be particularly difficult because of the cramped and badly lit space in which you will have to work. It may prove better to disconnect the water supply and waste pipes and pull the bath forward to give yourself more room to work.

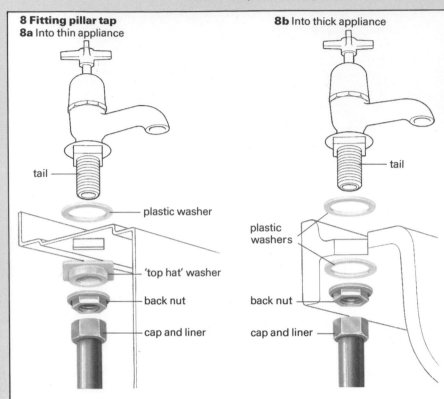

8 Fitting pillar tap
8a Into thin appliance

8b Into thick appliance

tail

tail

plastic washer

'top hat' washer

back nut

cap and liner

plastic washers

back nut

cap and liner

Pillar taps When fitting new pillar taps slip a plastic washer over the tail of the tap and insert the tail into the hole provided for it in the top of the appliance. Slip another plastic washer over the tail as it protrudes through the appliance and follow it with the retaining back nut. Where the tap is being fitted into an appliance of thin material, such as a stainless steel sink or an enamelled steel fitted basin, a 'top hat' or spacer washer must be used under the appliance to take the protruding shank of the tap (**see 8a**).

With an appliance of thick material, such as a ceramic wash-basin, a flat plastic washer can be used (**see 8b**). When fitting a tap into a basin of this kind do not overtighten the back nut, since the ceramic is very easily damaged by rough handling.

Pillar taps are connected to their water supply pipes by means of a 'tap connector' or 'cap and lining' joint. This incorporates a fibre washer that ensures a watertight connection.

equipment

pipe wrench
adjustable spanner
cranked basin spanner
screwdriver, penknife
coarse file
penetrating oil
wool, vaseline
PTFE plastic thread
    sealing tape
jumper, washer and
    seating parts (as
    needed)

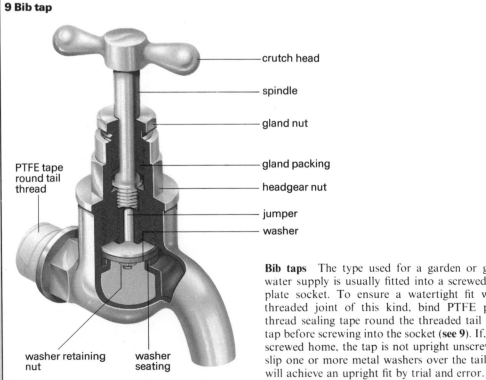

9 Bib tap

crutch head

spindle

gland nut

gland packing

headgear nut

jumper

washer

PTFE tape round tail thread

washer retaining nut

washer seating

Bib taps The type used for a garden or garage water supply is usually fitted into a screwed wall-plate socket. To ensure a watertight fit with a threaded joint of this kind, bind PTFE plastic thread sealing tape round the threaded tail of the tap before screwing into the socket (**see 9**). If, when screwed home, the tap is not upright unscrew and slip one or more metal washers over the tail. You will achieve an upright fit by trial and error.

Stopcocks and gate valves

Stopcocks and gate valves enable you to control and stop the flow of water through the pipes in your house. You should know where they go in your water supply system if you intend to carry out plumbing repairs and which ones to turn off in the event of an emergency.

Stopcocks
Every household water supply system has one stopcock provided by the water authority. This is installed in a pit with a hinged metal lid, usually under the pavement outside the house, but sometimes just within the boundary of the property.

Types of stopcock and gate valve found in domestic water supply systems
Left Water authority stopcock. This may have a specially shaped shank that can be turned only with the authority's key
Below Mini stopcock or regulating valve
Bottom left Screw-down stopcock
Bottom right Gate valve

Modern houses also have one or more screw-down stopcocks inside. These are manufactured with a variety of inlets and outlets so they can be fitted to plastic, copper, iron or lead pipe. The main internal stopcock is located just above the point at which the rising main enters the house, often under the kitchen sink. It is set into the rising main and usually has a crutch or capstan head like an ordinary tap. The stopcock is normally kept fully open; to close it to stop the flow of water, you turn the handle or head in a clockwise direction – this pushes a washered valve or jumper firmly onto the valve seating.

Renewing washers Since stopcocks are rarely turned off, their washers have a long working life and only occasionally have to be renewed. When this is necessary, turn off the water supply to the stopcock (you may have to get the help of the water authority to arrange this) and unscrew and remove the headgear to gain access to the jumper and washer. Unscrew the small retaining nut, pull off the old washer and fit a new one. If you have trouble unscrewing the retaining nut, fit a new jumper and washer set; these are available from DIY shops.

Gland packing failure A more common fault in screw-down stopcocks, this is indicated by water dripping from the stopcock spindle. It should be dealt with immediately since constant dripping of water onto a timber floor in the usually confined and ill-ventilated position in which a stopcock is situated can result in dry rot. To prevent the drip you may find it sufficient to tighten the first nut through which the stopcock spindle passes; this is known as the gland adjusting nut. If this does not work, you must repack the gland. You need not cut off the water supply to the stopcock to do this; simply turn the stopcock off. Unscrew and remove the small grub screw which retains the head or handle and pull the handle off. Then unscrew and remove the gland adjusting nut to gain access to the gland. Using the point of a penknife, pick out all existing gland packing material and replace it with wool soaked in petroleum jelly. Pack this down tightly and reassemble the stopcock.

Jammed stopcocks The most common fault in stopcocks is jamming through disuse. If you cannot move the handle, apply penetrating oil to the spindle; usually after about a week of applying oil and trying to turn the handle, the stopcock will operate normally. It is, of course, best to prevent jamming by opening and closing the stopcock a few times at least twice a year.

Fitting new stopcocks Make sure the new stopcock is the same size as the pipe into which it is to be fitted. If, for example, you fit a 15mm (or ½in) stopcock into a 22mm (or ¾in) pipe you are effectively reducing the diameter of the pipe to 15mm (or ½in). Also check the stopcock is fitted the right way round: screw-down stopcocks have an arrow engraved in the body which must point in the direction of the flow of water. If the stopcock is fitted the wrong way round, water pressure will force the jumper onto the valve seating and prevent water flowing even when the stopcock is fully open.

Mini stopcocks
These are fitted at the point where a water supply pipe connects with a ball valve or the tail of a tap. They are opened and closed with a screwdriver and enable you to renew tap or ball valve washers or replace taps and ball valves without affecting the rest of the plumbing.

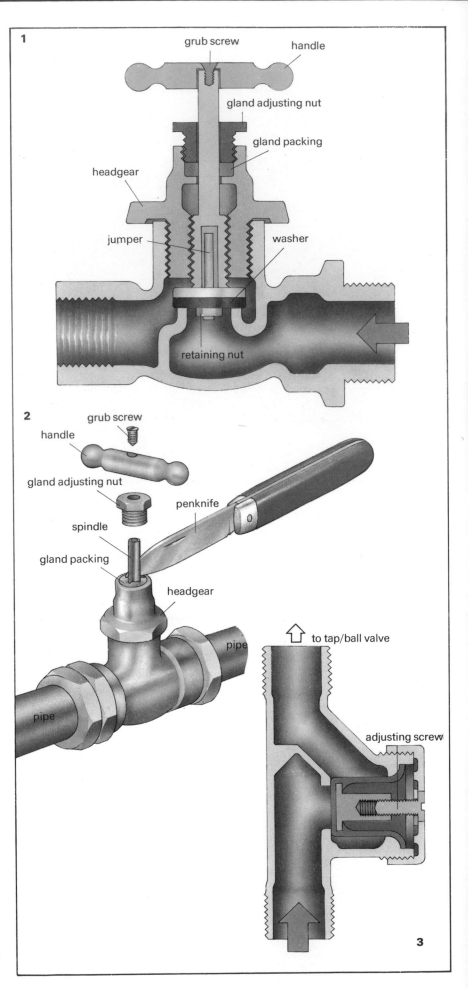

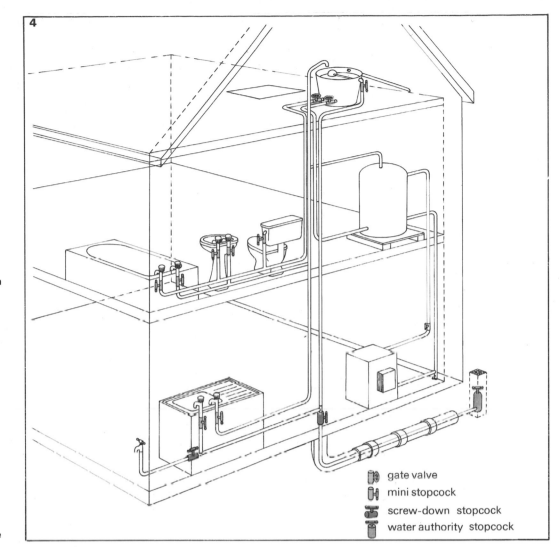

1 Features of a screw-down stopcock; the water flows from right to left
2 If water drips from the spindle of a screw-down stopcock, remove the gland packing and replace it with wool soaked in petroleum jelly
3 Features of a Markfram regulating valve (or mini stopcock); the water flows up through the valve
4 Refer to our standard house layout to locate the stopcocks and gate valves in your own home
5 Features of a gate valve; the water is cut off by screwing down a metal gate

gate valve
mini stopcock
screw-down stopcock
water authority stopcock

Gate valves

Gate valves are used where water pressure is low and where it is important there is an unrestricted flow of water. They are normally fitted into the supply pipe from the storage cistern to the bathroom cold water taps and are often placed immediately below the storage cistern; this allows part of the plumbing system to be isolated for repair or maintenance without affecting the rest of the system.

A gate valve has a larger body than a screw-down stopcock and usually a wheel, rather than a crutch or capstan, head. When you close the valve a metal plate, or gate, screws down to block the pipe; when the valve is open the plate is withdrawn to allow water to flow freely. Because this type of valve has a metal-to-metal seal it does not give as complete a cut-off of water as a screw-down stopcock, although this is not important in the situations in which gate valves are used. You can fit them either way round but, like stopcocks, they must be the same size as the pipe into which they are fitted.

Warning In normal use gate valves must be kept fully open. A partially closed valve on the supply pipe from the cold water cistern to the hot water cylinder is a common cause of recurring airlocks.

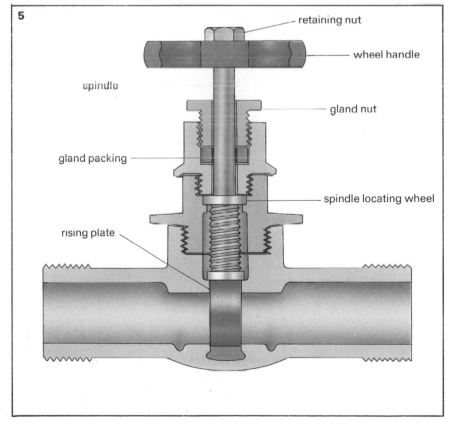

retaining nut
wheel handle
spindle
gland nut
gland packing
spindle locating wheel
rising plate

Taps, mixers and draincocks

Taps, which provide the practical outlet for your water system throughout the home, come in a variety of shapes and mechanisms – and include mixers, which enable you to control the temperature of water whether in a basin, bath or sink. One type of tap often overlooked is the draincock, which serves a more functional purpose in plumbing repair work.

Taps

The four most common types of tap are the pillar, bib, shrouded-head and Supatap, all of which we referred to on pages 59, 60, 61 and 62 in the section dealing with repairing leaks.

Pillar tap This vertical inlet tap is generally used

One difference in this type of tap is the method of connecting hoses – for example when filling a washing machine. Because the nozzle turns as the tap is operated, a special connector is necessary. It is secured in position by means of clips fitted over the ears of the tap; the body of the connector turns with the tap, while the swivel outlet designed for a hose connection remains stationary.

Mixers

These are simply two taps with a common spout and are often fitted to basins, baths or sinks, enabling you to use exactly the temperature of water you want.

Bath mixers These are now often supplied with a

1 Bib tap with hose union outlet
2 Supatap and hose connector
3 Section through basin mixer with pop-up waste
4 Sink mixer
5 Section through bath/shower mixer
6 Draincocks in the home; draincock in closed position (**inset**)

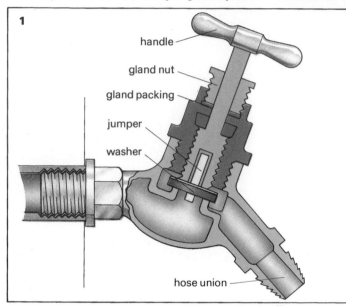

handle
gland nut
gland packing
jumper
washer
hose union

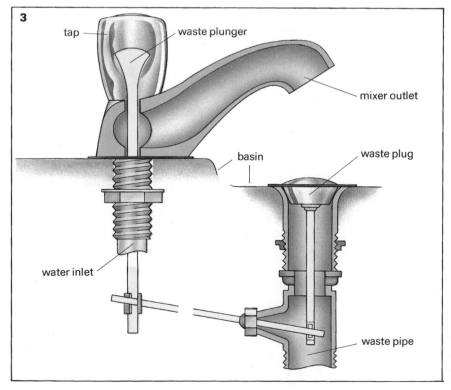

gland nut
automatic check valve
plastic ears
'O' ring seal
'O' ring seal
anti-splash nozzle
swivel outlet
rotating nozzle
hose

inside the home. A 15mm (or $\frac{1}{2}$in) tap is normally fitted to sinks and wash-basins and a 22mm (or $\frac{3}{4}$in) tap to baths. The metric sizes relate to the copper tubing to which they are fitted – not to the taps themselves. These taps fit into holes already provided in the appliances they are to serve.

Bib tap This type has a horizontal inlet and in modern homes is most commonly used to provide an outlet for the garden or garage water supply. A bib tap used for this purpose should ideally have a threaded nozzle onto which a hose connector can be screwed. It is also important to have the tap angled away from the wall or post to which it is fitted to prevent knuckles being grazed or knocked when turning the handle.

Shrouded-head tap This type has a handle specially designed to cover the headgear and was originally developed to prevent gland failure through detergent dripping from the handle of the tap into the mechanism. It has since become popular because of its neat and attractive appearance.

Supatap This tap works on a totally different principle from other taps, since it is controlled by turning the nozzle of the tap. Earlier models had the disadvantage of being too hot to touch, since the heat from the water transferred to the metal ears comprising the handle. Recent models are made with special plastic ears which do not conduct heat.

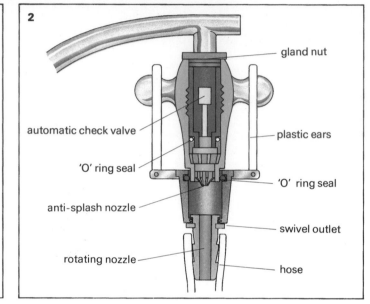

tap
waste plunger
mixer outlet
basin
waste plug
water inlet
waste pipe

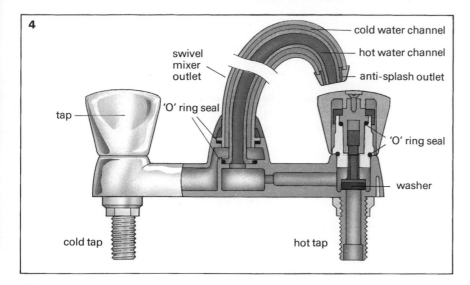

4

- tap
- cold tap
- swivel mixer outlet
- cold water channel
- hot water channel
- anti-splash outlet
- 'O' ring seal
- 'O' ring seal
- washer
- hot tap

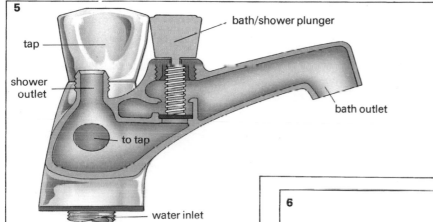

5

- tap
- shower outlet
- to tap
- bath/shower plunger
- bath outlet
- water inlet

water could be contaminated by coming into contact with the stored water.

To get over this problem, a special sink mixer has been developed which, although resembling bath and basin mixers in appearance, has in fact separate channels for the hot and cold water within its body. The two streams of water mix in the air after they leave the nozzle. Sink mixers frequently have a swivel nozzle, which enables you to direct the required temperature of water to any part of the sink – or, where there are twin sinks, to either sink. To make sure the nozzle is cool to the touch, cold water flows through the outer of the two channels within the mixer.

Draincocks

The simplest tap of all is the draincock, which should be fitted wherever any section of a hot or cold water or central heating system cannot be drained from an ordinary tap. Draincocks are closed by means of a washered plug which can be turned with a spanner or, in emergency, with a wrench or pair of pliers. A hose connector outlet is provided to enable easy drainage of the system. Draincocks should be fitted in the following places:

● Immediately above the main stopcock to enable the rising main to be drained.

● On the return pipe and close to any hot water cylinder storage system heated by an electric immersion heater only – and on any indirect hot water cylinder system.

● At the lowest point of any part of a central heating system which cannot be drained from the draincock beside the boiler.

flexible shower hose and sprinkler; the water, which can be mixed to the required temperature, is diverted from the spout to the shower sprinkler at the flick of a switch.

Basin mixers Some of these incorporate a pop-up waste, which eliminates the rather unsightly, traditional basin plug and chain. Pressure on a knob situated between the handles of the mixer activates the waste plug, which pops up to allow the basin to empty.

Sink mixers These are rather different in design, since water authorities prohibit the mixing of water from the rising main and water from a storage cistern within any plumbing system. This affects the sink since the hot water is supplied via the hot water storage cylinder (which in turn is supplied from the cold water storage cistern), while the cold water is supplied directly from the rising main. This means the hot and cold supplies are under unequal pressure and therefore mixing would be difficult. Apart from this, there is a possibility the mains

Inset

- to water pipes
- threaded plug
- washer
- fixing nut
- hose connector outlet

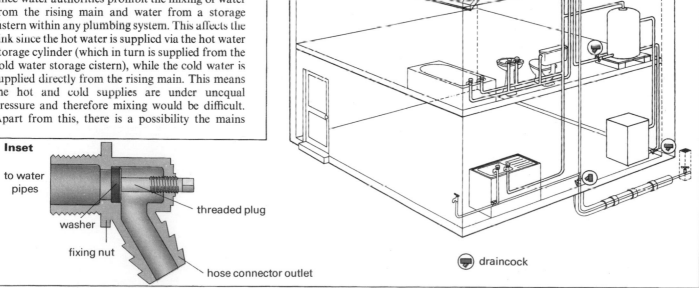

6

draincock

Ball valves

Ball valves are vital parts of the plumbing system in the home, since they control the amount of water in your cold water storage and WC cisterns. They must operate efficiently, otherwise the cisterns will overflow – or not fill up correctly.

The purpose of the ball, or float, valve is to maintain water at a constant level in cold water storage and WC flushing cisterns. All ball valves have a metal or plastic arm terminating in a float (not necessarily a ball) that rises or falls with the level of the water in the cistern. As the water level falls the movement of the float arm opens the valve to allow water to flow through it; as the level rises the arm closes the valve.

The older types of ball valve – the Croydon and the Portsmouth – control the flow of water by a washered metal plug. The main disadvantage of these is that failure of the washer or dirt or corrosion on the parts can cause leaks. Modern ball valves, which have a rubber diaphragm instead of a washered plug, are designed to overcome these problems.

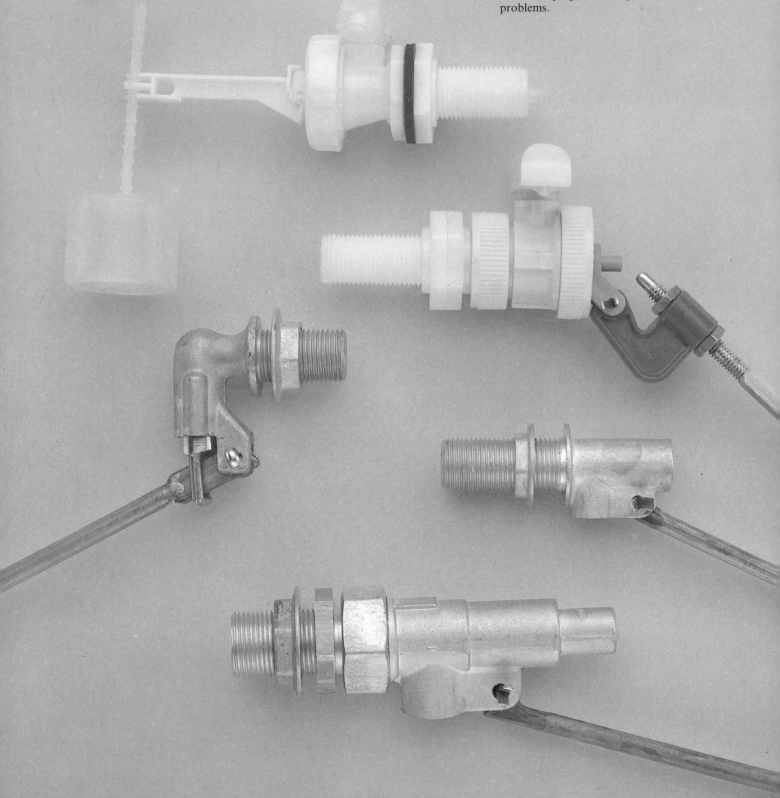

Croydon and Portsmouth valves

On both these valves a washered metal plug is forced tightly against the valve seating to prevent a flow of water when the cistern is full. The plug of a Croydon moves vertically within the valve body. When the valve is open, water splashes into the cistern via two channels built into either side of the body of the valve. Croydon valves are always noisy in action and, for this reason, are now rarely, if ever, installed in homes.

The Portsmouth valve is the one now most likely to be found in installations, particularly new ones. Its plug moves horizontally within the valve body and the end of the float arm is bent over to fit within a slot built into the plug. The noise of these valves used to be reduced by fitting a silencer tube into the valve outlet. This is a plastic or metal tube that delivers incoming water below the level of the water already in the cistern; it eliminates splashing and reduces the ripple formation that is a common cause of noise and vibration in ball valves. Unfortunately water authorities no longer permit the use of these silencer tubes, since in the event of water pressure failure they could cause water from storage and flushing cisterns to siphon back into the main.

Dealing with leaks A steady drip from the cistern's warning pipe indicates a worn washer – a common fault on the Croydon and Portsmouth valves. It may be possible to cure the leak, at least temporarily, without changing the washer simply by lowering the level of the water in the cistern. There is no need to cut off the water supply to do this: remove the cover from the cistern, unscrew and remove the float from the end of the float arm. Take the arm firmly in both hands and bend the float end downwards, then reassemble. This will keep the water below the normal level, which is about 25mm (1in) below the warning pipe in a cold water storage cistern and 13mm ($\frac{1}{2}$in) below the warning pipe in a flushing cistern. (If you need to raise the water level in a cistern, bend up the float end of the arm.)

Changing the washer If lowering the level of the water does not cure the leak, you will need to change the ball valve washer. First cut off the water supply at the nearest stopcock. Some Portsmouth valves have a screw-on cap at the end of the valve body: this must be removed.

Straighten and pull out the split pin on which the float arm pivots and remove the float arm, insert the blade of a screwdriver in the slot in the base of the valve body from which the float arm has been removed and push out the plug.

The plug has two parts: a body and a cap retaining the washer, but it may be difficult to see the division between these parts in a plug that has been in use for some time. To replace the washer you will need to remove the retaining plug: insert the blade of a screwdriver through the slot in the body and turn the cap with a pair of pliers. This can be very difficult, so don't risk damaging the plug. If the cap will not unscrew easily, pick out the old washer with the point of a penknife and force a new washer under the flange of the cap, making sure the washer lies flat on its seating.

Cleaning It is important to remove any dirt or scaling on the metal parts as this can also cause leaks. Before reassembling the plug, clean it with fine abrasive paper and smear with petroleum jelly.

When to replace the valve Continued leaking after renewal of the washer may indicate the valve seating of the plug has been scored by grit from the main or

a low pressure valve has been fitted where a high pressure one is required. In either case, a new valve will be needed.

Ball valves are classified as high pressure (HP) or low pressure (LP) depending on the diameter of the valve seating and are usually stamped accordingly on the valve body. High pressure valves are usually installed where the water supply is direct from the main and low pressure valves where the water supply is from another storage cistern, as is usually the case with WC flushing cisterns.

Using the wrong kind of valve will result in either constant leaks or a long delay in the refilling of the cistern. Where a WC flushing cistern is supplied from a cold water storage cistern only a metre (or 3ft) above the level of the WC suite, it may be necessary to fit a full-way valve – which has a wider orifice – to ensure the cistern refills rapidly after it has been flushed.

Equilibrium valve

In some areas water pressure may fluctuate considerably throughout a 24-hour period. In such cases, the provision of an equilibrium valve is

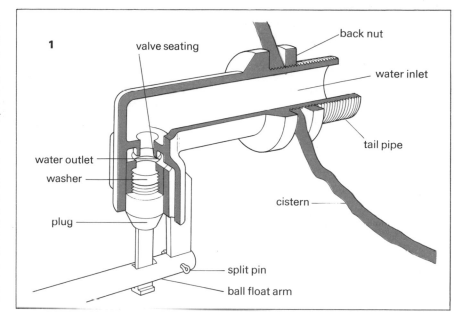

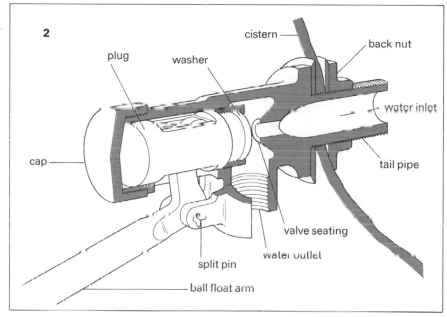

Opposite page Types of ball valve: Torbeck (**top left**), diaphragm (**top right**), Croydon (**centre left**), Portsmouth (**centre right**) and equilibrium (**bottom**).

1 The Croydon ball valve: the plug moves vertically in the valve body and water enters through channels on either side

2 The Portsmouth ball valve: the plug moves horizontally and water enters through a single channel

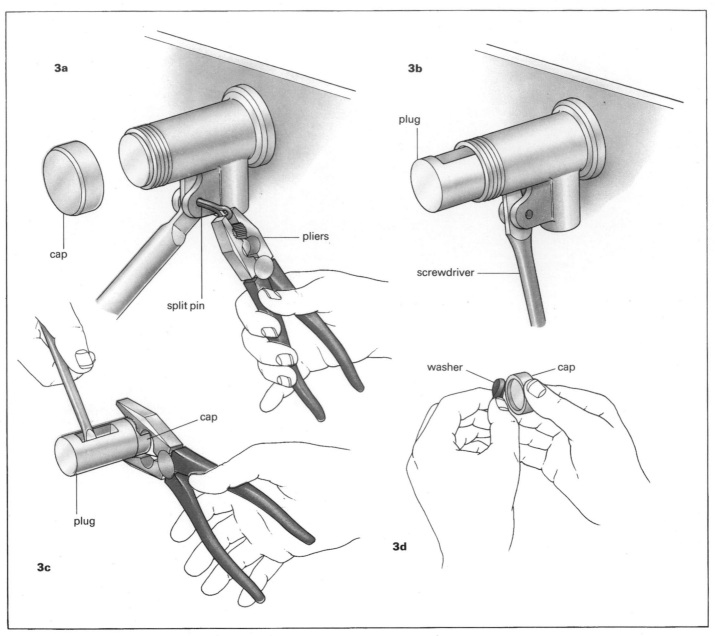

3a

cap

split pin

pliers

3b

plug

screwdriver

washer   cap

3c

cap

plug

3d

recommended. This valve has a wide nozzle orifice but is closed by a special plug with a channel bored through its centre: this allows water to pass through to a sealed chamber behind the valve. The plug is therefore in a state of equilibrium: water pressure is equal on each side of the plug and the valve opens only at the prompting of the float arm – not partly as a result of the pressure of water in the rising main trying to force the valve open.

An equilibrium valve is also useful in preventing water hammer – shock waves produced when the conflict between water pressure in the rising main and the buoyancy of the float result in the valve bouncing on its seating.

Diaphragm valves

A new type of ball valve – the diaphragm valve (also known as the Garston or BRS as it was developed at the Government's Building Research Station at Garston) – has been designed to reduce noise and eliminate other common ball valve problems. It may be made of brass or plastic and has a tough, score-resistant nylon nozzle that is closed, when the cistern is full, by a large rubber or plastic dia-

phragm. This diaphragm is pushed against the nozzle by a small plunger actuated by the float arm. All diaphragm pattern valves have some means of adjusting water level without having to bend the float arm.

To adjust the Garston valve, turn off the water supply to the cistern and flush the WC fully. On the opposite side to the valve there is a steadying screw, which should touch the side of the cistern. If it does not, slacken the lock nut and turn the screw till it does. If this does not work, the float valve probably needs adjusting.

The float arm is fixed to a pivot bracket with a lock nut on either side. Slacken the lock nut furthest from the valve half a turn and tighten the other one to take up the slack. Repeat this adjustment until you achieve the correct level of water in the cistern.

If this does not cure the problem, you will have to replace the diaphragm. Undo the large serrated-edged nut nearest the float to remove the dia-phragm. If the plastic seating against which the diaphragm presses is damaged, replace this by unscrewing the other large nut on the valve body.

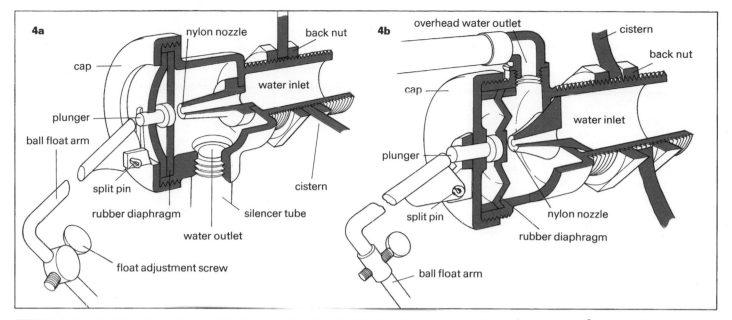

4a

cap

plunger

ball float arm

split pin

rubber diaphragm

nylon nozzle

back nut

water inlet

cistern

silencer tube

water outlet

float adjustment screw

4b

overhead water outlet

cistern

back nut

cap

water inlet

plunger

split pin

nylon nozzle

rubber diaphragm

ball float arm

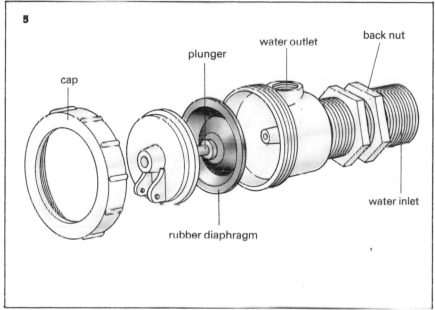

5

cap

plunger

water outlet

back nut

rubber diaphragm

water inlet

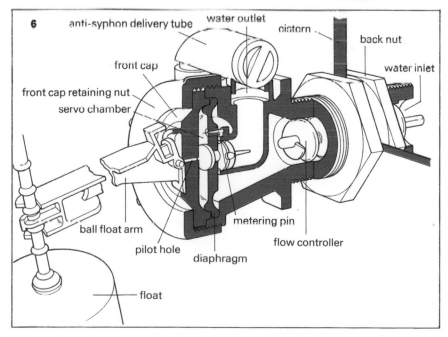

6

anti-syphon delivery tube

water outlet

cistern

back nut

water inlet

front cap

front cap retaining nut

servo chamber

ball float arm

pilot hole

diaphragm

metering pin

flow controller

float

Fit the new diaphragm, using a little petroleum jelly on the screw threads before refitting the nuts, which should be hand-tight only.

An important feature of this kind of valve is that it has few moving parts. These are anyway protected from the water by the rubber diaphragm, so the valves cannot jam as a result of scale or corrosion.

Early models of diaphragm valves were fitted with silencer tubes, but since these have fallen out of favour, manufacturers have developed overhead outlets with a distributing device that can be directed at the side of the cistern to ensure silent action. Modern diaphragm valves also have a detachable nozzle which allows them to be changed quickly from high pressure to low pressure.

Poor flow from a diaphragm valve is usually due to the diaphragm jamming against the nozzle or, more likely, to debris from the rising main accumulating between nozzle and diaphragm. The valve can be easily dismantled for cleaning and servicing: to release the nozzle simply turn by hand the large knurled retaining cap – but remember to cut off the water supply first.

Torbeck A more recent development is the Torbeck valve, which has some of the features of the diaphragm valve and some of the conventional equilibrium valve. It operates solely by water pressure acting on both sides of the diaphragm and has been found to be very efficient. It is also silent in action, unlike the other types of valve.

3a To change washer on Portsmouth or Croydon valve, pull out split pin holding ball arm (having cut off water supply). **3b** Push out plug with screwdriver. **3c** Insert screwdriver through slot in plug body and turn washer cap with pliers. **3d** Remove washer and fit new one. **4a** Early diaphragm valve fitted with silencer. **4b** Modern diaphragm valve with overhead outlet; spray delivery ensures silent action. **5** To dismantle diaphragm valve, unscrew cap and remove components. **6** Torbeck valve includes features from diaphragm and equilibrium valves.

The WC cistern

The fittings plumbed in to any home are in constant use and it is therefore important they are not only installed correctly but also properly maintained. You should know how each works to be able to tackle any jobs yourself.

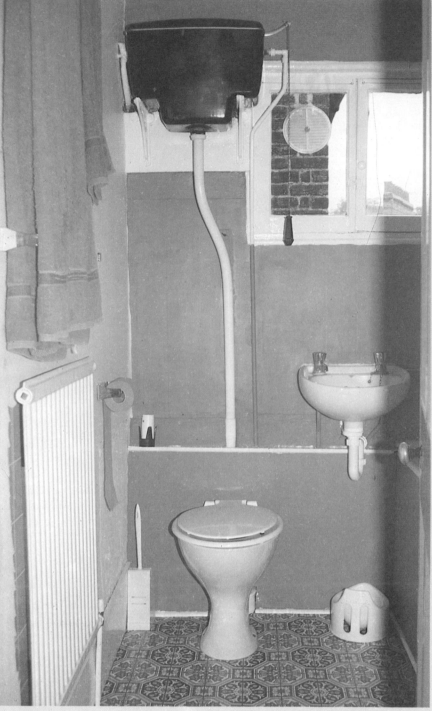

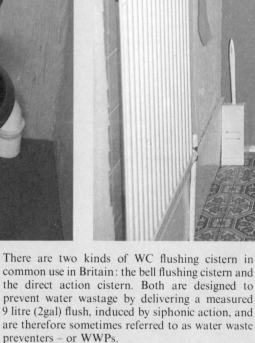

The direct action, low-level cistern (**above**) has now largely replaced the bell flushing type (**above right**) because it is quieter and more efficient in action, as well as looking neater

There are two kinds of WC flushing cistern in common use in Britain: the bell flushing cistern and the direct action cistern. Both are designed to prevent water wastage by delivering a measured 9 litre (2gal) flush, induced by siphonic action, and are therefore sometimes referred to as water waste preventers – or WWPs.

Bell flushing cisterns
This type of cistern is no longer installed when a house is built; but there are still many of them in use in older houses, particularly when the WC is outside. It is made of heavy hard-wearing cast iron and has a well in its base through which the flush pipe is continued open-ended to a point about 25mm (1in) above full water level. A heavy iron bell, with three or more lugs built into its rim, stands on the base of

the cistern, covering the flush pipe extension.

The flush is operated by raising the bell by means of a lever and chain and then releasing it suddenly. As the bell falls, its wedge shape forces water trapped within it over the open end of the flush pipe and in falling it takes air with it, creating a partial vacuum. In this way a siphon effect is produced and the pressure of the atmosphere pushes the contents of the cistern under the rim of the bell and down the flush pipe. The siphon effect is broken and the cistern refills when it has emptied sufficiently to allow air to pass under the rim.

Faults Bell flushing cisterns are prone to noise, corrosion by condensation, and continuous siphonage where, after flushing, the cistern fails to refill and there is a continuous flow of water down the flush pipe until the chain is pulled for a second time.

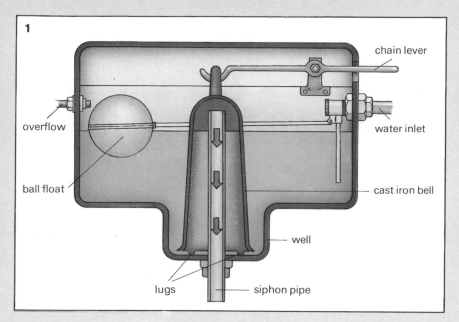

1

overflow

ball float

chain lever

water inlet

cast iron bell

well

lugs — siphon pipe

1 An old-fashioned bell
flushing cistern – noisy and
prone to corrosion and
continuous siphonage
2 A modern direct action
flushing cistern – the most
common fault is failure of
the diaphragm

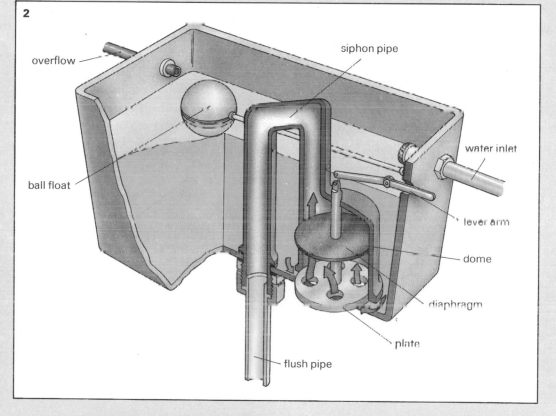

2

overflow

ball float

siphon pipe

water inlet

lever arm

dome

diaphragm

plate

flush pipe

has a flat base and may be made of plastic or ceramic material. A stand-pipe, which serves as a continuation of the flush pipe, rises to above water level and is then turned over and extended to form a dome with an open base about 25mm (or 1in) above the base of the cistern. A circular metal plate is raised within the dome when the flushing lever is operated and this throws water over the inverted 'U' bend into the flush pipe to start the siphonic action. This plate has a number of holes in it to allow water to pass through freely when the flush is operating. When the plate is raised these holes are closed by a valve – usually a plastic disc known as a siphon diaphragm, a siphon washer or a flap valve.

Faults Failure of the diaphragm is the most common fault in direct action cisterns. It is usually indicated by increasing difficulty in operating the flushing mechanism – two or three sharp jerks on the flushing lever may be required. If your cistern is displaying this symptom, remove the lid and check the cistern is filling to the correct level. There may be a mark to indicate this level inside the cistern wall; if not, adjust the ball valve by bending the

Continuous siphoning results from debris accumulating in the well of the cistern, often coupled with a too rapid refill of water through the ball valve, and the lugs on the rim of the bell wearing away. To solve the problem, clear out the debris, reduce the flow by partially turning off a stopcock control and build up the lugs with an epoxy resin filler. You cannot, however, eliminate the problem of noise.

The ideal solution is to replace the old cistern with a modern direct action one.

Direct action cisterns
For new and replacement work in modern homes direct action cisterns, sometimes called low level cisterns despite the fact they may be installed at high level, are most often used. This type of cistern

float arm upwards to give a full level about 13mm (½in) below the overflow outlet.

If the water level is correct, it is almost certainly the diaphragm which is at fault. Cisterns vary in construction but the following is the usual way of replacing the diaphragm. Tie up the ball valve arm to prevent more water flowing in and flush to empty the cistern. Unscrew the nut connecting the threaded tail of the siphon to the flush pipe and disconnect the flush pipe. Unscrew the large nut immediately beneath the cistern. Hold a bowl under the cistern as you do this since it will still contain about ½ litre (or 1pt) of water. Withdraw the siphoning mechanism to reach the diaphragm.

When you buy a replacement diaphragm it is unlikely you will know the right size, so buy the largest available and you can easily cut it to the

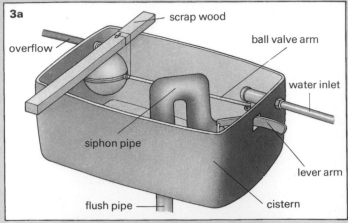

3a
overflow
scrap wood
ball valve arm
water inlet
siphon pipe
lever arm
flush pipe
cistern

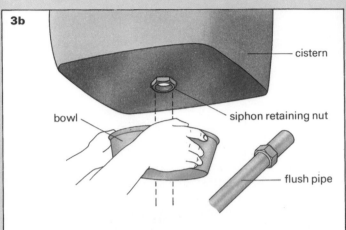

3b
cistern
bowl
siphon retaining nut
flush pipe

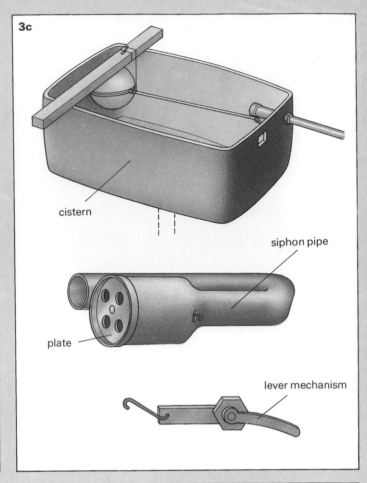

3c
cistern
siphon pipe
plate
lever mechanism

correct size and shape with a pair of scissors. Remove the old diaphragm and place the new one so it covers the circular metal plate completely and touches, but does not drag on, the walls of the siphon dome. Reassemble the cistern and reconnect the flush pipe. After flushing, the cistern should refill and be ready for use within two minutes. Slow refilling may be due to a sticking ball valve, an accumulation of debris behind the rubber diaphragm of a BRS pattern valve or the use of a high pressure valve where water is supplied under low pressure from a storage cistern.

Condensation can also be a problem in direct action cisterns as well as in the bell flushing type. Ceramic cisterns, cisterns of toilet suites situated in bathrooms and cisterns supplied direct from the main are particularly likely to be affected. Beads of moisture appear on the outside of the cistern below the water level and may give the impression the cistern has become porous.

Where a cistern is in the bathroom you should avoid drip-drying clothes over the bath and always fill the bath with cold water about 25mm (1in) deep before turning on the hot tap. Another way of combating the problem of condensation is to provide a radiant heat source and improved ventilation, for example by installing an electric extractor fan. In extreme cases, you can line a ceramic cistern with strips of expanded polystyrene sheet of the kind used under wallpaper. Before you do this, empty the cistern and make sure it is completely dry. Use an epoxy resin adhesive to fix the polystyrene sheeting and leave the cistern empty until the adhesive has set thoroughly.

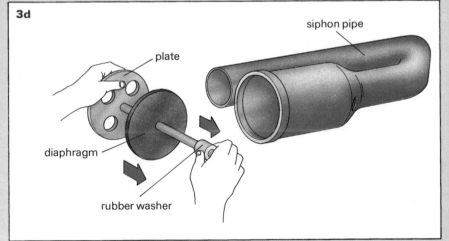

3d
plate
siphon pipe
diaphragm
rubber washer

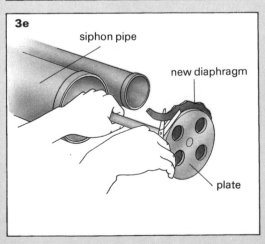

3e
siphon pipe
new diaphragm
plate

3a To replace the diaphragm in a direct action cistern, first tie up the ball valve arm and flush the cistern to empty it
3b Disconnect the flush pipe and catch any remaining water in a bowl
3c Remove the siphon mechanism and detach the operating lever
3d Withdraw the plate from the siphon and take off the diaphragm
3e Slide a new diaphragm onto the plate, trim it to fit if necessary and reassemble the cistern

Plumbing it in

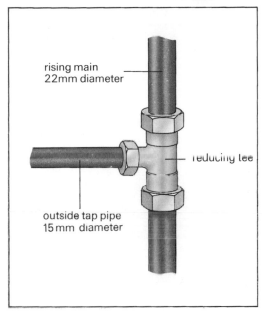

rising main
22mm diameter

reducing tee

outside tap pipe
15mm diameter

Plumbing in a washing machine or dishwasher

Plumbing in a washing machine or dishwasher involves tapping an existing water supply pipe and taking a branch from it. This can be done using a conventional compression tee; but if you are plumbing into hot and cold water, as is necessary with many machines, you will have to bend a pipe. An alternative and easier method is to use a thru-flow valve which connects directly to the flexible hose of the machine. Or you can fit a control valve, which is even easier since it does not involve cutting a section out of the supply pipe.

Whichever method you choose, you must first turn off the main stopcock and drain the water from the supply pipes you are going to use.

Using a compression tee

Cut out a 19mm ($\frac{3}{4}$in) section from the drained supply pipe and insert a 15mm ($\frac{1}{2}$in) compression tee. From the outlet of the tee take a short length of 15mm ($\frac{1}{2}$in) pipe to terminate in a stopcock to which the outlet of the flexible hose of the machine is connected. Special washing machine stopcocks with a back plate for fixing to the kitchen wall are available for this purpose.

If you are connecting to the hot and cold water supply pipes of the kitchen sink, you will probably find these run down the kitchen wall parallel to each other and about 100mm (4in) apart. This means the branch pipe from the further supply pipe will need to be bent to pass the nearer one. Make two bends within a short distance of each other so the pipe bypasses the other supply pipe.

Fitting a thru-flow valve

The Kontite thru-flow valve provides a simple means of tapping a 15mm ($\frac{1}{2}$in) copper water supply pipe for connection to a washing machine, dishwasher or garden hose. The valve incorporates its own 15mm ($\frac{1}{2}$in) tee junction and one end of the tee has no tube stop.

Before fitting, cut off the water supply and drain the pipe to which the valve is to be connected. Decide on the level at which you want the connection to be made and, with a hacksaw, cut out a section of pipe 28mm (or 1$\frac{1}{8}$in) long. Cut squarely and file away any burr.

Unscrew the cap nuts and remove the olives from the two compression couplings of the tee: slip the cap nuts, followed by the olives, over the two cut ends of the pipe. You can clip sprung clothes pegs onto the pipes to prevent them slipping down. Apply boss white to the pipe ends and olives.

Pull out the upper length of pipe enough to allow the end of the tee without the tube stop to be pushed over it. Then push back the pipe and allow the valve to slip over the lower section of pipe until

1 Plumbing in the machine to a single stack system using compression tees. The outlet can discharge over a yard gully or (**inset**) into the main stack pipe. With a two pipe drainage system, the outlet discharges into the main waste pipe (or over a yard gully)

2a To fit a thru-flow valve, a section of existing pipe has to be removed

2b Push the end of the valve without the tube stop over the upper length of pipe; slip the valve over the lower pipe and tighten the coupling nuts

2c Section through the fitted thru-flow valve

3a Marking the hole for the Opella plumbing-in kit

3b Fitting the back plate

3c The pipe inlet fits into the drilled hole

3d Section through the fitted plumbing-in kit

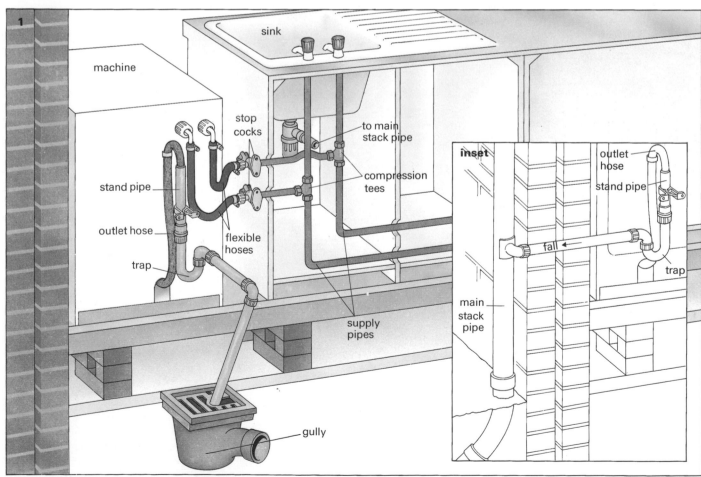

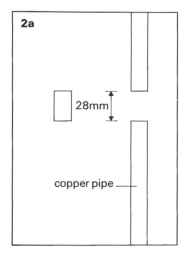

2a

28mm

copper pipe

held by the tube stop. Tighten up the two compression coupling nuts with a spanner. Make sure the plastic control knob is turned to the 'off' position and turn on the main stopcock.

Fitting a control valve

The Opella plumbing-in kit (control valve) is an alternative method of connecting a washing machine or dishwasher to a 15mm ($\frac{1}{2}$in) copper supply. It is a relatively easy method since it does not involve cutting the supply pipe – you simply drill a hole in it.

First cut off the water supply and drain the pipes to which the machine is to be connected. Decide on the point at which the hose connection is to be made and remove any paint from the pipe at this point, then clean with fine emery cloth.

Mark the centre of the hole on the front of the pipe with a centre punch, tapping the punch lightly with a hammer to avoid kinking the pipe. Carefully drill an 8mm ($\frac{5}{16}$in) hole at this point, making sure the hole is central, and do not allow the drill bit to pass through the pipe to damage the back. Place the back plate of the fitting behind the hole in the pipe, checking it is correctly positioned by inserting the pipe inlet in the front plate in the hole and ensuring the screw holes align. Check the rubber seal round the pipe inlet is in position; tighten the fixing screws and fix the back plate to the wall, using the screws and wall plugs provided. To complete the operation, screw the tap body into the front plate. You can adjust the position of the outlet if necessary by removing one or more of the washers on the tail of the tap.

This simple method does to some extent restrict the flow of water through the hose. If you wish to

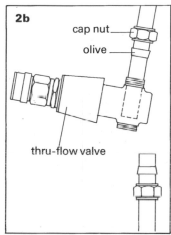

2b

cap nut
olive
thru-flow valve

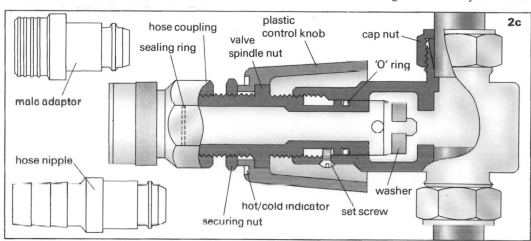

hose coupling
sealing ring
plastic control knob
valve spindle nut
cap nut
'O' ring
male adaptor
hose nipple
hot/cold indicator
set screw
washer
securing nut

2c

use this type of fitting but want a more conventional connection to the water supply pipe, you can cut the pipe and insert a 15×15mm ($\frac{1}{2} \times \frac{1}{2}$in) compression tee with a 15mm ($\frac{1}{2}$in) female iron threaded outlet into which the tap body can be screwed. Wrap PTFE thread sealing tape round the threads of the tap tail to make a watertight joint.

Fitting a self-drilling valve

The great advantage of this type of valve is that you can fit it to the existing system without having to turn off and drain the water supply. First fit the backplate to the wall behind the point on the pipe at which you want to fit the valve. You may have to pack this out to ensure the pipe fits in the groove of the backplate. Then fit the saddle over the pipe onto the backplate and finally screw the valve into the saddle to make the connection into the pipe. Full instructions are supplied with the valve.

Providing drainage

You can dispose of the water from a washing machine or dishwasher by hooking the outlet hose over the kitchen sink. If the machine is not near a sink, however, install a stand pipe outlet and hook the outlet hose of the machine permanently into it. Make the stand pipe with 38mm ($1\frac{1}{2}$in) PVC tubing at least 600mm (or 2ft) long. A trap should be provided at the base and the outlet taken either to an external gully or, where the kitchen is on an upper floor, to the main stack pipe of a single stack drainage system. Remember to consult the building control officer of your local council before making any connection to a single stack drainage system.

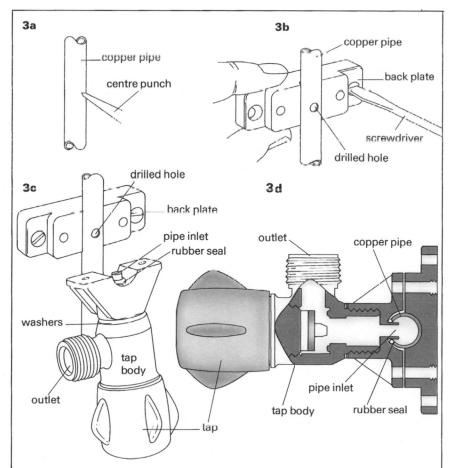

3a
copper pipe
centre punch

3b
copper pipe
back plate
screwdriver
drilled hole

3c
drilled hole
back plate
pipe inlet
rubber seal
washers
tap body
outlet
tap

3d
outlet
copper pipe
pipe inlet
tap body
rubber seal

Fitting an outside tap

An outside tap, with a hose connector, is virtually essential for the gardener or car owner. It saves connecting a hose to the tap over the kitchen sink, which can involve an inconvenient suspension of other kitchen activities and, by creating back pressure within the tap, may lead to early gland failure – indicated by water round the spindle.

Fitting an outside tap is a job you can easily do yourself, particularly if you use a proprietary garden tap kit – you should be able to obtain one of these from your local builders' merchant or DIY stockist. Before you begin work you should get in touch with your local water authority to find out whether, and under what conditions, they will permit the connection of an outside tap to the rising main. Normally this will be allowed, but the authority will probably make an extra charge on the water rate for the use of the tap.

Preparing for installation

Drill a 25mm (1in) diameter hole through the external wall to within 350mm (or 14in) of the rising main and about 75mm (3in) above the level at which the tap will be fitted. You can use a cold chisel and club hammer to make the hole, but an electric drill with a 25mm (1in) bit will, of course, make the job easier – particularly if the drill has a hammer action.

Turn off the main stopcock and drain the rising main from the tap over the kitchen sink – if there is a draincock immediately above the stopcock, drain from this as well. Use a hacksaw to cut a 19mm (¾in) piece out of the rising main at the same distance from the floor as the hole which you have cut through the wall. Make sure your cuts are made squarely and remove any burr from the pipe ends with a file.

An outside tap is a useful addition to the home's plumbing system since it will ease the demand on the kitchen tap when watering the garden or washing the car. You will also be saved the inconvenience of wet feet messing up the floor, buckets slopping water or hose pipe trailing over the kitchen sink

Carrying out installation

Unscrew the cap nuts and olives from the two ends of the crosspiece or run of the tee junction supplied with the kit. Smear the pipe ends with boss white and slip first a cap nut and then an olive over one of the cut ends of the pipe. Smear the olive with boss white. To make fitting easier the tee junction has no pipe stop at one end; pull out the pipe end and slip this end of the tee over it. Push the olive up to the tee and loosely screw on the cap nut – don't tighten it. Fit the cap nut and olive over the other pipe and apply boss white as before, then push the tee up over this pipe end until the pipe end is firmly against the pipe stop. Move the olive up to the tee and screw on the cap nut. Make sure the outlet of the tee is directed, parallel to the wall, towards the hole you have cut in the wall. Hold the body of the tee with an adjustable wrench and tighten the cap nuts with a spanner – this will help prevent overtightening.

Screw-down stopcock Although not included in the garden tap kit, you should fit a screw-down stopcock into the length of pipe inside the kitchen.

During winter this can be turned off and the outside tap opened to preclude any risk of frost damage. Fitting this stopcock will also reduce the time the rest of the plumbing system is not in action: once it is in position – and turned off – the main stopcock can be opened so water flows through the rising main and all the domestic plumbing fittings can be brought back into use. This means you can take your time over fitting the outside tap and avoid possible mistakes from trying to get the job done too quickly.

Cut a 200mm (or 8in) length from the 330mm (13in) pipe without elbow; fit one end of this into the tee in the rising main using a compression joint (cap nut, olive and boss white) in the same way as for fitting the tee. Attach the free end of the pipe to the inlet side of the stopcock, again using a compression joint. Take the 330mm (13in) length of 15mm ($\frac{1}{2}$in) copper tube with elbow attached and push it through the hole in the wall, from the inside, so the fixed connection of the elbow is inside the wall. Carefully measure the distance between the outlet of the screw-down stopcock and

Making the tee junction:
1a Fit the cap nut and olive over the pipe end;
1b Push the body of the tee junction over the end of the pipe coated with boss white;
1c Fit the bottom pipe into the other end of the tee;
1d Tighten the cap nuts with a spanner, holding the body of the tee with an adjustable spanner

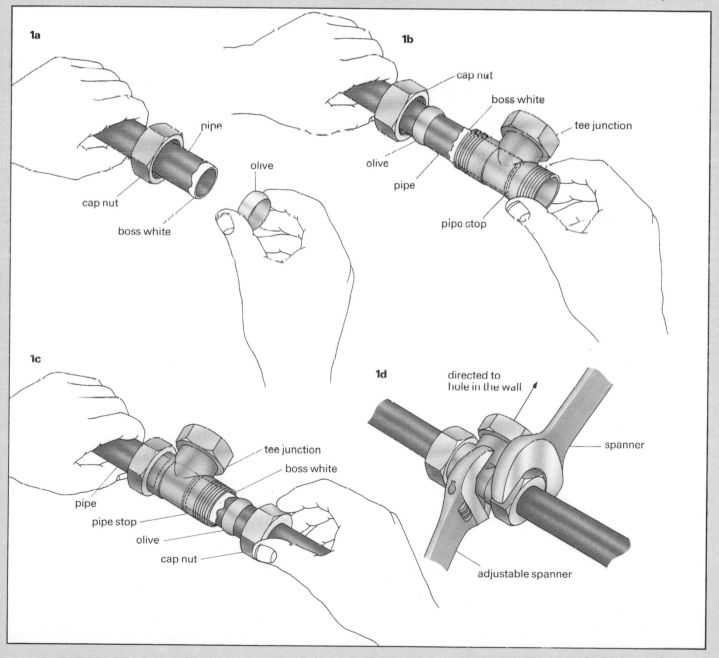

1a

pipe

olive

cap nut

boss white

1b

cap nut

boss white

tee junction

olive

pipe

pipe stop

1c

tee junction

boss white

pipe

pipe stop

olive

cap nut

1d

directed to hole in the wall

spanner

adjustable spanner

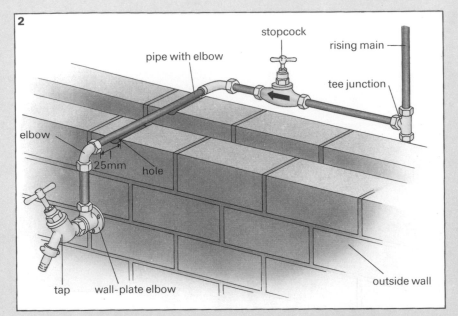

2

pipe with elbow

stopcock

rising main

elbow

25mm

hole

tee junction

tap

wall-plate elbow

outside wall

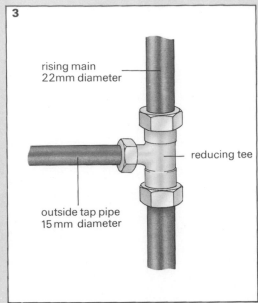

3

rising main
22mm diameter

reducing tee

outside tap pipe
15mm diameter

the outside end of this elbow and allow extra length
for the pipe which will be within the fittings. Using
a hacksaw, cut the remaining piece of copper tube
without elbow to the required length and connect
the two ends to the elbow and the outlet of the
stopcock with compression joints as before.

Finishing off Outside the house, cut the pipe end
so 25mm (1in) is projecting from the hole in the
wall. Connect the elbow joint to this pipe end so
the outlet of the elbow points downwards to the
position at which you want to fix the outside tap.
Place the wall-plate elbow against the wall, mark
the screw positions and drill and plug the wall.
Cut the short piece of copper tube to length, if
necessary, and connect the outlet of the elbow
projecting from the wall to the inlet of the wall-
plate. Then screw the wall-plate to the wall. To
ensure a watertight joint, bind PFTE thread sealing
tape round the tail of the tap and screw the tap into
the wall-plate elbow. If, when it is first screwed
home, the tap is not upright, add washers to the
tail until it comes to the right position. The tap
handle will be angled away from the wall so you
can turn it without grazing your fingers. Use an
exterior grade filler to repair the hole in the wall.

Warning These instructions for fitting an outside
tap apply only to houses with a 15mm ($\frac{1}{2}$in) copper
or stainless steel rising main. Some houses, where
water pressure is low, may have a 22mm ($\frac{3}{4}$in) rising
main and a reducing tee will be needed; this is
fitted in the same way as an ordinary tee. Also, in
older houses there may be a lead or heavy
galvanized steel rising main. To connect an outside
tap to a main of this kind, you should seek
professional help – at least for fitting the tee
junction to the rising main.

2 Section through wall showing connections
at the rising main, the stopcock inside and
the outside tap fittings
3 Reducing tee connection in rising main
Left A garden plumbing kit and optional
screw-down stopcock (**inset**)

Immersion heaters

One great advantage of an immersion heater fitted to your hot water cylinder is that it can be used to supply as much or as little hot water around the home as you need at any particular time. It can also supplement other heating systems such as gas, oil or solid fuel. With care, you can fit it yourself.

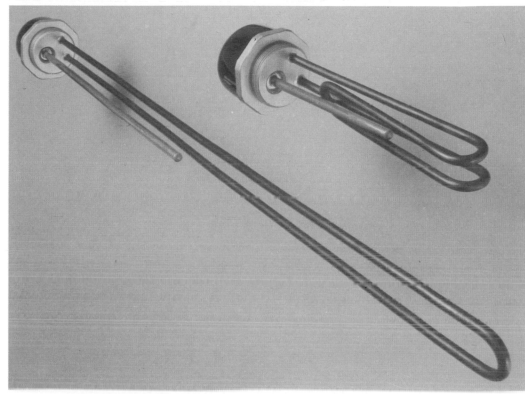

Left Immersion heaters are available in different lengths. You can buy a dual-element model, which heats either the top or all of the cylinder, or a single element one. If you decide on the single heater, you will find it is more economical to fit two, one at the top of the cylinder and the other lower down near the bottom
1 Types of immersion heater shown fitted into the hot water cylinder
1a Single element in varying lengths to suit different size cylinders
1b Separate heaters can be fitted so the top of the cylinder is heated for small amounts of water and all the cylinder heated when larger amounts are needed
1c The dual-element heater does the same job, but has the advantage of being a single fitting

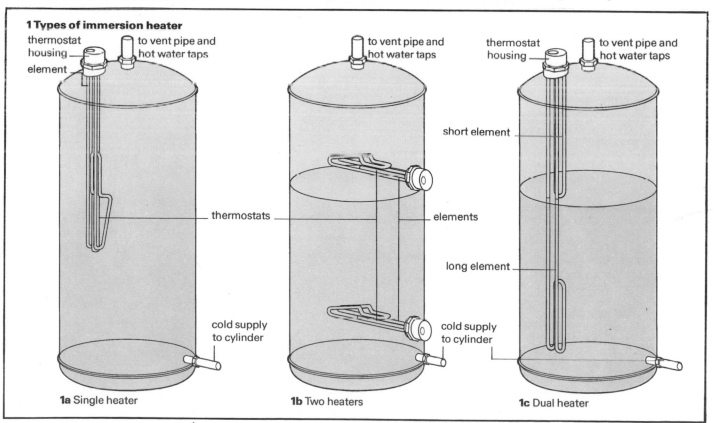

1 Types of immersion heater

thermostat housing — element — to vent pipe and hot water taps

thermostats

cold supply to cylinder

1a Single heater

to vent pipe and hot water taps

elements

cold supply to cylinder

1b Two heaters

thermostat housing — to vent pipe and hot water taps

short element

long element

1c Dual heater

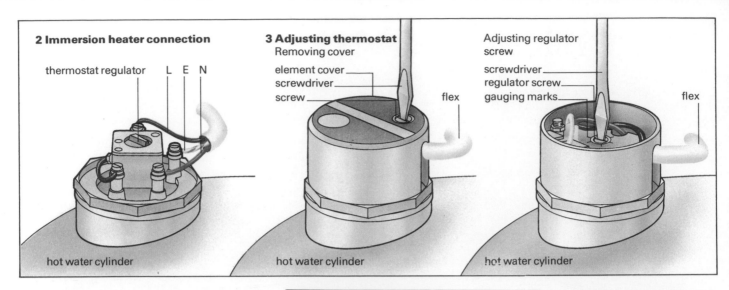

2 Immersion heater connection

thermostat regulator L E N

hot water cylinder

3 Adjusting thermostat
Removing cover

element cover
screwdriver
screw

flex

hot water cylinder

Adjusting regulator screw

screwdriver
regulator screw
gauging marks

flex

hot water cylinder

One of the most convenient methods of supplying hot water in the home is by installing an immersion heater in your hot water cylinder, although it is a fairly expensive form of heating to run if used constantly. Heaters are made in a range of lengths and loadings to suit the different types of cylinder and to give varying quantities of hot water. On some the heating element is coated with a titanium sheath; this is specially for use in hard water areas where corrosive substances in the water would adversely affect an ordinary element without a special coating.

The length of the heater can range from 245–914mm (10–36in). The type most commonly fitted is the single-element one which will heat the whole cylinder. It is, however, more economical to have two elements, one fitted near the top and the other about 50mm (2in) from the bottom of the cylinder. The top element heats enough water for hand or dish washing and the bottom one heats the whole cylinder, when for example you want a bath. There is also a dual heater, with a short and long element, which operates on the same principle. Both systems are independently switched so you can have either or both elements on at any time to suit your needs.

Special long heaters are needed for indirect and self-priming cylinders and for rectangular tanks. Hot water cylinders designed to work on the Electricity Board's White Meter tariff have either two heaters or a dual-element one to heat part or all of the water.

Wiring heaters
Common ratings for the heater are 1, 2 and 3kW, but because the immersion heater is considered to be a continuous load, whether you keep it switched on all the time or not, it must be supplied by its own circuit direct from the consumer unit using 2.5sq mm cable from a separate 20amp fuseway. The cable runs to a 20amp double pole switch (usually with a pilot light) which should be sited near the heater and close enough for anyone to operate if they are adjusting the thermostat. The wiring from the switch to the heater should be a 20amp rubber heat-resistant flex.

If you are installing two heaters in one cylinder, your double pole switch should incorporate a second switch which allows you to have either one or both heaters working. In this case a separate flex must run to each heater from the switch.

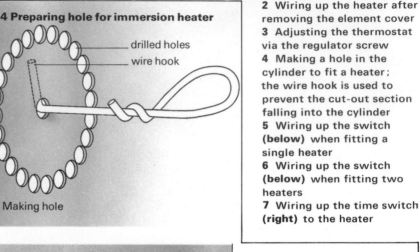

4 Preparing hole for immersion heater

drilled holes
wire hook

Making hole

2 Wiring up the heater after removing the element cover
3 Adjusting the thermostat via the regulator screw
4 Making a hole in the cylinder to fit a heater; the wire hook is used to prevent the cut-out section falling into the cylinder
5 Wiring up the switch **(below)** when fitting a single heater
6 Wiring up the switch **(below)** when fitting two heaters
7 Wiring up the time switch **(right)** to the heater

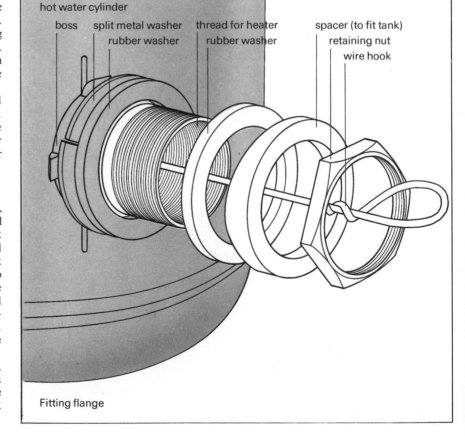

hot water cylinder
boss   split metal washer   thread for heater   spacer (to fit tank)
rubber washer   rubber washer   retaining nut
wire hook

Fitting flange

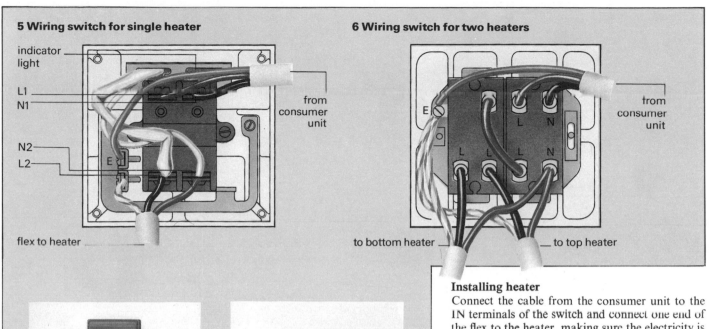

5 Wiring switch for single heater

indicator light
L1
N1
N2
L2
from consumer unit
flex to heater

6 Wiring switch for two heaters

E
L N
L L L N
from consumer unit
to bottom heater
to top heater

off ⊘ sink
on ⊖ bath

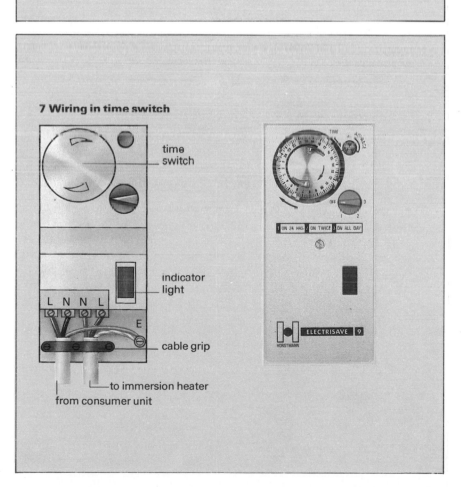

7 Wiring in time switch

time switch
indicator light
L N N L
E
cable grip
to immersion heater
from consumer unit

ELECTRISAVE 9
HORSTMANN

Installing heater
Connect the cable from the consumer unit to the IN terminals of the switch and connect one end of the flex to the heater, making sure the electricity is switched off at the mains. Turn off your water supply at the cold water storage cistern, drain the cylinder and remove the relevant boss, into which the heater will screw. The threads are sealed first by winding PTFE tape against the direction of turn, or by using hemp string and a non-toxic plumbing compound. Tighten the heater against its sealing washers, using a large wrench – but never over-tighten. Connect the free end of the flex to the OUT terminals of the switch, turn on the stopcock at the cistern and the electricity at the consumer unit and, after waiting for the cylinder to refill, switch on.

Warning Be sure to clamp the flex at both ends in the cord grips fitted to the heater and switch, and use the correct flex grips to secure it to the walls. Otherwise the flex might become entangled in linen (if in an airing cupboard) and be pulled away.

Cutting boss Most cylinders are now made with at least one boss fitting. However, if you have a direct copper cylinder, without a boss, in good condition you can cut a hole to take the heater. Mark out the required diameter hole and cut it with a hole saw fitted to an electric drill. Alternatively, drill a series of holes around the edge of the circle, knock out the centre and file the edge smooth. You can buy a patent fitting that includes the boss, a thread to take the heater thread, washers and a retaining nut. Don't try to cut a boss in an indirect self-priming cylinder.

Adjusting thermostat You must turn off the heater before attempting to adjust the thermostat setting. You reach it by unscrewing any screws holding the cap in place. Use a screwdriver to obtain the required setting, generally 60°, 71° or 82°C (140°, 160° or 180°F). In hard water areas scale tends to build up in cylinders at temperatures above 60°C (140°F) which is the lowest acceptable temperature for normal domestic purposes. The thermostat automatically turns off the power supply when the required temperature is reached.

Using a time switch An immersion heater can be controlled by a special time switch. This type of switch usually offers three on and off periods in each 24 hours.

Fitting sinks, basins and bidets

Installing a new sink, wash-basin or bidet may appear a daunting task, but it should be a job well within most people's capabilities as long as the correct procedures are followed. The general principles of fitting taps have been covered earlier – see pages 66, 67, 78 – but there are specific areas of fitting certain units which need explanation.

Fitting sinks

Whatever type of sink you choose, there is one general principle you should follow when fitting it: carry out as much work as possible before you place it in position. If your new sink has a sink mixer tap arrangement, you should fit flat plastic washers over the tails of the mixer before inserting them into the holes provided in the sink top. When you have inserted the tails, fit top-hat or spacer washers over them under the sink to accommodate the protruding shanks of the mixer before you screw home the back nuts.

A special sink waste facility incorporating a flexible overflow pipe is manufactured for modern sinks. Bed this into the outlet hole of the sink onto a layer of non-setting mastic and connect the open end of the flexible pipe to the overflow outlet on the sink, inserting a rubber washer between the frontpiece and the sink. Screw the trap, which has a 50mm (or 2in) seal for a two pipe drainage system or a 75mm (or 3in) seal for a single stack system, onto the slotted waste outlet. For a double sink, only the outlet from the section nearer to the drain is separately trapped and you should take the outlet from the other section to connect to this above the trap, using a 'banjo' fitting, or double sink set, to make this connection.

An electrically operated sink waste disposal unit provides a convenient means of disposing of soft household wastes such as vegetable peelings and dead flowers. If you are fitting one of these, check the size of the sink outlet: it should be 87.5mm (3½in) instead of the usual 38mm (1½in).

Fitting wash-basins

The three basic types of wash-basin – pedestal, wall-hung or countertop – each have their advantages. The water supply and waste pipes can be concealed within the pedestal basin, but a wall-hung type may be preferred where floor space is limited; the latter also gives you choice of fitting level. Usually these are installed with the rim about 812mm (or 32in) from floor level, but you can vary this by moving the hanging brackets. The waste outlet from the basin usually passes through a hole in the hanging bracket. To fix the basin to the bracket, bed the waste outlet into the basin outlet hole on non-hardening mastic, pass the waste outlet through the hole in the bracket and place a plastic washer over the waste outlet before screwing on the back nut. Countertop units take up more space, but conceal plumbing and provide room for storage. They should be sealed into the countertop (following the manufacturer's instructions) and plumbed in in exactly the same way as a sink unit, except the cold water supply is normally taken from the cold water storage cistern, not direct from the main.

Wash-basins are usually made of ceramic, but

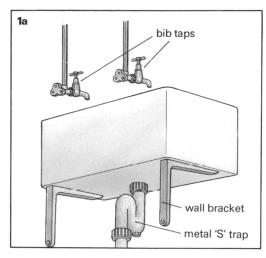

1a bib taps
wall bracket
metal 'S' trap

1a Typical old-fashioned ceramic sink
1b Modern sink unit with double drainer
1c Double sink unit with swivel mixer outlet

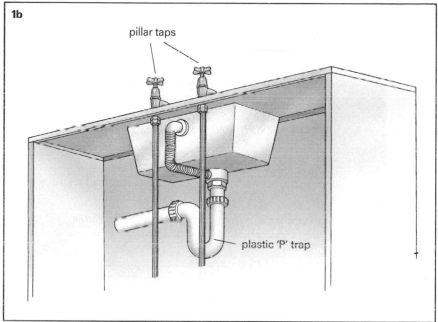

1b pillar taps
plastic 'P' trap

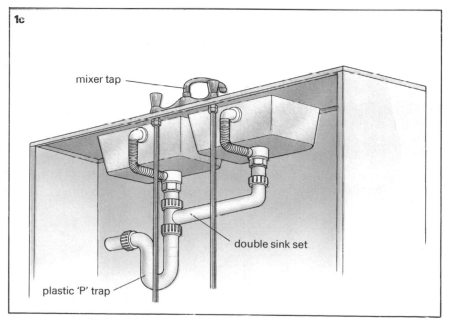

1c mixer tap
double sink set
plastic 'P' trap

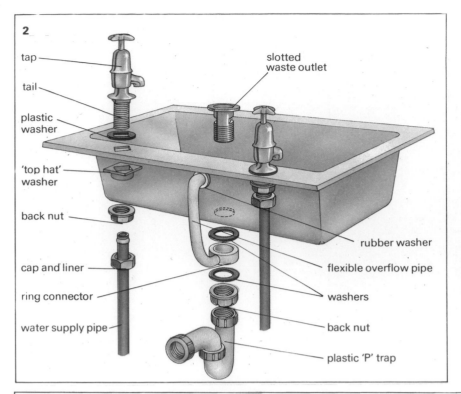

2

- tap
- tail
- plastic washer
- slotted waste outlet
- 'top hat' washer
- back nut
- cap and liner
- ring connector
- water supply pipe
- rubber washer
- flexible overflow pipe
- washers
- back nut
- plastic 'P' trap

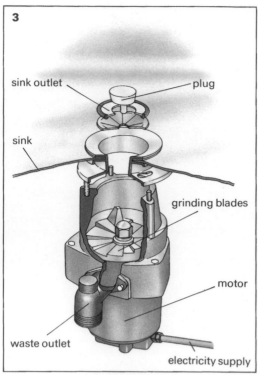

3

- sink outlet
- plug
- sink
- grinding blades
- motor
- waste outlet
- electricity supply

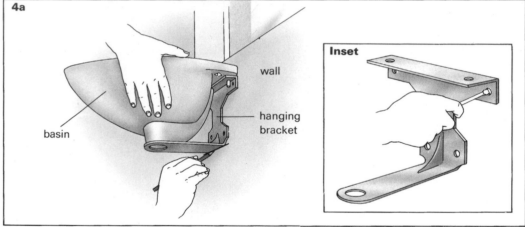

4a

- wall
- hanging bracket
- basin

Inset

2 Installing metal sink with slotted waste outlet
3 Electrically operated sink waste disposal unit
4a Marking fixing positions of concealed hanger for wall-hung basin and (**inset**) screwing hanger in place
4b Plumbing in wall-hung basin
5 Plumbing in ceramic basin
6 Plumbing in bidet with through-rim supply, ascending spray and pop-up waste
7 Installing bidet with rim supply and ascending spray

other materials such as plastic, stainless steel and enamelled pressed steel are also used. Since ceramic basins are made of relatively thick material you should not find it necessary to fit a top-hat or spacer washer under each tap. Use flat plastic washers between the back nuts and the basin and tighten the nuts sufficiently to hold the tap firmly, taking care not to overtighten. The overflow of the basin usually consists of a channel built into the appliance and a slotted basin waste outlet is bedded into the basin outlet hole on non-setting mastic. Make sure the slot in the waste fitting coincides with the outlet of the built-in channel. A conventional 'U' trap or a bottle trap may be provided between the basin waste outlet and the waste pipe. It is better to use either a chromium plated or plastic bottle trap for a wall-hung basin.

Warning Take care when carrying out work on ceramic basins since they are easily damaged.

Fitting bidets

The simplest and cheapest form of bidet – an 'over rim supply' type – resembles a ceramic wash-basin apart from the shape and the level at which it is fitted. It is supplied with water from a hot and

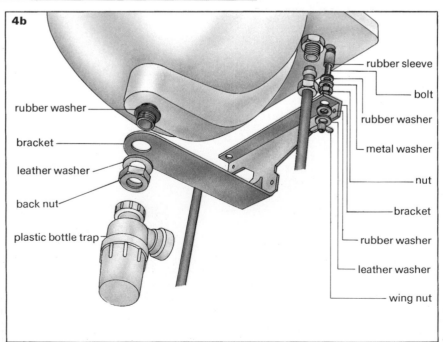

4b

- rubber washer
- bracket
- leather washer
- back nut
- plastic bottle trap
- rubber sleeve
- bolt
- rubber washer
- metal washer
- nut
- bracket
- rubber washer
- leather washer
- wing nut

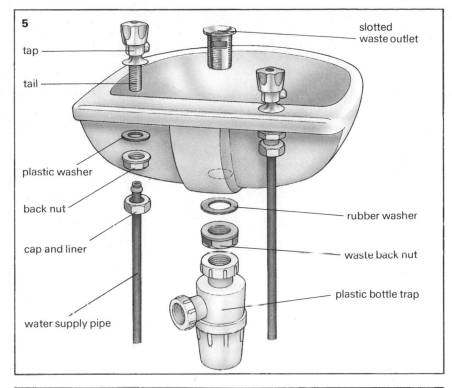

5

- tap
- tail
- plastic washer
- back nut
- cap and liner
- water supply pipe
- slotted waste outlet
- rubber washer
- waste back nut
- plastic bottle trap

cold tap or, more probably, a basin mixer and the waste is dealt with in exactly the same way as that of a wash-basin. You can provide the water supply by connecting 15mm ($\frac{1}{2}$in) pipes to the existing bathroom hot and cold water supply pipes using a 'T' joint.

The more complex and expensive 'rim supply with ascending spray' bidet presents special problems. In this type of bidet, mixed hot and cold water flows in via a rim similar to the flushing rim of a WC pan and this warms the rim and makes it comfortable for use. By pressing a knob you can divert the inflowing water into an ascending spray directed towards those parts of the body to be cleansed.

You must take special care with a submerged water inlet of this kind to prevent any possible contamination of the rest of the household water supplies. Using a 15mm ($\frac{1}{2}$in) distribution pipe, take the cold water supply directly from the cold water storage cistern and take a 15mm ($\frac{1}{2}$in) hot water supply pipe directly from the vent pipe above the hot water storage cylinder. Never connect the hot or cold water supply as a branch from a distribution pipe supplying any other fitting. As a final precaution, make sure the water inlet to the bidet is at least 2.75m (or 9ft) below the level of the base of the cold water storage cistern.

6

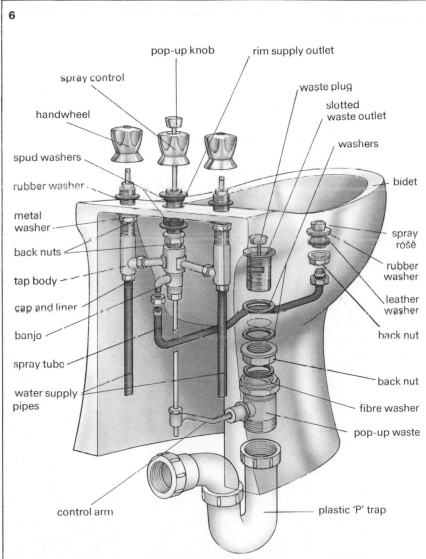

- spray control
- pop-up knob
- rim supply outlet
- handwheel
- waste plug
- slotted waste outlet
- spud washers
- washers
- rubber washer
- bidet
- metal washer
- back nuts
- spray rose
- tap body
- rubber washer
- cap and liner
- leather washer
- banjo
- back nut
- spray tube
- water supply pipes
- back nut
- fibre washer
- pop-up waste
- control arm
- plastic 'P' trap

7

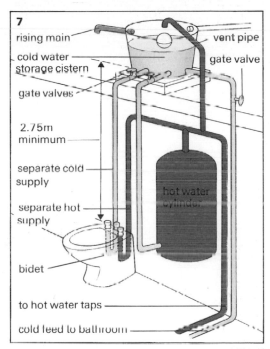

- rising main
- vent pipe
- cold water storage cistern
- gate valve
- gate valves
- 2.75m minimum
- separate cold supply
- hot water cylinder
- separate hot supply
- bidet
- to hot water taps
- cold feed to bathroom

Warning Don't make the mistake of assuming that, because of the use to which it is put, a bidet should be regarded as a soil fitting and connected directly to the drain or soil pipe in a two pipe system of above-ground drainage. A bidet is an ablution fitting and its waste should be dealt with in the same way as that of a bath or wash-basin.

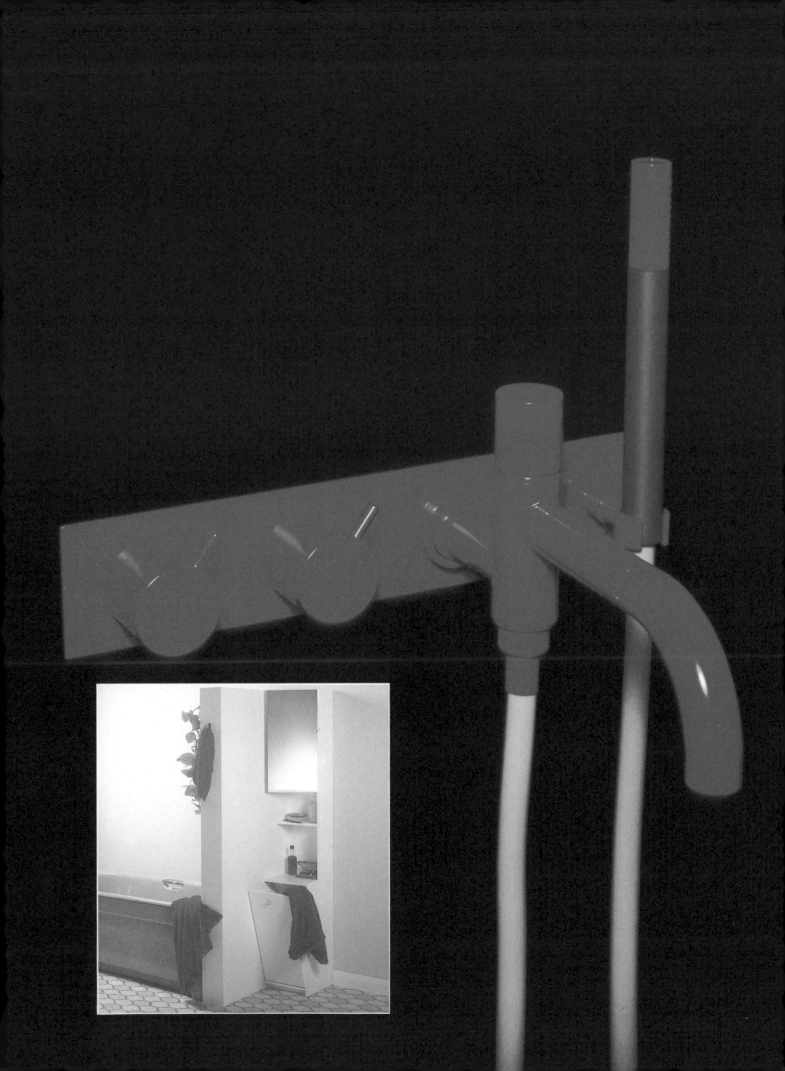

Fitting showers

Showers are a useful addition to your washing facilities, particularly since they are so economical with water. Whether you want a unit over the bath or a cubicle, you can fit it yourself.

A shower cubicle can be installed practically anywhere in the home: squeezed into a corner of a bedroom, onto a landing or even into the cupboard under the stairs. You will require a space about 2m (or 6ft) high and 1m (or 3ft) square. Shower units can, of course, be fitted above a bath using a fixed wall attachment or a flexible arm which connects to a mixer tap set and can also be hung on a wall; in this case the plumbing is simplified since the drainage is already installed.

Plumbing requirements

Most types of shower can be installed in conjunction with a hot water cylinder storage system, but there are a number of plumbing requirements necessary to ensure a safe and successful system.

Water pressure There must be enough water pressure to provide sufficient spray and this depends on the height between the shower sprinkler and the base of the cold water storage cistern. The best results will be obtained if the vertical distance between these points is at least 1.5m (or 5ft). It may be possible to reduce this 'head' to an absolute minimum of 1m (39in) where pipe runs are short and there are few bends.

Where this amount of head is not available, the cheapest and simplest solution is to raise the cold water storage cistern onto a platform in the roof space (if there is room) and lengthen the rising main and the distribution pipes by means of compression fittings.

If you live in a flat or ground floor maisonette, it may not be possible to raise the cistern; but you can boost pressure by installing an electrically operated pump: this does, however, substantially increase the cost of providing a shower.

Hot and cold supply You must have hot and cold water supplies which are mixed manually or thermostatically to give a comfortable temperature – and the supplies to the mixer must be under equal pressure. The hot water will be under constant pressure from the main cold water storage cistern and the cold must be taken from the same cistern and never directly from the main supply.

It is not only illegal to mix water from the mains with water from a storage cistern, it is also impractical and dangerous. If you try to do this, the shower will run cold until the cold supply is turned

Top right Pre-fabricated cubicles enable you to install showers easily in virtually any room in the home. They can stand in a corner or, as here, fit unobtrusively into a suitable cupboard

1 The plumbing requirements for a shower

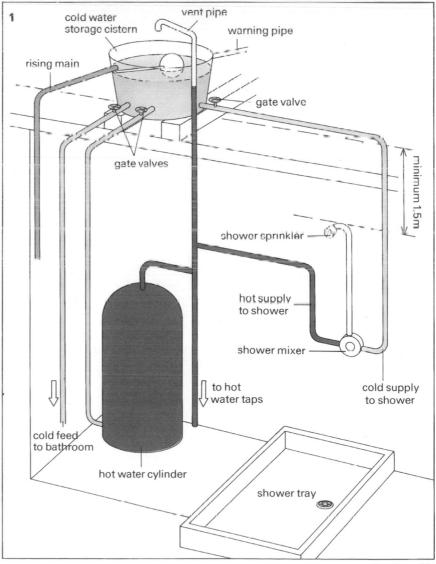

1 cold water storage cistern · vent pipe · warning pipe · rising main · gate valve · gate valves · minimum 1.5m · shower sprinkler · hot supply to shower · shower mixer · to hot water taps · cold supply to shower · cold feed to bathroom · hot water cylinder · shower tray

off, then it will run scalding hot. For safety reasons, the cold supply must be taken to a mixer in its own separate distribution pipe from the cistern and must not be a branch from a pipe supplying other fittings; otherwise flushing a WC or running the cold tap of a wash-basin, for example, could reduce the pressure on the cold side of the shower and seriously scald someone using it.

Bath/shower fittings

When fitting a shower over a bath, the simplest method is to use a rubber tube taken from an over-head sprinkler and connected to the two bath taps by push-on rubber connectors. Such cheap and simple fittings can work satisfactorily if you do not mind adjusting the taps until you get the required temperature.

Alternatively you can use a bath/shower mixer which you buy as a set and fit it in place of the ordinary hot and cold taps. Water flows into the bath while you adjust the taps to the required temperature; you divert the flow upwards to the shower sprinkler by operating a lever or switch.

Showers fitted over baths need either a plastic shower curtain or panels of rigid glass or translucent plastic to prevent water splashing onto the floor. Shower curtains are cheaper, but rigid panels are more effective and give a more professional appearance.

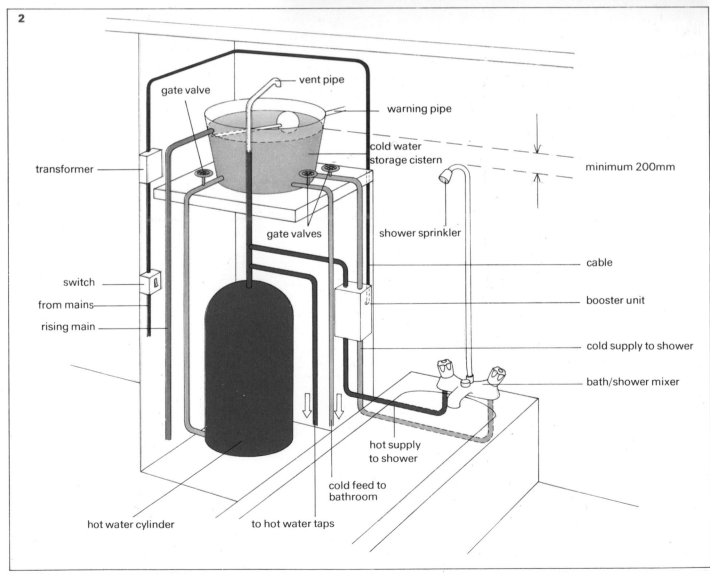

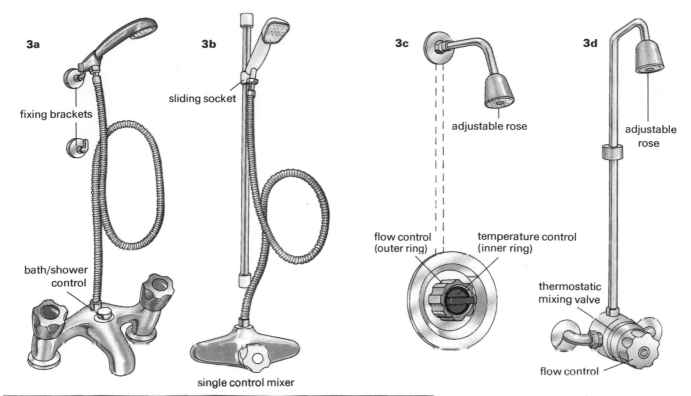

3a

fixing brackets

bath/shower control

3b

sliding socket

single control mixer

3c

adjustable rose

flow control (outer ring)

temperature control (inner ring)

3d

adjustable rose

thermostatic mixing valve

flow control

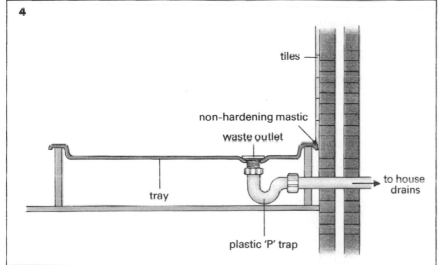

tiles

non-hardening mastic

waste outlet

to house drains

tray

plastic 'P' trap

Top left This shower unit fits snugly over one corner of the bath; a plastic shower curtain prevents water splashing into the room when the shower is in use
2 If the necessary amount of pressure is not available, fit an electric booster pump on the hot and cold supply pipes to the shower mixer
3a Bath/shower mixer with flexible hose
3b Single control shower mixer with adjustable height
3c Dual control mixer with concealed plumbing
3d Thermostatic mixer with fixed riser
4 A shower tray and its plumbing connections

Instantaneous shower heaters

Lack of cylinder-stored hot water, or the presence of other plumbing problems, need not rob you of a shower, since you can install an instantaneous gas or electric shower heater. There are a number of models available and they need only be connected to the rising main by means of a 'T' joint and to the electric or gas supply. Instantaneous heaters are reliable, but do increase the cost of a shower. The flow rate is lower than that of a shower run off a storage cylinder and hard water scale can present problems in some areas.

Installing a shower

You can buy a prefabricated cubicle which includes a shower tray or fit a tray enclosed by curtains. You can also fit the shower in a corner and use the existing walls for two sides; angled tube can then be fitted to the walls to carry the curtains. In any case, the walls and floor of the shower area should be made of waterproof materials such as ceramic tiles or plastic or stainless steel. If using tiles, make sure the fixing adhesive and grouting is water-resistant, otherwise water will seep behind the tiles and cause them to lift from the surface.

Most independent cubicles are fitted with manual mixing valves which mix water to the temperature required by turning a single knurled knob; some also incorporate a flow control. Thermostatic mixing valves are also available; these are designed to maintain the temperature despite fluctuations in either hot or cold water pressure, but will not accommodate the difference in pressure between a mains cold water supply and a hot supply under pressure from a storage cistern.

First cut off the water supply by closing the stopcock serving the cold water storage cistern or by tying up the ball valve serving the cistern and running the taps until water stops flowing. Connect the water supply to the shower mixer using 15mm (½in) copper tubing. Make sure the joints are watertight by wrapping PFTE plastic thread sealing tape round the fittings before tightening them. From an appearance point of view you should conceal the pipes in channels cut into the wall plaster or box the pipes in with panels.

To fit the waste outlet to the shower tray, bed it in non-hardening mastic and secure it with a back nut over a plastic washer. For connection to a two-pipe drainage system use a shallow seal trap of 50mm (2in); with a single stack drainage system, use a deep seal trap of 75mm (3in).

Warning With the exception of the bath mixer type of shower, all shower installations require the approval of the local water authority, who may impose certain conditions, such as increasing the size of the cold water storage cistern to cope with the extra demand on the water supply. Make sure you check this out first, before you make a start on the work.

Fitting a waste disposal unit

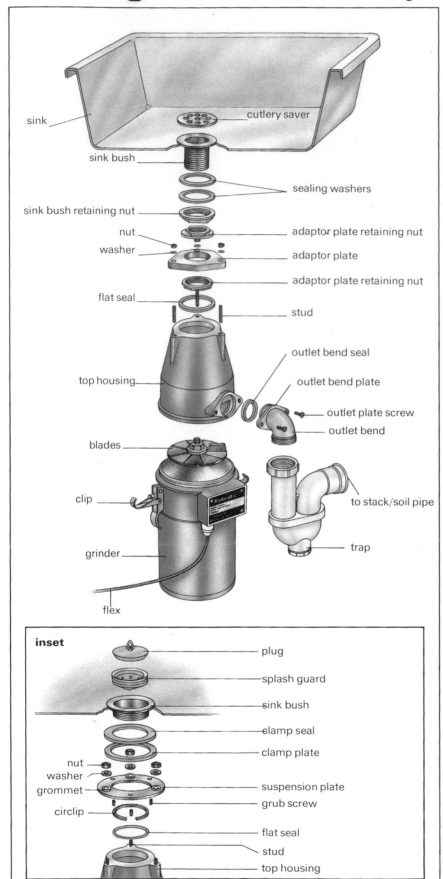

sink

cutlery saver

sink bush

sealing washers

sink bush retaining nut

nut

adaptor plate retaining nut

washer

adaptor plate

flat seal

adaptor plate retaining nut

stud

outlet bend seal

outlet bend plate

top housing

outlet plate screw

outlet bend

blades

clip

to stack/soil pipe

grinder

trap

flex

inset

plug

splash guard

sink bush

clamp seal

clamp plate

nut

washer

grommet

suspension plate

circlip

grub screw

flat seal

stud

top housing

A waste disposal unit fits under the sink and is plumbed permanently into the sink outlet and the waste pipe. Installation of the unit is relatively simple, provided you are fitting it to a stainless steel sink. Models generally fit an 89mm (3½in) diameter outlet hole, although one model is now made to fit the standard 38mm (1½in) outlet – and in another case a modification kit is available. Waste disposal units can be fitted to vitreous enamel sinks, but great care must be taken since the enamel will craze very easily.

Methods of installation vary according to the type of waste disposal unit you buy; detailed instructions are included with each model. It is, however, worth bearing in mind several general points. When fitting the unit, plan the plumbing carefully; never fit pipes where they will hinder access to the unit or any of its controls and avoid tight bends, kinks, tee junctions and stopped ends wherever possible. The waste pipe should not be shared with any other appliance and the waste outlet should be below the gully grating. Bottle traps should never be used with this unit. Make sure the bore of the trap and the waste pipe are readily accessible and check the fall on the waste pipe is at least eight degrees to the horizontal.

Motor Most models have a 420 watt (½hp) capacitor-start induction motor. This type of electric motor, with no carbon brushes or commutator, has a solid rotor (armature); it is characteristically robust and, being a brushless machine, needs no periodic attention and is unlikely to fail in service. The motor should last at least 20 years.

Being a capacitor-start motor, it will start immediately on full load. Some waste disposal units have motors of lower power, but these are adequate for the specific duties they are to perform. Some have both forward and reverse facilities; reverse is normally used to release a jammed disposal unit, although one type operates alternately in forward and reverse – to prolong the life of the disposer's cutting blades, it is claimed.

A self-reversing actuator is available with one model; this can be surface-mounted or flush-fitted to the wall or other suitable surface near the disposal unit itself. The actuator is pneumatically operated and has no electrical connections; the sheath containing the fibre-optic light-guide and pneumatic tube will have to be recessed in a channel if the actuator is flush-fitted to the wall.

Power supply The electrical supply to a disposal unit can be taken from a 13amp outlet – either through a fused plug and socket or a switched fused connection unit. The fused connection unit is preferable, since it makes a permanent connection for the disposal unit and avoids flex and a plug lying loose under the sink when the socket is used for another appliance.

Making connections

Whether you connect the disposal unit through a switched fused connection unit or a socket outlet, the circuit can be a spur branching out from the ring circuit. The connection to the ring circuit can be made at one of the existing socket outlets in the kitchen. To save cable and work, choose the socket outlet nearest to the waste disposal unit provided it

Left Exploded view of a waste disposal unit which fits into a standard 38mm sink outlet; units normally fit sink outlets of 89mm diameter (**inset**)

Below Waste disposal unit adapted to fit a standard sink outlet

Below right Unit requiring 89mm sink outlet

Bottom right Unit with pneumatically operated self-reversing actuator; the sheath containing the fibre-optic light-guide and pneumatic tube connects the actuator to the unit

Bottom Cutaway of a self-reversing disposal unit showing the component parts

offers an easy run for the new cable. Before starting work, switch off the power at the mains and check the chosen socket is not itself a spur.

Run the new cable from this socket outlet to the position of the outlet for the waste disposal unit – which should be on the wall fairly close to the disposal unit, but conveniently placed for switching on and off. Use 2.5sq mm twin core and earth flat PVC-sheathed cable. If the cable is to be surface-mounted, choose white sheathing and knock out a thin section from a one gang plastic mounting box to make an entry hole for it; thread in the circuit cable and screw the box to the wall, using the appropriate wall or cavity fixings. For flush mounting, remove one of the knock-outs in a one gang steel box, fit a PVC grommet in the hole and thread the cable through this; sink the box into the wall flush with the plaster.

Strip about 125mm (5in) of sheathing from the end of the cable, leaving about 13mm ($\frac{1}{2}$in) of sheathing within the box. Slip a length of green/yellow PVC sleeving over the bare earth conductor and strip about 8mm ($\frac{5}{16}$in) from the end of the two insulated wires.

Socket outlet If you are wiring up a socket outlet, connect the red wire to the terminal marked L, the black wire to terminal N and the PVC-sleeved earth wire to terminal E. Lay the wires neatly in the box and fix the socket in place with the two screws supplied with it. All you need to do now is wire a 13amp fused plug onto the flex from the unit.

Fused connection unit If you are wiring up a switched fused connection unit, prepare the ends of the cable as for the socket, but connect the red wire to the mains terminal L, the black wire to the mains terminal N and the earth wire to an E terminal in the unit (some have two E terminals). Thread in one end of the three core sheathed flex and strip off about 100mm (4in) of sheathing. Fix the end of the sheathing under the flex grip and strip off about 8mm ($\frac{5}{16}$in) of insulation from the end of each of the three cores. Connect the brown wire to the load terminal L, the blue wire to the load terminal N and the green/yellow wire to an E terminal. Lay the six wires in the box and fix the connection unit onto the mounting box with the screws supplied.

Remove the terminal cover of the waste disposal unit and thread the other end of the flex through the cable entry grommet. Check the length of the flex; if necessary, cut it to length but allow sufficient slack to lower the motor housing if ever necessary and about 150mm (6in) within the terminal box. Strip off about 150mm (6in) of the sheathing and secure the end of the sheathing under the flex grip. Strip off about 8mm ($\frac{5}{16}$in) of insulation from the end of each of the three cores. Connect the brown wire to terminal L, the blue wire to terminal N and the green/yellow wire to terminal E. Place the wires neatly in the box and replace the cover.

Loop-in socket Turn off the power at the mains, release the socket from its box and knock out another cable entry hole in the box. If this is metal, you will have to knock out a metal blank and fit a PVC grommet. With the circuit cable from the disposal unit outlet neatly laid and fixed, push the end of the cable through the knock-out hole into the mounting box; cut the cable, leaving about 125mm (5in) in the box. Strip off the sheathing, leaving about 13mm ($\frac{1}{2}$in) within the box. Bare the ends of the two insulated wires and enclose the earth wire in PVC sleeving. Loosen terminal L of the existing socket and insert the end of the red wire into the terminal alongside the other two red wires; tighten the terminal screw. Connect in a similar way the black wire to the N terminal and the earth wire to the E terminal. Lay the nine wires in the box and refix the socket to its box.

Releasing jammed unit
The most likely trouble to be experienced with the waste disposal unit is when waste jams up in it. With a reversible action model you simply flick the reversing switch and restart the motor. Since the jamming stalls the motor, however, this will run hot and operate a thermal cut-out. Wait about five minutes for the motor to cool and the cut-out to reset. With a non-reversible action disposal unit a key is used for releasing the jammed unit. Switch off the connection unit or pull the plug out of the socket; by the time the release has been accomplished, the motor will have cooled and the cut-out reset. Switch on and restart the machine.

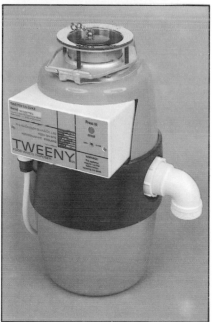

Installing a bath

If you want to replace an old bath with a modern pressed steel or plastic one you can do the job yourself, provided you have help to move the old bath out. Modern baths are much lighter than the traditional cast-iron ones and an acrylic plastic bath is particularly suitable for DIY installation, since one strong person can easily carry it upstairs and plumb it in. Pressed steel baths are liable to accidental damage in storage and installation, so care is needed in handling them. This drawback, however, has been largely overcome by the introduction of the 'super-steel' bath, made from material 50 percent thicker – and so much tougher – than ordinary pressed steel baths.

If you choose a bath with taps in the same position as those in the old one, fitting will present few problems.

Removing the old bath

As with many plumbing projects, removing the old fitting is more difficult than installing the new one. Your bath is likely to have been installed many years ago and the plumbing fittings – connected in the cramped, ill-lit space between the end of the bath and the wall – may be difficult to undo. You will almost certainly need a bath tap spanner which can be used in a vertical position in the limited space behind the bath.

Cut off the water supply to the bath taps by closing the stopcock on the cold water storage cylinder or, if there is no stopcock, by tying up the ball valve serving the cistern and running the taps until water ceases to flow. Remove the bath panels (where they exist) and apply penetrating oil to the nuts securing the water supply pipes to the taps and the waste pipe to the bath trap. (An aerosol of penetrating oil is easier to use and more effective than rubbing on oil.) Use the bath tap spanner to undo the nuts connecting the tails of the taps to the water supply and the nut connecting the trap to the waste pipe. If it is impossible to undo these nuts in this way, you can cut through the tap tails and the trap with a hacksaw and the nuts can be turned once the bath has been moved.

The overflow pipe may be connected directly to the bath trap; but in an old installation, it is more likely to be taken straight through the wall to discharge into the open. In this case cut through the pipe and block the hole to prevent draughts.

If the bath has adjustable feet, you can lower them before moving the bath and probably avoid damaging glazed wall tiles around the bath. Either get someone to help you remove the bath or cover it with a blanket (to prevent metal flying) and go to work on it with a sledge-hammer, so you can take it out piece by piece.

Plumbing in the new bath

Do as much of the plumbing as possible before moving the bath into place. Fit the taps or bath mixer into the holes, using a flat plastic washer between the base of the tap and the surface of the bath. Underneath you will probably need to fit a top-hat washer before screwing on and tightening the back nut. Make sure your 22mm ($\frac{3}{4}$in) hot and cold water supply pipes are the right length to

connect to the tap tails and that they are fitted with tap connectors or 'cap and lining' joints.

Bed the 38mm ($1\frac{1}{2}$in) bath waste outlet down, in non-hardening mastic, into the hole provided at the bottom of the bath. Fit a plastic washer over the protruding threaded end of the waste outlet and secure with the waste fixing nut. Fit the bath trap (which will almost certainly have a flexible overflow pipe fitted) to the waste, using a non-hardening mastic and hand-tighten the coupling nut. If you choose a trap without a built-in overflow pipe, you should

1

- adjustable feet
- spreader batten
- water supply pipes
- metal 'P' trap
- overflow pipe

2

- mixer tap
- back nut
- cap and liner
- flexible overflow pipe
- plastic 'P' trap with built-in overflow
- water supply pipe
- plastic washer
- 'top hat' washer
- waste outlet

1 The plumbing of a traditional cast-iron bath
2 Plumbing in a new bath with a flexible overflow pipe built into the trap
3 Two types of bath wrench; the adjustable one (**top**) is particularly useful for reaching into tight corners
4 Before plumbing in an acrylic bath, turn it upside down and assemble the frame and cradle
5 The tile-on-tile method is one way to close the gap between an existing tiled area and the bath rim

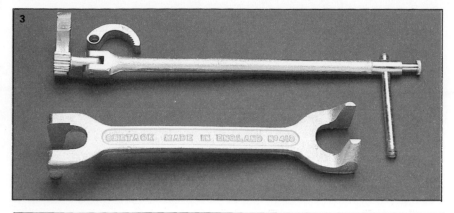

3

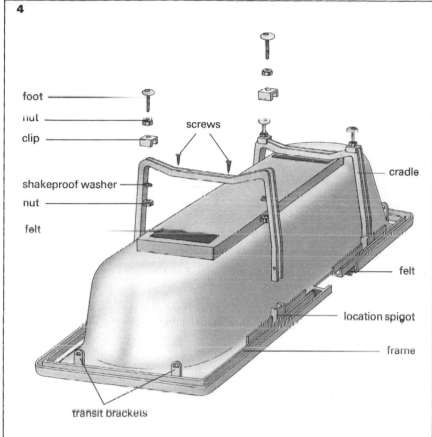

4

foot
nut
clip

screws

shakeproof washer
nut
felt

cradle

felt

location spigot

frame

transit brackets

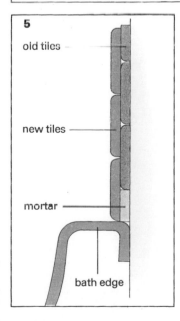

5

old tiles

new tiles

mortar

bath edge

---

connecting the trap to the waste pipe; but if you are doubtful about fixing, say, plastic to lead, change the waste pipe (and connections) to a material which is compatible with your bath plumbing. This is quite straightforward, especially if, in the case of an older house, you are discharging into a hopper head set in a rainwater downpipe.

Acrylic baths These are fitted in felt-lined frames and cradles to prevent them moving in use. Begin by assembling and fixing the frame and cradle according to the manufacturer's instructions.

If you are using soldered capillary joints for the bathroom water supply pipes, keep the blowtorch well away from the bath and shield it with a piece of asbestos as you work. Use a PVC rather than a metal trap and waste pipe because the thermal expansion which takes place when the bath is filled with hot water could result in the acrylic being damaged.

Coping with settlement

The type of floor in your bathroom is important because baths often take months – and frequent use – before they settle and find a permanent level. Settlement is more noticeable when a bath is placed on a timber floor and sinks into the softwood; it is often accentuated when softwood pieces are used as spreader battens to distribute the load on the feet over a larger area of floor, or as a means of adjusting the height of the bath (this applies even on a concrete floor). Settlement is rarely more than about 3mm ($\frac{1}{8}$in), but may be greater than this if the floor gives under its increased load. Some settlement of the feet into the floor (or battens) does have the advantage of anchoring the bath if it is otherwise unfixed. Alternatively you can use hardwood battens or quarry tiles as packing to avoid settlement. Drill holes in the feet of the bath and screw through these and the packing into the floor.

If the bath area is tiled, any settlement will leave a small gap between the bath rim and the bottom course of tiles; this is not only unsightly, but also provides an entry point for insects and moisture (which can build up and cause rot in the fabric of the building).

Sealing the gaps

If you are tiling above the bath and have not taken precautions against settlement, wait until the bath has settled then lay the bottom course of tiles as close to the bath rim as possible to allow the minimum grouting line. You may want to retile the whole area, particularly if your new bath is lower than the old one; this you can do with the tile-on-tile technique. First fill the gap flush to the existing tiles with a mortar mix of three parts sand to one part cement, then lay the first course of new tiles close to the bath rim, again allowing a small gap for grouting. If you do not want to retile the bath area, you can close any gap below the existing tiles by raising the bath with packing or by adjusting the feet (as described above). Alternatively bridge the gap using quadrant tiles or fill the cavity with a non-hardening mastic.

Quadrant tiles These are available in sets consisting of straight lengths, mitred internal corners and rounded external ends, together with the appropriate adhesive.

Lay out the tiles without adhesive to see whether any have to be cut. If so, always cut the centre tile in each row. Cut them by scoring across the glazed convex surface in the required cutting place, bend-

---

fit a slotted waste outlet and the overflow pipe must be fitted with the appropriate ring connector. This is slipped over the waste, using a plastic washer between it and the bath, and secured with the waste fixing nut.

Before you move the bath into position, make sure the branch waste pipe that is to connect to the trap is the right length. When you are satisfied all the plumbing will connect properly, move the bath into place and ensure it is level by placing a straight-edge across the rim (widthways and lengthways) and checking with a spirit level. Adjust any fall by screwing or unscrewing both feet on one side or end respectively. The fall of the bottom of the bath towards the waste outlet is built in and need not be taken into account. Make the connections, starting with the supply pipe to the furthest tap, then the flexible overflow pipe (which may be connected with a jubilee clip or a nut and bolt through the overflow outlet), then the near tap and finally the waste pipe to the bath trap.

A number of permutations exist when it comes to

6a If you need to cut a quadrant tile, score across the glazed surface and tap the waste piece with the end of a cold chisel
6b Alternatively score the cutting line and snap the tile with a pair of pincers
6c You can also use a hacksaw to cut halfway through the tile; then snap the tile by hand
6d Always start laying tiles at an internal corner
7a When using non-hardening mastic, apply an even pressure to the tube while pushing it forwards slowly
7b Trim and lift off any surplus mastic with a knife

ing a piece of stiff card around the curve as a guide; tap the waste section with the flat end of a cold chisel to form a clean break. Alternatively, use a pair of pincers to snap the tile. Another method is to saw part way through the back surface with a hacksaw and snap the tile from the front, using glasspaper to clean the broken edge.

Start tiling with an internal mitred corner and continue until you reach nearly midway on that edge. Lay the corner tiles at the other end and again work towards the middle. If necessary the last tile can be cut to fill the gap. Keep your joints uniform for an overall balanced look. Before you stick the tiles down, make sure the top edges of the bath are clean and dry; apply adhesive to the flat back edges of the tiles and press them into position. Don't slide the tiles into place and keep adhesive off the glaze.

Trim any surplus adhesive away with a sharp knife and wipe over the glaze with a rag dipped in white spirit. When the adhesive is dry, grout between the tiles in the usual way.

Mastic sealant This remains firm but pliable so it can expand or contract in the cavity and, unlike a cellulose filler, it will not shrink and fall away. It is available in a range of colours to match popular sanitary ware and is easily applied from tubes. One

large tube is usually sufficient to fill a gap up to 3mm ($\frac{1}{8}$in) wide, providing the depth of the cavity is not too great. If the cavity is deep, pack it with sand and cement mortar if you can do so without it falling to the floor behind the bath. This will save a considerable amount of mastic.

Your tube may have a tapering nozzle, which can be cut at marked positions to correspond with the width of the gap. To master the technique of applying it, remember the tube must be pushed forward slowly during application and you should squeeze it out at an even pressure to produce a clean concave line. Ideally the depth of the mastic should be 6mm ($\frac{1}{4}$in). Any surplus mastic left on the bath or tiles can be trimmed off with a knife. Make sure the blade is not too sharp, otherwise it will score the surface of the bath or the tiles.

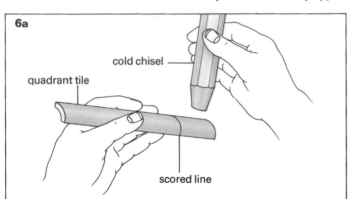

6a
cold chisel
quadrant tile
scored line

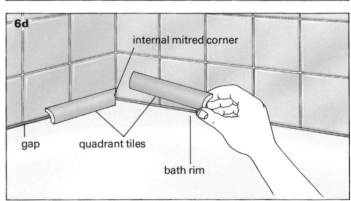

6b
scored line
pincers

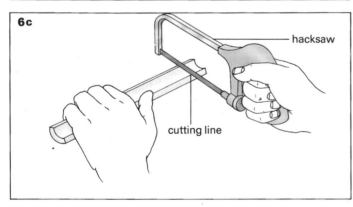

6c
hacksaw
cutting line

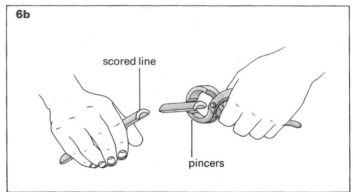

6d
internal mitred corner
gap   quadrant tiles
bath rim

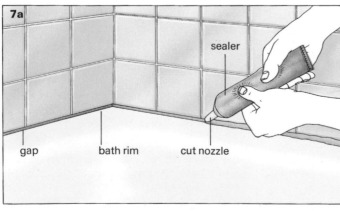

7a
sealer
gap   bath rim   cut nozzle

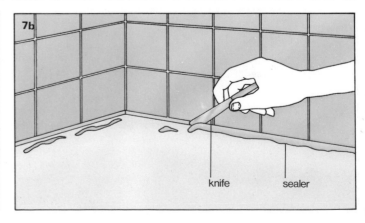

7b
knife   sealer

Central heating

Fitting a gas or solid fuel back boiler

Although the installation of back boilers and room heaters involves a considerable amount of work, there is no reason why a competent DIY worker should not tackle it provided the proper tools are available and certain essential factors are considered. There are three types of appliance generally installed in the home – the solid fuel-fired back boiler, the solid fuel room heater and the combined gas-fired space heater and back boiler unit.

Solid fuel back boiler This appliance utilizes the surplus heat from an open fire. One type basically supplies domestic hot water since its heat output is insufficient to supply radiators with adequate heat to guarantee room temperatures. A second type, which has side cheeks, has a high output and will supply radiators as well in an average size house.

Solid fuel room heater This is an extremely popular appliance with householders who wish to use solid fuel to supply their total hot water requirements, since it has a high enough output to provide full central heating and hot water for an average size house.

Combined gas-fired space heater/back boiler This type of appliance is also extremely popular since gas is a cleaner fuel than coal; it is capable of providing an inexhaustible supply of hot water for washing, cooking and central heating. The gas space heater provides a source of heat which can be operated independently of the back boiler unit. This means it can be used to heat a single room when the weather is not so cold and full central

heating is unnecessary. However the back boiler unit will have to be used if hot water is required. Normally, when the appliance is used for central heating, the hot water is automatically supplied to the cylinder via gravity circulation.

Checking the chimney
It is imperative the chimney is swept before the boiler is installed, since a blocked chimney will cause fumes to come into the room. If you decide to sweep the chimney yourself, lay down plenty of dust sheets to avoid damage to furnishings. Although you can easily hire the necessary equipment, the cost of employing a sweep is comparatively low and this is a job which might be best left to the professional. Even if the chimney is clear, you must test it to ensure there is a good updraught for fumes to clear properly. The chimney is best tested with the fire surround in position as follows:
● Cover the fireplace opening with a damp sheet of newspaper.
● Make a small hole, not larger than 50mm (2in) in diameter, in the centre of the sheet.
● Close all doors and windows in the room where the fireplace is situated and in any adjoining rooms.
● Light a match and place it in front of the hole, taking care not to set the paper alight. If the flame is drawn towards the opening, the chimney is clear. But if the flame remains upright or blows into the room, the chimney is defective or inadequately cleaned; any faults must be rectified before any

Below Solid fuel back boiler
Bottom left Inset room heater
Bottom Gas-fired heater with back boiler

1 Before installation, check for correct updraught in the chimney so fumes will clear properly
2a Minimum depth of recess required for most appliances
2b The recess can be deepened by using a hollow surround
2c With a shallow recess, or where you do not wish to remove the existing fireback, use a free-standing heater
3 Where a back boiler is to supply central heating, it must be connected to an indirect hot water system; all pipe dimensions given here are minimum sizes

98

appliances are fitted. If the flue is in poor condition, you can line it; but for solid fuel installations the job should be done by a professional.

Checking the water system
Once the chimney has been checked it is advisable to examine the existing water system; it must conform to water board regulations with regard to pipe size and methods of connection. Remember back boilers must be connected to an indirect water system if needed to supply a central heating system. If you need to purchase a new cylinder, it might be worth considering one with a special boss so an immersion heater can be fitted in the system at the same time as the other appliances. This will be a useful standby for providing hot water should the main appliance be shut down for any reason.

Estimating boiler size
To determine what size boiler you need to fit, you must assess the total heat loss of the area the boiler is intended to supply. Relative heat loss is easily measured by checking with the manufacturer as to the output of each radiator. The outputs are added together, with an additional 1–2kW to compensate for hot water requirements, to give you the total output.

If you have no radiators, you must use a more

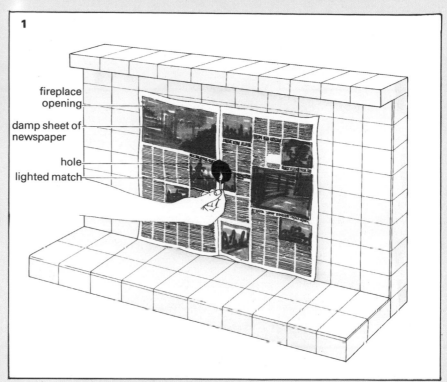

1

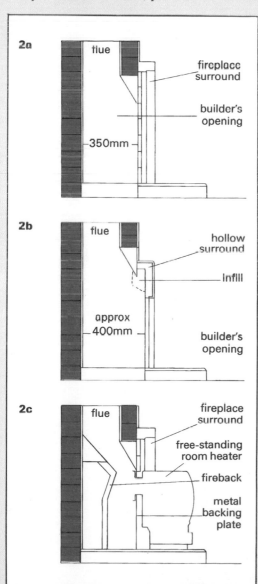

2a

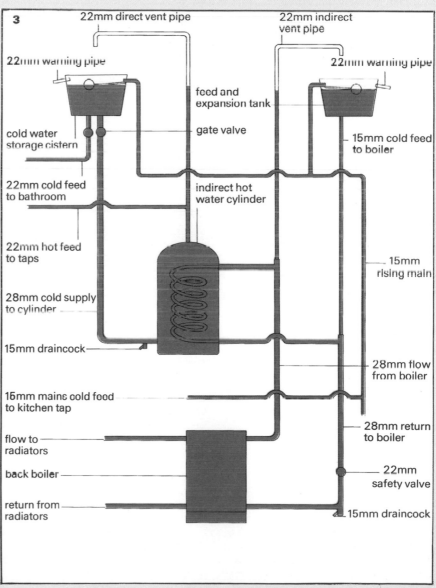

99

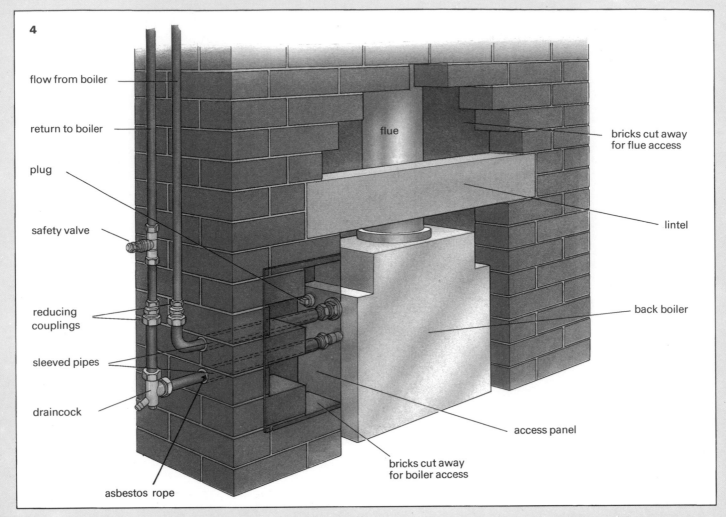

4

flow from boiler

return to boiler

plug

safety valve

reducing couplings

sleeved pipes

draincock

asbestos rope

flue

bricks cut away for flue access

lintel

back boiler

access panel

bricks cut away for boiler access

elaborate method of calculating heat loss. This involves a sound knowledge of basic mathematics, since you have to calculate the number of air changes per room or space and the heat loss that ensues, as well as the heat loss through the structure from each room or space. This will be covered on pages 105 and 106.

Since appliances are not 100 percent efficient, care must be taken to ensure a boiler with the correct input is installed to provide a sufficient output of heat to supply the system. As a rough guide, most modern gas-fired and high output solid fuel boilers are over 70 percent efficient, whereas solid fuel boilers supplying just hot water are only 45–50 percent efficient. If the size of the back boiler needed to heat a particular area is too large for the fireplace, another type such as the free-standing model is available. Installing an undersized boiler with insufficient output is bad economics.

Preparing the fireplace
You may need to remove the fire surround, in which case take care not to damage it if you intend to replace it. Each individual surround has to be treated differently since there are various types with a variety of fixing points. They are usually quite simple to remove and it is worth considering selling the surround to a second-hand furniture shop.

Once the surround has been removed, the fabric of the old existing fireback should be cleared away. (With some room heaters this is not necessary.) Break the firebrick with a club hammer and clear away all the backfill material to reveal a clean

builder's opening of square brickwork. The builder's opening is the structure that is left after the fire surround, the fire bricks and all the builder's rubble have been removed from the fireplace.

Since this operation will be very dusty, lay plenty of dust sheets around the fireplace and wear a protective mask. Check there is sufficient room in the builder's opening to take the boiler. The depth of the recess should be at least 350mm (14in), although some boilers require more space than this. If this is the case, a different type of fire surround can be fitted to increase the overall depth of the fireplace opening; where the space is still too small, a free-standing room heater may be fitted.

Connecting the water supply
Apart from slight variations in the positions of the tappings in the boiler, the method of connecting any boiler to the water supply is the same. Connections to the boiler itself should always be made with compression type fittings, since these are easy to disconnect should the need ever arise. The external thread on the fitting must be screwed into the internal thread on the boiler, using hemp and jointing compound to ensure a sound, watertight joint. PFTE tape should not be used since boiler tappings usually have deep thread forms which are not easy to seal.

The boiler tapping determines the size of pipes which must pass through the chimney-breast; you must sleeve these pipes by running them through a pipe one size larger than that being used and insulate between the two with asbestos rope. If the pipe

4 The connections for the water supply to the boiler. The pipes which pass through the chimney-breast must be sleeved in pipes one size larger and asbestos rope should be placed between the two. Where pipes must be reduced, this should be done on vertical runs by using reducing couplings. A draincock should be fitted on the lowest part of the system and a safety valve incorporated in the return pipe to the boiler. A removable panel will make access easier for maintenance of the installation later

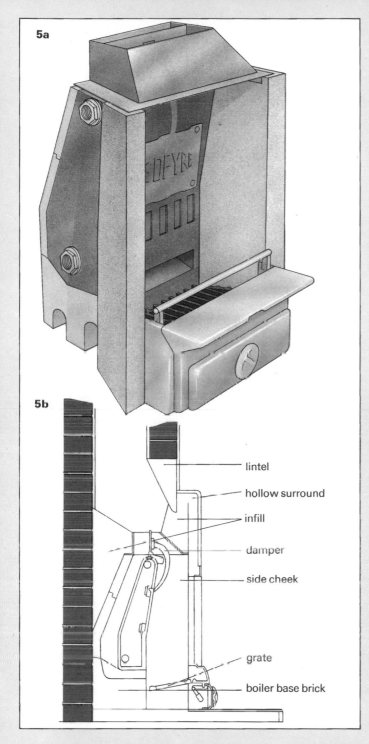

5a

5b

- lintel
- hollow surround
- infill
- damper
- side cheek
- grate
- boiler base brick

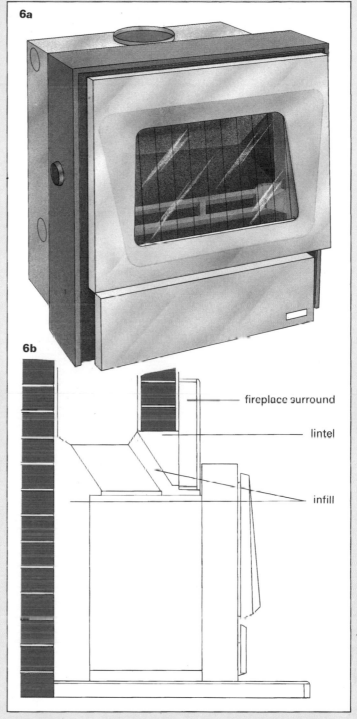

6a

6b

- fireplace surround
- lintel
- infill

size needs reducing, this should be done on a vertical piece of pipe, since this aids circulation.

To gain access to the pipework connections during installation, it may be necessary to cut away some of the chimney-breast. Once the water connections are made, any opening can either be bricked up or covered with a temporary panel which can be removed should inspection or maintenance be necessary. Do not forget to install a draincock in the system so it can be drained when necessary; this should be fitted onto the lowest part of the system. Fit a safety valve on the return to the boiler in a position which can be easily reached when carrying out maintenance.

Existing pipes should be connected with either compression or soldered capillary fittings, whichever is easier, although the latter are generally

cheaper to buy. Any tappings that are not used can be blocked off with brass plugs if a direct cylinder is used; with an indirect cylinder black iron plugs, commonly called gas plugs, should be used. Galvanized plugs should never be used.

Once the connections are made they must be tested by filling the system and any radiators with water and flushing through to ensure all pipes are clear. Failure to test the system at this stage may lead to difficulties later should the joints prove unsound. It is advisable to flush the system again after about six months.

Installing a solid fuel back boiler
Most modern back boilers take the place of the firebrick back. The boiler is usually supplied in parts and consists of a back, side cheeks and a flue

5a Solid fuel back boiler for use with open fires
5b Section through the installation
6a Inset room heater with back boiler
6b Section through the installation

damper assembly; all these must be assembled on site. Once assembled and correctly positioned, the water connections (as described above) can be made.

Once the water connections have been checked, fill in the space between the opening and the back of the boiler with infill (six parts vermiculite to one part lime) and refix the fire surround close up to the back boiler cheeks.

Warning When the fire is first lit, run the system at a low heat for at least 24 hours to allow the installation to expand and settle down slowly.

Installing a solid fuel room heater
There are two types of room heater available, one free-standing and the other inset. Both are available with or without a boiler attached. The inset type, although more difficult to fit, does not project as far into the room as the free-standing type and is therefore more likely to comply with Building Regulations.

Since the inset appliance is mostly hidden, the opening needs to be exposed by removing the fire surround, while part of the chimney breast at the side will need to be cut away to gain access to the pipework and flue connections, as described above.

Once the builder's opening has been cleared and the brickwork exposed, you can replace the surround. It is essential the surround is replaced perfectly level and upright in relation to the hearth, which must also be level, otherwise the appliance will be poorly sealed; this will affect both the performance and the efficiency of the appliance.

Ease the appliance into position and secure it to the hearth with screws; make sure the wall plugs you use are non-combustible. Fixing points vary

7a Free-standing room heater with back boiler
7b Section through the installation and detail of the flue connection (**inset**)
8a Gas-fired space heater and back boiler
8b Section through the installation
9a Ventilation for a gas-fired appliance may be provided by metal ducting under the floor; the ducting should lead from the side of the chimney-breast to an airbrick in an outside wall
9b Alternatively ventilation may be provided by an

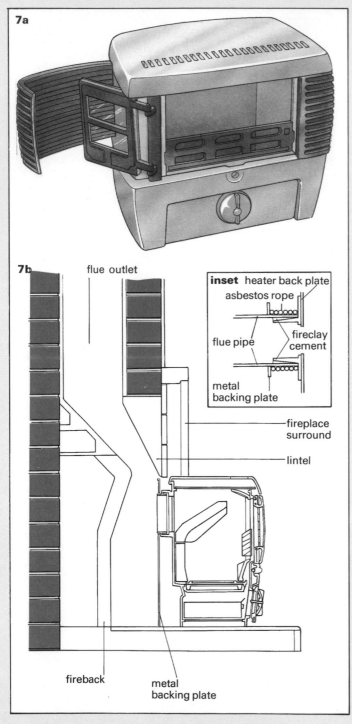

7a

7b
flue outlet

inset heater back plate
asbestos rope
flue pipe
fireclay cement
metal backing plate

fireplace surround

lintel

fireback

metal backing plate

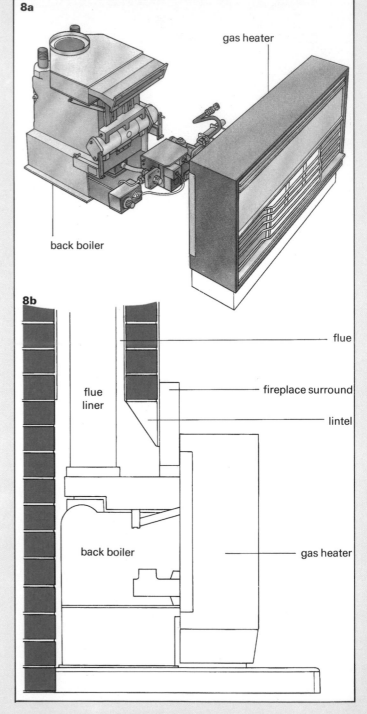

8a

gas heater

back boiler

8b

flue liner

flue

fireplace surround

lintel

back boiler

gas heater

airbrick set into the chimney-breast and covered with a fixed grille

10a Before fitting a flue liner, measure the length required by lowering a piece of weighted string down the chimney; the liner must protrude 150mm above the chimney

10b Pass the liner down the flue

10c At the top of the stack, clamp the liner into position and fit a cowl terminal; at the bottom, fit the liner onto the flue spigot of the boiler

from one appliance to another, but the manufacturer's instruction sheet should clarify the method of fixing. Connect up the pipes and test, as described above.

Appliances are available with either a back or top flue socket which is also the flue outlet. Top outlets are usually more suitable and certainly easier to attach to the main flue, although the type best suited to any particular situation will depend on the way in which the main flue is constructed. The top outlet on the boiler is extended into the main chimney stack; a piece of cast iron or mild steel can be used for this. The flue extension must be sealed to the main stack and the flue outlet on the appliance. The gap between the appliance and the builder's opening should now be filled after a final check for water leaks. Finally, fill the opening at the side of the chimney-breast.

Installing gas-fired space heater/back boiler

The installation of this type of appliance involves the following sequence of work: installing the flue liner, positioning the boiler, connecting the water supply, wiring, making the final gas connection and testing the installation.

Flue liner A gas appliance produces carbon dioxide and water vapour. Both are harmless provided the appliance is adequately ventilated and care is taken to prevent condensation occurring in the flue. The question of ventilation is most important and provided it is adequate no problems will arise; your local gas board will tell you how much you need. Condensation, however, will occur if a flue liner is not placed in the chimney.

The flue liner is installed in two stages: the liner is first passed down the flue from the roof, before the boiler is positioned; then the final sealing and

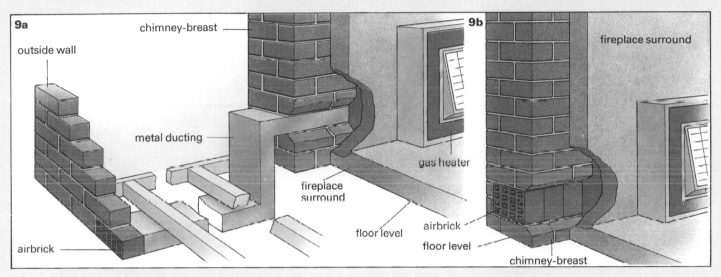

9a
outside wall
chimney-breast
metal ducting
fireplace surround
floor level
airbrick

9b
fireplace surround
gas heater
airbrick
floor level
chimney-breast

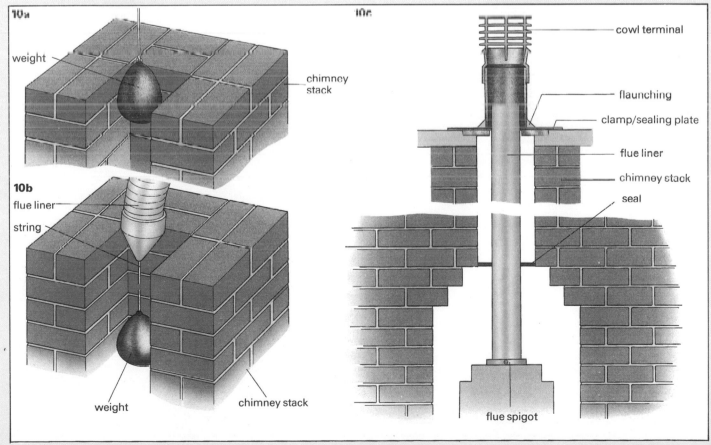

10a
weight
chimney stack

10b
flue liner
string
weight
chimney stack

10c
cowl terminal
flaunching
clamp/sealing plate
flue liner
chimney stack
seal
flue spigot

connection to the boiler is made, when the boiler is positioned and connected to the water supply. Before inserting the flue liner, remove the chimney pot and make sure the flue is clear. Lower a weighted piece of string down the chimney in order to measure the exact length of the flue liner required, bearing in mind the flue liner must protrude 150mm (6in) above the chimney at the top and must fit onto the flue spigot of the boiler at the bottom. Pass the liner down the chimney, using the string as a guide and preferably having someone at the bottom to hold it. When connecting the flue liner to the boiler it is essential all the air seals are maintained since these prevent condensation.

Positioning boiler Once the flue liner is in its approximate position, the boiler can be placed in the fire opening. Whether or not the surround needs to be removed depends upon the make of boiler being fitted; whatever the type, however, it is necessary to remove the fire bricks and clear the builder's opening, since this facilitates the connection to the water supply which is installed in the same way as for the solid fuel appliances. Once the appliance has been tested for water leaks, the flue liner can be attached to the appliance and the installation of the flue completed at roof level.

Wiring The use of electrical controls on gas appliances is now universal and it is impossible to buy a domestic gas fired boiler without them. The method of wiring up a system depends on the make of boiler and the type and number of controls incorporated in the system. It is therefore essential to examine thoroughly the maker's data sheets on the boiler and any controls used to determine how the system is wired. The installation must be wired in accordance with IEE regulations, using heat resistant cable of the correct loading. The cable must not touch any hot surfaces or pipes and all controls – including the boiler – must be earthed to the common earthing point provided by the local Electricity Board.

Making final gas connection Under the 1972 Gas Regulations Act it is illegal for anybody other than a qualified gas engineer to interfere with or fix any part of a gas installation. Severe penalties are imposed for contravention, including imprisonment. Therefore at this stage of the installation it is essential you contact a qualified gas engineer to run the gas supply, make the final gas connections to the boiler and space heater, check the installation and test it for correct operation. Under no circumstances tackle this part of the work yourself.

You will have to replace the fire surround before the space heater is finally fixed.

Following regulations

All the installations described must be carried out in accordance with the relevant section of the Building Regulations and must also comply with Gas, Electricity and Water Board regulations where applicable. The manufacturer's instructions should be strictly adhered to at all times.

11 The wiring from the mains to a gas boiler via a froststat, time clock/programmer and room thermostat

12 The minimum dimensions for fireplaces stipulated by the Building Regulations

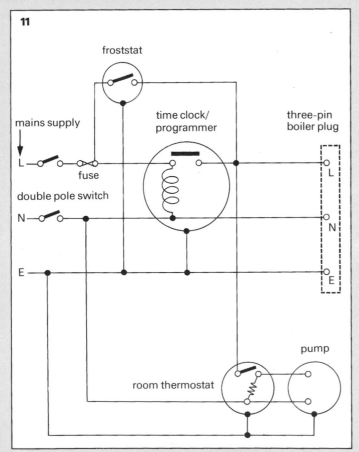

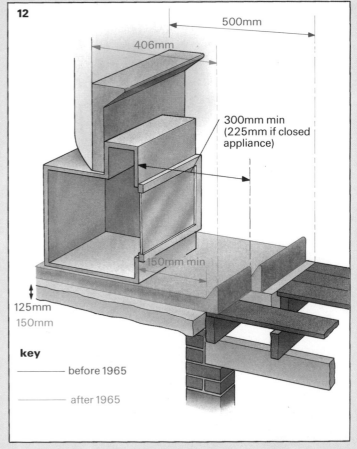

Calculating heat loss and boiler size

Heat is a form of energy which always flows from a hot place to a colder one until an even temperature is reached; the greater the difference in temperature, the greater the rate of heat loss. Insulation can slow down the rate of loss, but will never stop it completely; so the lost heat has to be replaced.

In a central heating system the boiler has to provide enough heat to compensate for all the losses. For a hot water cylinder the boiler has to replace the losses and also heat up water which is drawn off for use. It is possible to calculate these heat losses and from there to find the size of boiler necessary for a particular installation.

Calculating boiler size for hot water cylinder

The water in the cylinder is heated by the boiler to a temperature suitable for domestic purposes – usually 60°C. A calculation based simply on this demand would, however, lead to a much larger boiler size than necessary; hot water is rarely drawn off continuously and therefore a heating-up period can be allowed for. A boiler which has twice as long to heat a given amount of water need only be half as powerful – and therefore smaller and less expensive. It is important to strike a balance between usage and heating-up time to avoid having to wait for hot water, but generally a two to three-hour period can be allowed. The total heat requirement is calculated by adding together three factors:

A The heat required to raise the water to the right temperature.
B The heat lost from the pipes.
C The heat lost from the cylinder.

A The heat required to raise the water to the right temperature depends on the quantity of water to be heated and the difference in temperature between the cold water and the desired hot water. For calculations it is expressed in the formula:
$$Q = M \times SH \times (t_h - t_l)$$
where Q is the heat required (in kilojoules), M is the quantity of water to be heated (in litres), SH is the amount of heat required to raise 1kg of water 1°C (known as the specific heat of water – normally 4.2), t_h is the desired temperature of hot water and t_l the temperature of cold water.

B The heat loss from the pipes depends on the length of the pipe run between the cylinder and the boiler and on the temperature difference between the hot water and the air in the surrounding room. This can be estimated from the graph.

C The heat loss from an adequately lagged cylinder can be taken as 145 watts per second.

Example The volume of the cylinder is 400 litres. The cold water is at 10°C and the required temperature of the hot water is 60°C. The total length of 28mm diameter pipe is 20m and the temperature of the room is 10°C. The pipes are painted, but not insulated. (1 litre of water weighs 1kg).

A Using the formula above:
$$Q = 400 \times 4.2 \times (60 - 10) = 84000 \text{ kilojoules}$$
To get the answer in kilowatts (kilojoules/sec) to heat the water in one hour, divide by 3600:
$$Q = \frac{84000}{3600} \text{ kW/hr} = 23.34 \text{ kW/hr.}$$

B From the graph (line ABC) the heat loss from the pipes is 62 watts per metre per hour. The total length of the pipes is 20m, so the total loss is $62 \times 20 = 1240$ watts per hour = 1.24kW/hr.

C The heat loss from the cylinder is 145 watts or 0.145kW. The total heat requirement for the boiler is therefore the sum of A, B and C:
$$23.34 + 1.24 + 0.145 = 24.785 \text{kW/hr.}$$
If the boiler has a two-hour heating-up period, the boiler output needs to be:
$$24.785 \div 2 = 12.39 \text{kW/hr.}$$
If the boiler has a three-hour heating-up period, the boiler output needs to be:
$$24.785 : 3 = 8.26 \text{kW/hr.}$$

Boiler rating These figures give the output required from the boiler, but unfortunately most manufacturers quote the input figure for the rating. To convert the output rating to the input, an allowance must be made for the boiler efficiency. In addition, an overload factor of 20 percent must be included in the case of any fuel other than gas to allow for

1 Use this graph to estimate how much heat is lost from your pipes: find the temperature difference between the hot water in the pipes and the air in the room (A), draw a line vertically to the curve for the pipe diameter (B), then draw a line horizontally and read off the heat loss (C)

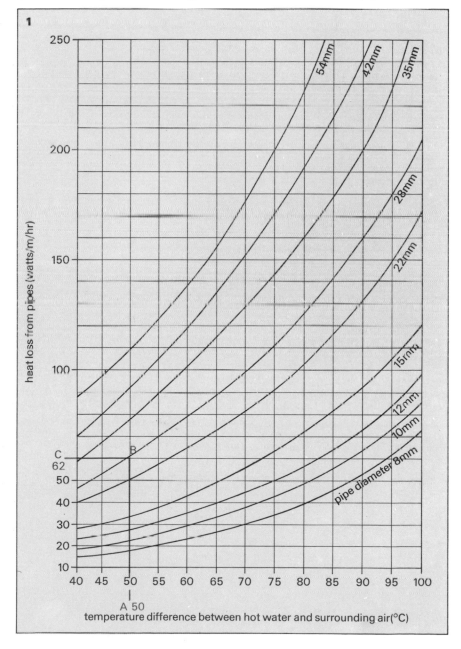

1

heat loss from pipes (watts/m/hr)

temperature difference between hot water and surrounding air(°C)

variations in output. Therefore the total input rating for a two hour period becomes:

$$12.39 \times \frac{100}{55} \text{ (efficiency)} \times \frac{120}{100} \text{ (overload)}$$
$$= 27.03 \text{kW/hr.}$$

The boiler needed for this installation would therefore be one with an input rating of not less than 27.03kW/hr.

Calculating boiler size for central heating and hot water

To determine the size of boiler required to provide central heating and hot water for a particular property, you must calculate initially the heat loss from the relevant area. Heat is lost in two ways:

A Through the fabric of the building.
B By ventilation.

A The rate of heat loss through the fabric depends on the thermal transmittance (or 'U' value), the area of the surface and the temperature difference between the inside and outside air. The 'U' value is a property of the material – or combination of materials – in the construction and can be found from specially prepared tables (such as in the *Institution of Plumbing: Data* book, which should be available through your local library). An area of different material, such as a window, has a different 'U' value and must be calculated separately from the rest of the wall. For calculations the heat loss through the fabric is expressed in the formula:

$$Q = A \times U \times (t_h - t_l)$$

where Q is the heat loss, A is the area of each separate material, U is the 'U' value of the construction, t_h the desired room temperature and t_l the outside air temperature.

The outside air temperature is taken as $-1°C$ in Britain. For an internal wall of a room, t is taken as the temperature on the other side of the wall; if this is the same as the temperature in the room – or higher – there is no heat loss.

B Heat loss through ventilation depends on the volume of the room, the number of air changes per hour and the difference in temperature between the room air and the outside air. For calculations the heat loss is expressed in the following formula:

$$Q = M \times N \times SH \times (t_h - t_l)$$

where Q is the total heat loss, M is the volume of the room, N is the number of air changes per hour (see table), the specific heat of air ($1.21kJ/m^3/°C$ at $16°C$), t_h the desired room temperature and t_l the outside air temperature.

Example The dimensions of the room are as shown on the plan. The ceiling height is 2.8m and the window is 2m high and 2.5m wide. The floor is timber on joists, with an airbrick below. The ceiling is plasterboard on joists, with a timber floor above and a temperature of 16°C in the room above. The rooms are of average exposure. Rooms are said to be exposed when the building is on a hillside, at the coast or on the riverside – and when it has an outside wall facing north, north-east or east. The 'U' value tables give two sets of readings – for average and exposed rooms.

A Using the formula above:

$$Q = A \times U \times (t_h - t_l)$$

the heat loss must be calculated for all the surfaces in the room. You must first list the relevant surfaces and work out their areas:

outside wall $A = 4.0 \times 2.8 = 11.2m^2$
outside wall $B = (3.5 \times 2.8) - (2.5 \times 2) = 4.8m^2$
window $C = 2.5 \times 2 = 5.0m^2$

partition wall $E = 4.0 \times 2.8 = 11.2m^2$
floor $= 3.5 \times 4.0 = 14.0m^2$
ceiling $= 3.5 \times 4.0 = 14.0m^2$

The partition wall D is not included in the calculations since the temperature is the same on both sides. The 'U' values for each surface can be found from the specially prepared tables (see above). The room temperature required is 21°C and the outside temperature is $-1°C$. The heat loss for the outside wall A will therefore be:

$$Q = 11.2 \times 1.5 \times [21 - (-1)] = 369.6 \text{ watts}$$

Follow the same procedure for all the surfaces and add the amounts together. The total heat loss for the room will be:

$369.6 + 158.4 + 473.0 + 98.0 + 187.88 + 119.0$
$= 1405.88$ watts

B The volume of the room is $39.2m^3$ ($3.5 \times 4.0 \times 2.8m^3$). The number of air changes per hour is taken as 2 (see table). The required room temperature is 21°C and the outside temperature is $-1°C$, as above. The heat loss through ventilation will therefore be:

$$Q = 2 \times 39.2 \times 1.21 \times [21 - (-1)] = 2087.01 \text{kW/sec}$$
or 0.58kW/hr

Therefore the total heat loss from the room is:
$1.406kW + 0.58kW = 1.99kW$.

The heat losses from each room have to be added together to give the heat loss for the whole house – and hence the boiler output rating. The boiler input rating is derived from this in the same way as for the hot water cylinder.

If there is a combined boiler for central heating and hot water, it is only necessary to calculate the requirements for the central heating and add on an extra 1kW for the hot water, if the hot water cylinder is no larger than 140 litres.

2 This room has been taken as an example from which to work out heat losses through the fabric of the building
3 The recommended number of air changes for particular rooms and the temperatures which should be maintained in those rooms when the outside temperature is $-1°C$

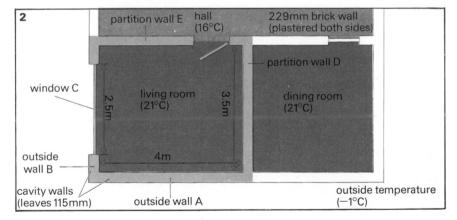

2 partition wall E | hall (16°C) | 229mm brick wall (plastered both sides)
window C | 2.5m | living room (21°C) | 3.5m | partition wall D | dining room (21°C)
outside wall B | 4m
cavity walls (leaves 115mm) | outside wall A | outside temperature (−1°C)

Room	**Desired temperature**	**Air changes/hr**
Living room		1½-2
Dining room	21°C	1½-2
Bedsitter		1½-2
Bathroom		2
Hall or landing		2
Toilet	16°C	1½
Bedroom		1
Kitchen	18°C	2

What fuel?

If you are going to install a central heating system, one of the first decisions you will have to make is what fuel to use. This involves a choice between an all-electric system and systems using solid fuel, gas or oil. Each type of fuel has advantages and disadvantages to be considered when you are deciding which system will best suit your requirements. Bear in mind all systems, apart from the solid fuel gravity-fed type, depend on electricity, for example to operate the pump which drives the hot water through the pipes and, in some cases, to power a programming device so appliances are not in operation 24 hours a day; this means they are all susceptible to electrical breakdown and power cuts.

Solid fuel

If you decide to use solid fuel and install an appliance in a fireplace where it can be seen, it provides a source of radiant heat giving physical warmth and a comforting glow with a distinct psychological benefit. Also, modern technology has developed ways of reducing the problems of dirt, smoke and work associated with the use of solid fuel. Some types of solid fuel can be treated to remove some of the volatile matter which makes them burn with a smoky flame; other types such as anthracite are termed smokeless and can be burned in certain appliances without further treatment. A number of appliances can burn a selection of the variety of solid fuels available, so if one fuel is temporarily unavailable another will serve. In some cases, however, selection of the correct fuel is critical if the appliance is to work at maximum efficiency.

There must be adequate space for storing the fuel.

The problem of storage can be considered a chief disadvantage of solid fuel, although once the fuel is delivered and stored you will have the advantage of an independent fuel supply. The more storage space you have the better, so you can buy coal in the summer when it is usually cheaper and store it for use in the winter when it may be in short supply and more expensive. Fuel must be taken from the storage area to the boiler or furnace and ashes must be removed. Appliances with self-feed hoppers cut the need for hand-stoking and eliminate the need to carry fuel through the home; but this does not overcome the problems caused when fuel is delivered, if you do not have a side or back entrance to your house. You will have to remove ashes and clinker, but riddling devices and large ash-pans make this less of a dirty and laborious job.

It is important to ensure the flue is sound before the appliance is installed; if flue defects occur, fumes containing carbon monoxide may enter the room. The flue should be swept at least once a year; but apart from this, if the flue is in good condition and the appliance properly installed, little maintenance is required. Problems may arise where there is an old, oversize chimney flue; in this case a great deal of air is drawn up into the flue causing the loss of useful heat from the room and making draughts likely. With a modern appliance and a standard-sized flue, draughts are minimal and the loss of heat from the room greatly reduced. If there is any doubt about the soundness of the chimney, it would probably be best to choose a gas-fired system since the flue would have to be lined in any case.

Because of the nature of the fuel and the way it

Below left Solid fuel cooker with integral back boiler to provide hot water and heating
Below Pressure jet oil-fired boiler

burns, a solid fuel system cannot operate fully automatically and an element of manual control is needed to adjust flue dampers or temperature regulators. Often the boiler operates for 24 hours since the appliance's response to output demands is too slow to allow programming to take place without overheating; this problem can lead to periods of either over or underheating of the house.

Installation of the appliance itself can be costly in terms of man hours and more difficult when compared with the installation of appliances using other fuels. On the other hand, solid fuel is one of the cheaper fuels.

Gas

This is a clean, economical fuel which does not require storage space on site. Temperature and time control systems are easily applied to gas-fired central heating systems so they will run automatically. The appliances should be serviced regularly; the supply and heat content of the fuel is fully guaranteed by law at certain minimum standards of pressure and quality.

Wherever possible gas appliances with balanced flues should be fitted and these must be installed on an outside wall. With this type of flue the air for combustion is drawn from outside the home and the harmless products of combustion are returned to the same source.

When compared with solid fuel appliances balanced flue gas appliances are easier to install. Bear in mind, however, a gas engineer must make the final gas connection and test the system.

Oil

Appliances fuelled by oil have some of the advantages of both gas and solid fuel appliances. For example, once the oil is delivered you will have an independent fuel supply, as with solid fuel. Oil is cleaner in use than solid fuel, but since oil-fired appliances are more difficult to adjust than gas appliances they are not quite as efficient or as clean as gas ones. Balanced flue type appliances are

available and oil is a controllable fuel which can be programmed in the same way as gas.

A large fuel tank is needed to store the oil; this can represent a formidable fire hazard which may affect house insurance premiums. If you are considering an oil-fired system, remember the storage tank must be accessible when deliveries are made.

Setting up an oil-fired system is more difficult than those powered by other fuels. Also, it is advisable – though not legally necessary – to ask a qualified engineer to check your installation before firing the appliance and systems for the first time.

Electricity

This is a clean and efficient fuel and appliances do not require a flue. You do not need space for storage, and time switches and thermostats can be fitted to make a system fully automatic.

Electricity can, however, be an expensive fuel and the running cost may be a disadvantage. Off-peak rates do reduce the cost of operating storage heaters and other forms of electric heating and, if efficiently installed and controlled, an electric system can be competitive to run. Some electric systems can be installed by the home handyman; others require a professional installation.

Top Thermostat for gas-fired wall boiler
Above Control panel for oil-fired boiler
Left Electric storage radiator
Below left Solid fuel gravity feed boiler
Below Gas-fired boiler

Choosing systems and appliances

Having chosen which fuel to use to fire your central heating system, you must decide on the type of system to install and the type of appliance which will be used to fire that system. There are various systems and appliances available which can be fired by solid fuel, oil or gas; there are also various electric systems available.

Warm air systems

Central heating systems can be either dry and based on ducted hot air or wet and based on piped hot water. Warm air systems rely on the distribution of heat using air as a transfer medium which is made to circulate through ducts of an appropriate size by a fan enclosed in the appliance. These systems have the advantage that they ensure a quick build-up of desired temperatures since air is forced to circulate and is constantly reheated; also the systems promote air change and thus ventilation. There are no radiators or pipework and significantly, these systems are cheaper to install in a new property than a wet system of comparable size. Warm air systems are also cleaner than their wet-type counterparts in that problems such as wall staining above radiators do not occur.

While warm air systems are very efficient, they are seldom fitted in an existing property because of the difficulties involved in installing them. A major problem is how to conceal the ductwork; it can be hidden behind false walls or under false ceilings, but this reduces room sizes and makes installation very expensive. These systems do not provide radiant heat, which is sometimes regarded as a disadvantage, and an additional appliance must be provided to supply hot water.

Wet systems

Most of the systems installed in existing properties utilize water as a transfer medium with the associated pipes and radiators. Gravity systems do not have a pump, but large diameter pipes are needed to give adequate circulation. Small bore systems never use copper pipe of an outside diameter smaller than 15mm (or $\frac{1}{2}$in) whereas mini or micro bore systems do incorporate pipes of smaller diameters than this for some runs. Some types of system have become quite complicated with regard to electrical control installation; you will find it easier to install a simple small bore system with pumped circulation to the radiators and gravity circulation to the hot water cylinder, since the design criteria and installation techniques demanded by this type of system are less complicated than with a mini bore system. If the system is to be connected to an existing hot water system, it is worth considering using one appliance to heat hot water and the radiators at the same time; make sure the existing pipework system complies with local Water Board requirements and is of the indirect type.

Small bore Where a small bore system is installed with one appliance heating both hot water and the radiators, the radiator circuit utilizes tappings on one side of the boiler while the hot water circuit

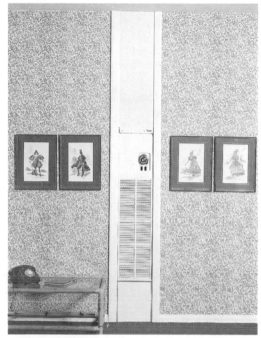

Left This unit, used to heat a warm air central heating system, is gas-fuelled; other fuels may also be used to fire this type of unit
1 A typical warm air central heating system. Heated air passes along ducts and is released through registers in the rooms; air returns into the system through grilles to be reheated and recirculated

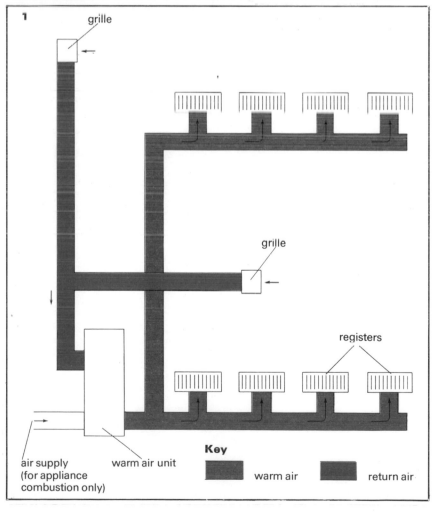

1

grille

grille

registers

warm air unit

air supply
(for appliance
combustion only)

Key

warm air   return air

109

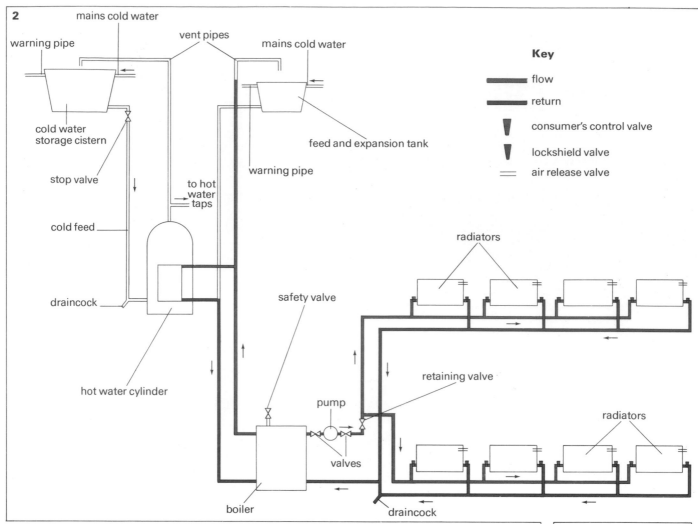

2

warning pipe
mains cold water
vent pipes
mains cold water

cold water storage cistern

feed and expansion tank

warning pipe

stop valve

to hot water taps

cold feed

radiators

draincock

safety valve

hot water cylinder

retaining valve

radiators

pump

valves

boiler

draincock

utilizes other tappings. Some form of temperature control should be fitted to the cylinder to safeguard against overheating of the hot water drawn off at taps, especially if the appliance is gas or oil-fired. If you are intending to utilize the existing hot water system for central heating, you should check the current boiler output; if it is insufficient you will have to replace it with one of the correct size.

If the appliance is to supply central heating only, special attention should be paid to the location of the pump relative to the open vent and cold feed. The open vent must tee-off from the flow pipe before the pump is fitted and the cold feed must be placed in the return pipe as close to the appliance as possible. Where the appliance supplies domestic central heating and hot water, the pump must be located on the flow as close as possible to the appliance before any tees are placed on the flow pipe and must pump water away from the appliance in the direction of the arrow stamped on the pump casing.

A retaining valve, sometimes called a check or non-return valve, should be fitted on all oil and gas-fired installations whether the appliance heats hot water and the radiators or just supplies heating. This is a mechanical weight-loaded non-electrical valve which stops gravity circulation when the pump is not running in the heating circuit.

Extra circuits can be run from the heating flow and return pipes if necessary; but whichever way a system is installed, always make sure it can be totally drained of water to facilitate maintenance.

Mini bore Apart from smaller pipe sizes, this is similar to the small bore system except that the flow and return connections on the radiators are fed with pipes from a manifold. It may be an open system or of a closed type with a sealed expansion tank. The mini bore system has the advantage of less water content than a small bore system and is sometimes cheaper to install. Since the pipe sizes are small a mini bore system is less obtrusive and can be run on top of skirting boards without looking unsightly. The use of copper bending tools is reduced because the pipe is fully annealed and can be bent easily with the fingers; when a system is run under the floorboards, less structural damage is caused to joists since they do not need to be so deeply notched. It is customary to run a manifold tapping to a radiator connection with one piece of 6, 8, 10, or 12mm outside diameter pipe without any joints in it apart from where it joins the manifold and the radiator valve; since there are fewer joints there is less risk of water leakage. Special radiator valves have been designed for mini bore systems.

Types of appliance

Where small and mini bore systems are concerned, appliances can be fired by either gas, oil or solid fuel and can be either free-standing, wall-mounted or back boiler types.

Free-standing boilers, fired by gas, oil or solid fuel, can be conventionally flued or gas and oil-fired types may have a balanced flue. A conventionally flued appliance can be fitted to an existing stack

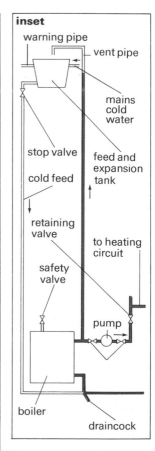

inset

warning pipe

vent pipe

mains cold water

stop valve

feed and expansion tank

cold feed

retaining valve

to heating circuit

safety valve

pump

boiler

draincock

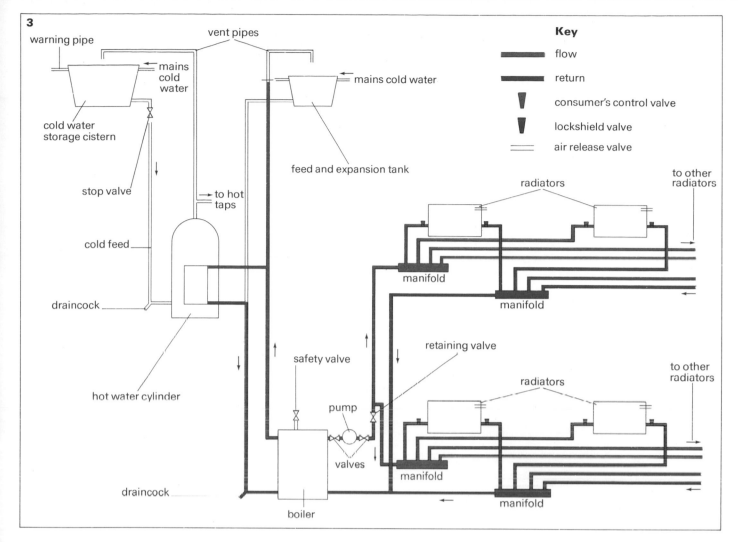

3

warning pipe

vent pipes

mains cold water

mains cold water

cold water storage cistern

feed and expansion tank

Key

━━━ flow

━━━ return

▼ consumer's control valve

▼ lockshield valve

═ air release valve

stop valve

to hot taps

radiators

to other radiators

cold feed

manifold

manifold

draincock

hot water cylinder

safety valve

retaining valve

to other radiators

radiators

pump

valves

manifold

draincock

manifold

boiler

2 A typical small bore system. Pipework carries heated water to radiators throughout the home; the boiler heats both the central heating system and the domestic hot water supply. A small bore system can be installed, where the boiler serves the central heating system only (**inset**)

3 A typical open-type mini bore system. Radiator flow and return connections are fed with pipes from manifolds

with a flue liner inserted. Some source of permanent ventilation must be supplied in the room where the appliance is fitted since both the appliance and the flue require adequate fresh air to work efficiently. If possible, it is best to use an appliance with a balanced flue since this results in more efficient running.

Gas or oil-fired wall-mounted boilers with balanced or conventional flues have the advantage that they can be more easily concealed than other types of appliance. Take care when selecting a model of this type since some manufacturers specify complicated pipework systems with the appliance and these are usually too difficult for the average DIY enthusiast to tackle. Also, because this type of appliance is small in size, the output is limited. Oil-fired wall-mounted boilers should be positioned carefully to ensure fumes (which can be more pungent than those from a gas-fired appliance) do not find their way back into the house – for example through a nearby window.

Back boilers have already been covered; oil-fired back boilers for central heating systems are not available.

Which system to choose

Small bore systems are easier to plan and install compared with other types of system. A mini bore closed-type system, for example, is relatively difficult to plan and is best left to the expert, especially since the finished system operates under pressure and this can cause problems at the planning, installation and running stages.

Selection of appliances depends on personal preference, the position of flues and outside walls, the position of the hot water cylinder and the amount of space available. It is best to avoid the use of existing flues by installing a balanced flue appliance; but if this is not possible, always line the flue irrespective of the fuel. Remember that balanced flue appliances must be fixed to an outside wall. Any hot water vessel fed by gravity circulation must be fixed in relation to the appliance so gravity circulation is not impaired. Sometimes there are occasions when there is only one place where the boiler can be located; if this is the case, normally only one kind of boiler can be selected irrespective of the other factors involved.

Warning Whatever system you decide to install it should always comply with any legal requirements applicable – the Building Regulations and local by-laws, for example – and any instructions given by the manufacturer. Gas equipment and supplies must be finally connected to the gas installation and tested by a qualified gas engineer.

Controlling a small bore system

If you are installing a central heating system your-self, it is likely you will choose a small bore system because this type is less complex and involves a relatively small capital outlay compared with other systems. At the design stage it is essential to consider the type of temperature control which will be used on the system to maintain maximum standards of economy and safety. Most appliances, especially those which are gas or oil-fired, have integral controls fitted to them to ensure minimum standards of safety; but care must be taken when installing the system and wiring up the controls to make sure these inbuilt safety factors do not mal-function or are not overridden.

Types of control
With a system which has gravity circulation to the hot water storage cylinder and pumped water to the radiators and where there is a gas or oil-fired boiler, three factors need to be controlled; the time you want the system functioning, the temperature of the water stored in the hot water storage cylinder and the temperature of the rooms and living spaces in the house. With a solid fuel boiler only two factors need to be controlled: the ambient temperature and the water temperature in the hot water storage cylinder. Time control on a solid fuel appliance is not feasible since the boiler runs continuously. Methods of control can be either mechanical or electrical.

Mechanical controls If you choose a mechanical method, you can control the hot water storage temperature by fitting a thermostatic control on the cylinder or the pipes which run to or from it. Some manual control of room or living space tem-

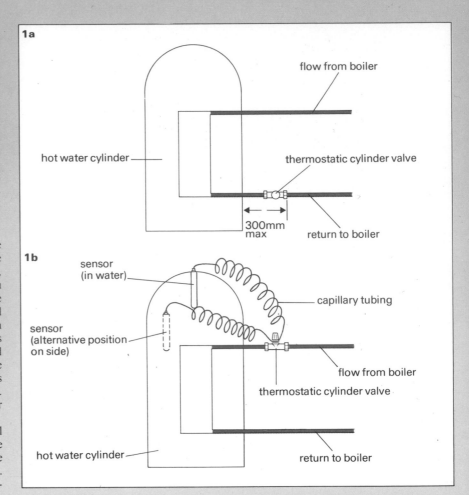

1a

flow from boiler

hot water cylinder

thermostatic cylinder valve

300mm max

return to boiler

1b

sensor (in water)

capillary tubing

sensor (alternative position on side)

flow from boiler

thermostatic cylinder valve

hot water cylinder

return to boiler

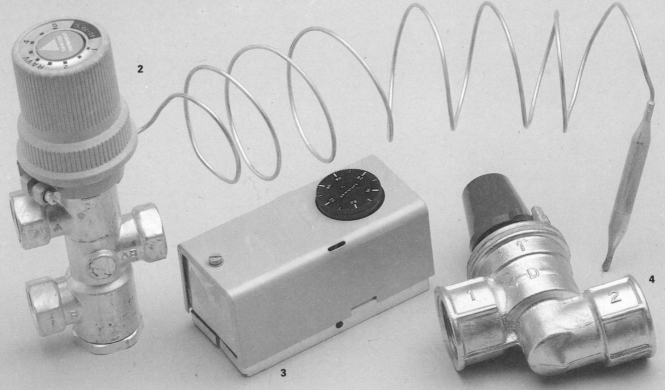

2

3

4

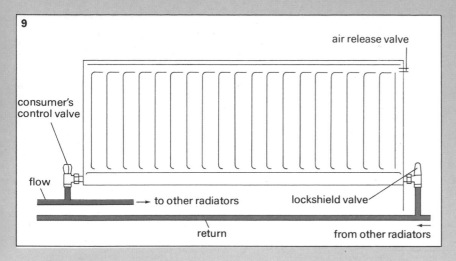

9

air release valve

consumer's control valve

flow

→ to other radiators

lockshield valve

return

from other radiators

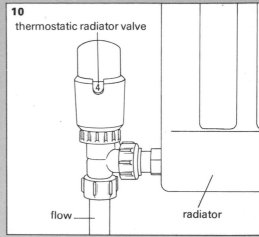

10

thermostatic radiator valve

4

flow

radiator

perature can be achieved by fitting a consumer's control valve to the flow pipe on each radiator; but this will only turn the radiator on or off. To achieve further control you can fit a thermostatic radiator valve in place of the control valve.

On the return pipe of each radiator there is a lockshield valve which is used by the installer to balance the system along with all the other lockshield valves in the system. An air release valve, which may be an integral part of the radiator or may need to be fitted to the radiator using PFTE tape or hemp, is used to remove air from the radiator, in particular when filling the system.

Electrical controls Systems of electrical control are more complex; but since either the boiler and/or the pump require electricity anyway, it can be more economical and functional to use electricity for control systems in most cases. A basic wiring system involving a boiler with electrical controls and a pump is where the pump and boiler are wired in parallel, usually through a switched fused connection unit. However, this type of system will not operate automatically and this could be inconvenient.

Remember earth connections must be made to all appliances and controls, unless otherwise stated by the manufacturer, to maintain maximum safety.

To provide time control in a simple system a clock can be used to turn a system on or off at pre-arranged times, while there is a separate manual control of the central heating pump. The temperature of the water is determined by the boiler's operational temperature and gravity circulation between the boiler and the hot water storage cylinder.

You can achieve improved control and a reduction in running costs by operating the pump automatically with a room temperature control thermostat. It is also worth fitting a clock with a selector, known as a programmer, which will allow you to choose different programmes related to your hot water and heating requirements. This type of control system provides adequate control of the heating circuit, but still leaves the domestic water supply stored in the cylinder to be heated to the operation temperature of the boiler of say 82°C (or 180°F). A hot water temperature of 60°C (or 140°F) is quite adequate for purposes of household

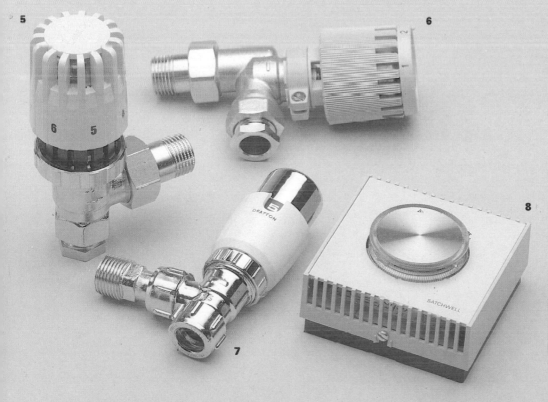

5

6

7

8

1a Thermostatic cylinder valve, with self-contained sensor, fitted on return pipe to boiler within 300mm of hot water cylinder
1b Thermostatic cylinder valve fitted on flow pipe from boiler with remote sensor in cylinder: the valve is pressure-operated and has a small by-pass connecting to the indirect vent pipe to prevent pressure build-up when the valve is closed
2 Thermostatic cylinder valve with remote sensor
3 Cylinder thermostat which straps onto the cylinder and should be wired to the boiler
4 Thermostatic cylinder valve with self-contained sensor
5, 6, 7 Thermostatic radiator valves
8 Room thermostat
9 Radiator connections
10 Thermostatic radiator valve with numbered ring fitted instead of consumer's control valve

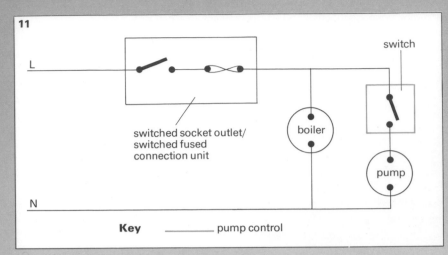

11

L

switched socket outlet/
switched fused
connection unit

boiler

switch

pump

N

Key _____ pump control

use, including general chores such as washing up.

You can partially overcome this problem by fitting a cylinder thermostat on the cylinder. This circuit also prevents the boiler switching on and off to make up its own rate of heat loss; since this is a common source of energy wastage in domestic systems, this addition results in substantial savings in running costs.

You may decide to use a combination of controls; for example, an electrical room thermostat to control the heating and a mechanical temperature control on the cylinder. Most manufacturers of control equipment provide detailed instructions on the application and installation of more elaborate control systems; but it is worth thinking carefully before you contemplate such systems since they may be too complicated for the average home handyman to install safely.

11 Basic wiring system which is operated manually (earth omitted)
12 Wiring system providing automatic time control with manual control of pump (earth omitted)
13 Wiring system with programmer and room thermostat to control the pump and hot water automatically (earth omitted)
14 Cylinder thermostat added to previous system to provide some temperature control for domestic hot water (earth omitted)
15 Time switch
16, 17, 18 Four types of programmer

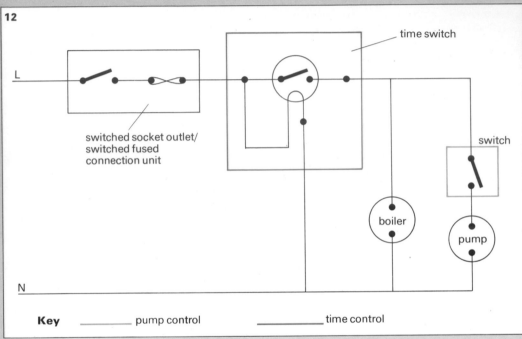

12

L

switched socket outlet/
switched fused
connection unit

time switch

boiler

switch

pump

N

Key _____ pump control _____ time control

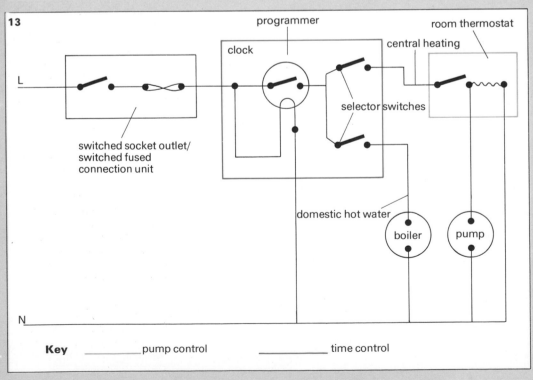

13

L

switched socket outlet/
switched fused
connection unit

clock

programmer

selector switches

central heating

room thermostat

domestic hot water

boiler

pump

N

Key _____ pump control _____ time control

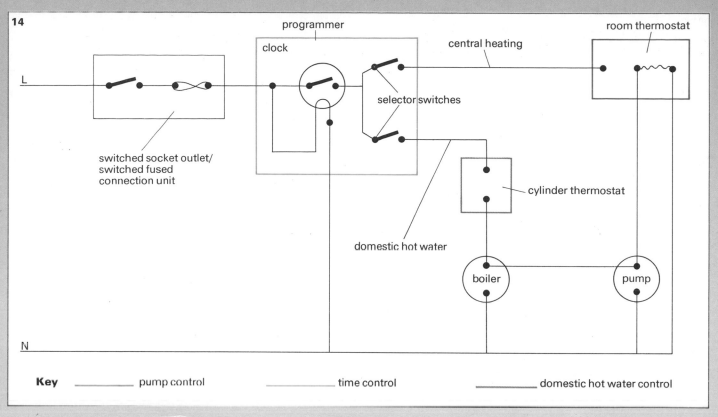

14

programmer

clock

central heating

room thermostat

selector switches

L

switched socket outlet/
switched fused
connection unit

cylinder thermostat

domestic hot water

boiler

pump

N

Key ———— pump control ———— time control ———— domestic hot water control

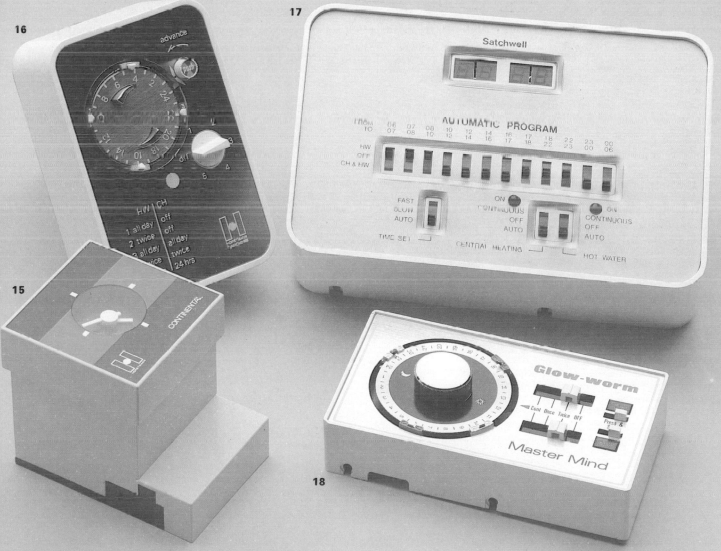

16

advance

push

HW | CH
1 all day | off
2 twice | off
3 all day | all day
| twice | twice
| | 24 hrs

17

Satchwell

AUTOMATIC PROGRAM

FROM 06 07 08 10 12 14 16 17 18 22 23 00
TO 07 08 10 12 14 16 17 18 22 23 00 06

HW
OFF
CH & HW

FAST
GLOW
AUTO

ON
CONTINUOUS
OFF
AUTO

ON
CONTINUOUS
OFF
AUTO

TIME SET

CENTRAL HEATING

HOT WATER

15

CONTINENTAL

Glow-worm

Cont Once Twice OFF

Press &

Master Mind

18

Designing a small bore system

After you have decided on the fuel and appliance you are going to use to fire your small bore central heating system, you can go ahead with designing the system. Care taken at this stage will prevent disappointment later.

Calculating equipment size

Draw a scale plan of your house showing the construction of exterior walls and their thickness, the area of window space in each room in square metres and whether windows are single or double glazed, the structure of floors and ceilings and the temperatures required in each room. Make heat loss calculations as described earlier; the sum of all the heat losses can be used to estimate the size of the boiler, while the heat losses from individual rooms indicate the size of radiator and the radiator heat output required for each space to be heated.

Radiator size In the example given (**see 1**) radiator A needs an output of 1750 watts to satisfy the heat requirements of the space in which it is fitted. By referring to manufacturers' information sheets on radiator dimensions, the dimensional size of a radiator with an output of 1750 watts can be determined. Remember long low radiators are preferable to high narrow ones since they give a better heat distribution when fitted under a window, which is the best place to locate radiators since they will warm cold down draughts which may enter through a window. Using this method of estimating radiator size means the radiators will be slightly oversize; but an oversize radiator can always be turned down, whereas the additional calculations required to obtain the exact size do not justify the extra benefit derived.

Pipe size Once all the radiator sizes have been estimated you can use calculating tables to work out the pipe sizes needed to connect the radiators to the boiler. You will need to calculate the equivalent heat flow in watts per degree Centigrade. This is obtained by dividing the radiator output by 20 (a standard figure for the temperature difference between the flow and return pipes on the radiator). For example, to work out the size of the pipes needed to supply radiator A (**see 1**) with a heat output of 1750 watts, the equivalent heat flow is: $1750 \div 20 = 87.5$ watts/°C; table A indicates 87.5 watts/°C can be served by a 15mm pipe and the water velocity can be kept below 1 metre per second (1m/s) with a pressure loss of 29 Newtons per square metre (29N/sq m). The water velocity must be kept below 1m/s or the noise of water passing through the system would become a nuisance. The pressure loss factor is also important since this is used later to estimate the size of pump required.

Mark the figures you have reached on the plan; the figures in the example given (**see 1**) indicate 15mm copper pipes can be used between radiators A and B upstairs ($3500 \div 20 = 175$ watts/°C). The pipe sizes are best calculated backwards from the furthest radiator in the system to the boiler. The pipe size from the tees at X to radiator C must be large enough to supply the joint outputs of radiators A, B and D: $1750 + 1750 + 2250 = 5750$ watts.

Table A indicates 15mm pipe will be sufficient; but at this stage, at 287.5 watts/°C, the pressure loss will be 230N/sq m.

When estimating the size of pipe from the boiler to upstairs, consider the outputs of all the upstairs radiators (A, B, C and D): $1750 + 1750 + 1750 + 2250 = 7500$ watts. By referring to the nearest value to 375 watts/°C, table A shows 22mm copper pipe is best at a pressure loss of 56N/sq mm.

You can follow the above procedure to calculate the size of all pipes in the circuit except those which supply the hot water storage cylinder; these are sized relative to cylinder capacity as shown in table B. When you are using table B, remember all

1 Typical design for a small bore central heating system in a house with a timber ground floor; if you have a solid ground floor, use a drop pipe system from the first floor

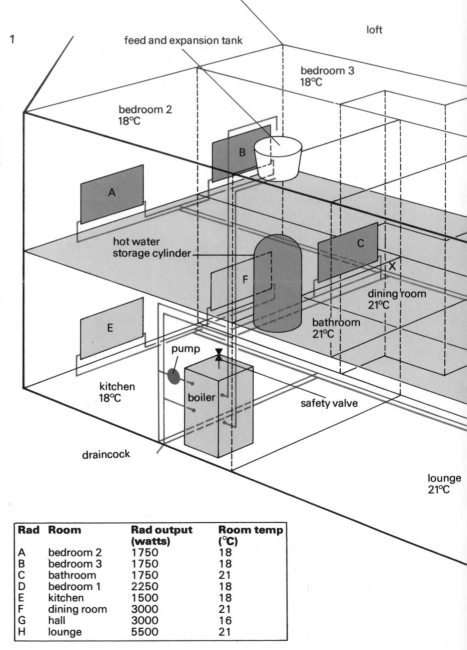

Rad	Room	Rad output (watts)	Room temp (°C)
A	bedroom 2	1750	18
B	bedroom 3	1750	18
C	bathroom	1750	21
D	bedroom 1	2250	18
E	kitchen	1500	18
F	dining room	3000	21
G	hall	3000	16
H	lounge	5500	21

cylinders in central heating systems are of the indirect type.

Once the pipes are sized the type and number of fittings can be estimated by direct reference to the plan; by taking measurements from the plan you can determine the amount and size of copper tube you will require.

Pump size To size the pump you should find the index circuit on the pipe run from the boiler to a radiator which creates the most resistance in N/sq mm to water flow. Use the pressure loss figures marked on the plan to determine this. In the example given (**see 1**) the index circuit runs between the boiler and radiator A; to find the pressure loss in this circuit the pressures indicated on the pipe runs are added together. This figure indicates the size of pump required and should not exceed 350N/sq m; if it does, you will have to use larger diameter pipes on runs with a high pressure drop. Reference is again needed to determine the water flow rate (kg/s) relative to this pressure loss, since pump manufacturers' specification sheets require both factors to be known when selecting the pump.

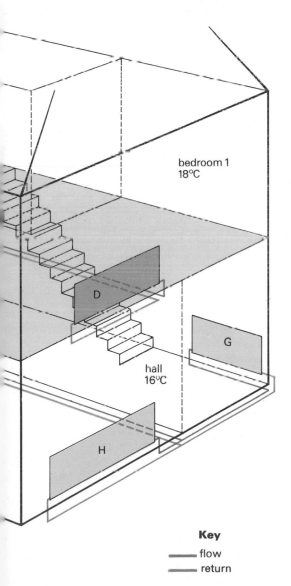

Key

—— flow

—— return

Table A

Pressure loss in N/sq m per metre run of pipe

flow rate kg/s	equivalent heat flow watts/°C	pipe diameter			
		15mm	22mm	28mm	35mm
0.010	42	9			
0.016	67	18	3		
0.020	84	27	4		
0.025	105	40	6		
0.030	125	54	8	2.5	
0.035	146	71	11	3.5	
0.040	167	90	14	4	
0.045	188	110	17	5	
0.050	209	132	20	6	
0.055	230	155	24	7	
0.060	251	181	28	8	
0.065	272	209	32	9	
0.070	293	237	36	11	
0.075	314	207	41	12	
0.080	334	299	46	14	
0.085	355	335	51	15	5
0.090	376	370	56	16	6
0.095	397	406	62	18	6.5
0.10	418	445	68	19	7
0.11	460	527	80	23	8
0.12	502	*1 m/s* 616	93	27	10
0.13	543	709	107	31	11
0.14	585	808	122	35	13
0.15	627	913	137	40	14
0.16	669	*1.2 m/s* 1025	154	45	16
0.17	711	1140	171	50	18
0.18	752	1263	190	55	19
0.19	794	*1.2 m/s*	210	60	21
0.20	836		230	66	23
0.21	878		250	72	25
0.22	920		271	78	28
0.23	961		294	85	30
0.24	1003		316	91	32
0.25	1045		340	98	35
0.26	1087		362	105	37
0.27	1129		390	113	40
0.28	1170		417	120	42
0.29	1212		443	128	45
0.30	1254		470	135	48
0.31	1296		500	144	51
0.32	1338		528	152	54

Table B

direct cylinder litre/s	indirect cylinder litre/s	pipe size mm
Up to 120	Up to 117	28
144–166	140–162	35
200–255	190–245	42
290–370	280–360	54

Installing a small bore system

When you have bought all the equipment for your central heating system, lay it out so you can easily identify the parts – particularly such fittings as tees, elbow joints and valves – when you start work.

Fittings Either soldered capillary or compression joint fittings can be used to make pipework connections. The soldered type is less expensive and neater in appearance; but it is advisable to fit compression type fittings on any part of the installation which may need to be periodically disconnected or removed for servicing, such as the boiler, pump, retaining valve or radiators.

Installing radiators

Place the radiators in position to check they will fit the space allocated. Usually they are secured to the wall with brackets held in position by screws and wall plugs; it is best to use No 14 screws and plugs even with small radiators since they will be reasonably heavy when filled with water. Wherever possible, fit the bottom of the radiator level with the top of the skirting board; try also to place the radiator in the centre of the space under a window so cold down draughts from the window are heated before they can circulate round the room.

To determine the position of the wall brackets, hold the radiator up to the wall with its weight resting on the floor; lean it slightly away from the wall and mark the bracket positions with vertical lines on the wall. Remove the radiator, place a bracket on it and measure the distance between the base of the radiator and the base of the bracket;

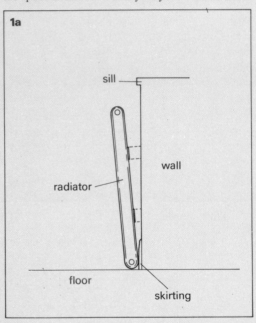

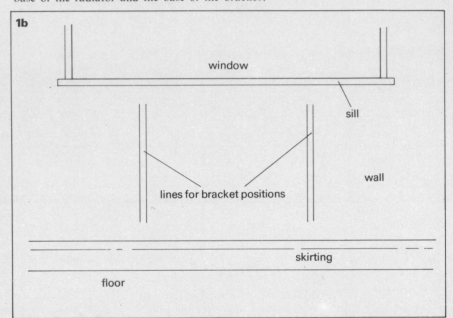

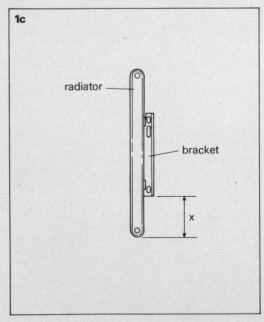

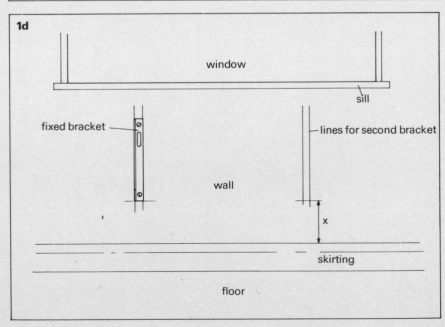

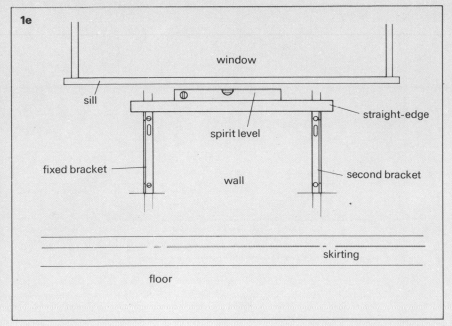

1e

window

sill

spirit level

straight-edge

fixed bracket

wall

second bracket

skirting

floor

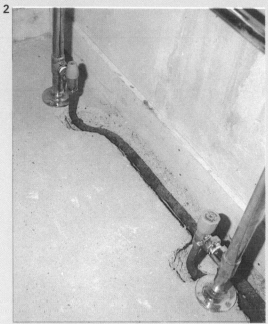
2

3

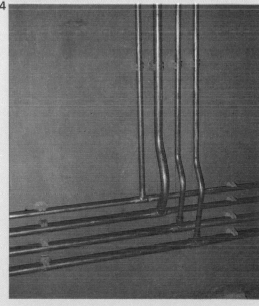
4

1a To find the position for the radiator brackets, rest the radiator on the floor so it leans slightly away from the wall; mark the position of the radiator bracket slots on the wall

1b Draw vertical lines on the wall to indicate the position of the brackets; if under a window, the radiator should be fitted centrally

1c Place a bracket on the radiator and measure the distance x between the base of the radiator and the base of the bracket.

1d Mark the distance x on the vertical lines on the wall and place the bottom of the bracket on the mark; fix the bracket in place

1e Follow the same procedure for the second bracket; before fixing it in place use a spirit level and a straight-edge to ensure it is level with the first

2 If you have a solid floor, you can channel out grooves in the surface to take the pipework (here connecting a heated towel rail)

3 Alternatively the pipes connecting up the radiator can be run along the wall

4 Use clips to hold pipes firmly in place

mark this distance on the vertical line on the wall, measuring from the top of the skirting. Place the bottom of the bracket on this mark and mark the position of the fixing holes; drill the holes and fix the bracket. Follow the same procedure for the second bracket, using a spirit level and straight-edge to ensure it is level with the first before finally fixing it in place.

Before finally hanging the radiator in position, fit the tails of the radiator valves in the radiators and fit the necessary air release valves. With the most common type of radiator valve the tail connection into the radiator should be made using PFTE tape or boss white and hemp.

While the compression nut and olive are put onto the copper pipe in the normal way, the nut tightens onto the main body of the valve and a water-tight joint is made via a ground seating on the valve and the boss.

Installing boiler and cylinder
You should now install the boiler and cylinder and carry out any work which needs to be done in the loft. Remember when you are installing the feed and expansion tank in the loft it should be on a firm base and the bottom of the tank should be fitted level with or lower than the base of the main cold water storage cistern. This ensures that, if a leak develops in the indirect hot water cylinder, the direct hot water will flow into the indirect system because of the greater head of pressure; otherwise the direct supply could be contaminated by any additives in the feed and expansion tank. This arrangement also has the effect of causing the feed and expansion tank to overflow through the warning pipe, giving audible and visual indication of a fault.

Take great care when attaching fittings to the cylinder. These must eventually be watertight; but since the walls of the cylinder are thin, force exerted in the wrong direction can easily cause the cylinder to collapse. Also remember cylinders full of water weigh a considerable amount, so they must be fitted on a firm floor or base which can support the weight. Be sure to fit an efficient cylinder jacket to prevent undue heat loss.

Installing the boiler is a relatively difficult part of

119

5 Any pipes which run under floorboards should be lagged as they are installed
6 With timber floors pipes can be run under the boards and fed up to connect with each radiator
7 Check with our chart to determine the spacing of the clips for the size of pipe you are using

the operation; make sure it is installed strictly according to the manufacturer's instructions. The appliance must be situated on a fireproof base; where there is a timber floor under the boiler, you should place a 25mm (1in) thick sheet of asbestos or similar fireproof material between the boiler and the floor as a safety requirement. Ideally the boiler should be of the balanced flue type and the flue should also be fitted exactly to the manufacturer's specification. Remember when you are positioning the boiler to allow yourself space to carry out any future maintenance work which might be required.

Installing pipework

When the radiators, boiler and cylinder are in place, the pipework to the radiators can be installed. Make sure pipes which are run under boards on the ground floor are lagged as they are installed; you will have to lift the floorboards to run pipes here and usually when installing pipework you will have to make holes in brick walls and ceilings. Where there is a solid ground floor you will have to channel out grooves for the pipes or lay them on top of the floor.

It is advisable first to lay out the fittings for a particular pipe run on the floor; this will help you to decide whether any fittings are missing and also to remember to fit items such as tees where they are required. When installing pipework, try to eliminate the use of fittings; these not only increase the cost of the installation, but also restrict the flow of water round the system.

Once you have decided on a pipe run, you can prepare the route. Lift any floorboards where necessary, make holes through walls and ceilings and channel out the tops of joists to take the pipes. Check the pipes can be run where you want them to go; if any obstacles are met which would prevent the chosen route being followed, select a new route to avoid wasting material, labour and time.

Checking system

Once all the pipework, including any safety valves, pumps or water controls, is installed, you should fill the system with water and check for leaks. If the system is watertight, empty it and repeat the filling and emptying process at least three times to remove any foreign matter which may be in the pipes or ancillary fittings. You can then finally fill the system with water and make the necessary electrical connections. Then fit the fuel supply; remember if the appliance is gas-fired, this work must be carried out by a qualified gas engineer.

It is worth leaving the initial commissioning and testing of the system to a professional heating engineer; heating systems are fairly complex and a professional will be able to detect any faults and set up the system for efficient operation quite quickly. Also remember to retain any technical information which applies to your system, since you will probably need this to sort out any future problems which may arise; it should also be passed on to the next owner should you decide to sell the property.

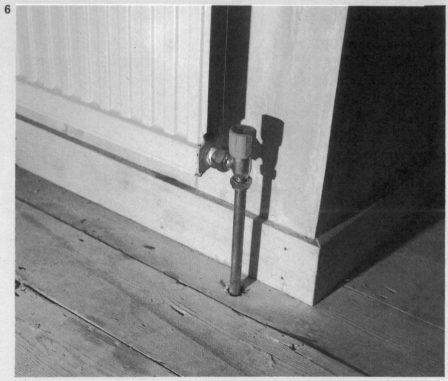

Spacings for copper pipe clips

Size of pipe (mm)	Intervals for vertical runs (m)	Intervals for horizontal runs (m)
15	1.9	1.3
22	2.5	1.9
28	2.5	1.9
35	2.8	2.5
42	2.8	2.5

Electric central heating

If you decide to install electric central heating in your home, there are various systems available from which you can choose the type most suited to your requirements. These include low intensity radiant systems incorporated in the building fabric, forced warm air systems, hot water radiator systems and individual radiant or convector systems.

Very good standards of insulation in the home should be maintained to ensure low operational costs of a central heating system; this is particularly important with electricity because of the higher cost per unit relative to other fuels. Wiring or connections on an electrical installation should comply with current safety regulations and it is advisable to have all wiring and electrical components checked by a qualified electrician.

Low intensity radiant systems

These systems are usually placed in the building fabric or inlaid in the floor and require professional installation. One type used at ceiling level consists of a flexible glass cloth membrane coated with impregnated conducting silicone rubber. It is fitted with copper strip electrodes and enclosed in an electrical insulating envelope. Another type uses an electrical element in the form of a metal resistance foil encased in an insulating envelope. Both of these systems span most of the ceiling area. It is advisable to place a layer of thermal insulation at least 100mm (4in) thick above the heating source to prevent unnecessary heat loss into the roof space or room above.

Ceiling heating systems are usually controlled by a wall-mounted air thermostat controlling the element in the room in which it is situated. Continuous 24-hour operation is recommended; this means in a 12-month period the system will consume 1600–2000kWh per kW of calculated heat

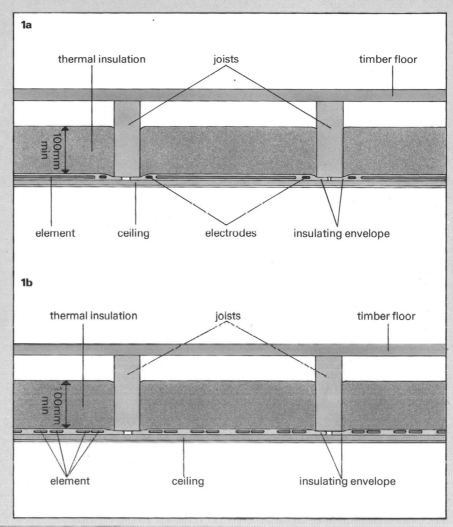

1a Section through a ceiling incorporating a low intensity radiant heating system of the flexible glass cloth element type; the elements, encased in insulating envelopes, are fixed to the undersides of joists (or laid between them when access is possible from above) and are concealed in the ceiling
1b This type of low intensity radiant heating system uses an electrical element in the form of a metal resistance foil; like the glass cloth element type, the whole unit is encased in an insulating envelope and concealed in the ceiling
2 Electric underfloor heating in a concrete ground floor; this system can also be used in a suspended concrete floor

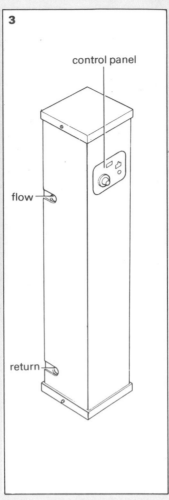

control panel

flow

return

loss. Systems are normally supplied by the standard electricity tariff, but where hot water is also heated by electricity it is usually advantageous to have an off-peak or Economy 7 meter installed and make use of the lower tariff at night.

Underfloor heating systems utilize an element consisting of insulated conductors laid zig-zag fashion in the concrete. It is advisable to place a layer of thermal insulation material at least 25mm (1in) thick under the heat source to prevent undue heat loss into the ground or the room below. The system is used at restricted times determined by the area Electricity Board by means of a time clock. Also, the consumer can control the system output temperature by means of a room thermostat. Floor warming systems consume 1800–2000kWh per kW of calculated heat loss over 12 months.

Forced warm air systems

Electric warm air systems are similar in construction to the warm air systems fuelled by gas, oil, or solid fuel described earlier.

Electricaire, as such a system is usually known, operates mainly on off-peak or Economy 7 tariff electricity; the night-time input of heat energy is limited by a charge control which can be adjusted to meet seasonal requirements. Usually this type of system consumes 1500–2000kWh per kW of calculated heat loss over 12 months.

The appliance itself is a thermal storage unit with a well-insulated core which has air passages in it. Air passed through the core by a fan in the unit is heated, mixed with cooler room air to maintain the desired temperature and then discharged into a ducted warm air heating system; this distributes the warmed air along the ducts and into each room through an open outlet register (open/closable grille).

The daytime output of heat from this type of system is determined by the quantity of air circulated by the fan, which is controlled by an air thermostat placed in a central position in the home. The fan speed is variable and can be increased by manual switching to provide a rapid temperature build-up over a short period if required.

Installing a system of this type can be a DIY

operation; but it is difficult, requires a great deal of competence and also involves a higher capital cost than one using storage heaters or panel radiators.

Hot water radiator systems

Pipework systems and radiators used in conjunction with electric 'boilers' are run and connected in the same way to the appliance as in a gas, oil or solid fuel-fired system as described earlier.

The heating appliance is different in design and fuel-firing principle; it consists of a small metal container in the form of a tube which is 80–150mm (or 3–6in) in diameter depending on the output required. At each end of the container there is a pipe connection to take the flow and return pipes of the radiator system. Inside the container there are one or more immersion heaters running its full length, a water temperature control thermostat and an overheat cut-out to prevent overheating. The container and its associated controls are mounted in a metal cabinet which houses switchgear and a circulating water pump. The flow heater is connected to the radiator circuit across the flow and return pipes in a similar manner to other wet systems.

Energy consumption in a system of this type is equal to 1500kWh per kW of calculated heat loss over 12 months. These systems are relatively easy to control since a room thermostat can be used to control the pump; if the pump stops, the immersion heaters will switch off as the appliance temperature rises. They are also suitable for DIY installation.

Individual radiant or convector systems

There are several types of appliance available which can be plugged into a standard 13amp power socket and used collectively or as independent units. There are also electric storage heaters; all these appliances are suited to DIY installation.

Above left Free-standing convector heater with teak finish

3 Electric 'boiler' or flow heater designed for use with a closed circuit indirect hot water central heating system; this type should be fixed to the wall at least 50mm above the floor to allow air to circulate freely

Above Wall-mounted
convector heater with heat
levels of 1 or 2kW and an
adjustable thermostat
Above right Panel
convector heater with hinged
mounting frame
Right Electric oil-filled
radiator with 'air sensitive'
thermostat; the radiator plugs
into a 13amp socket

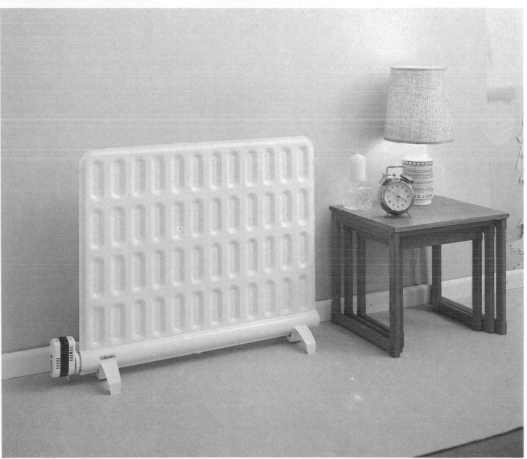

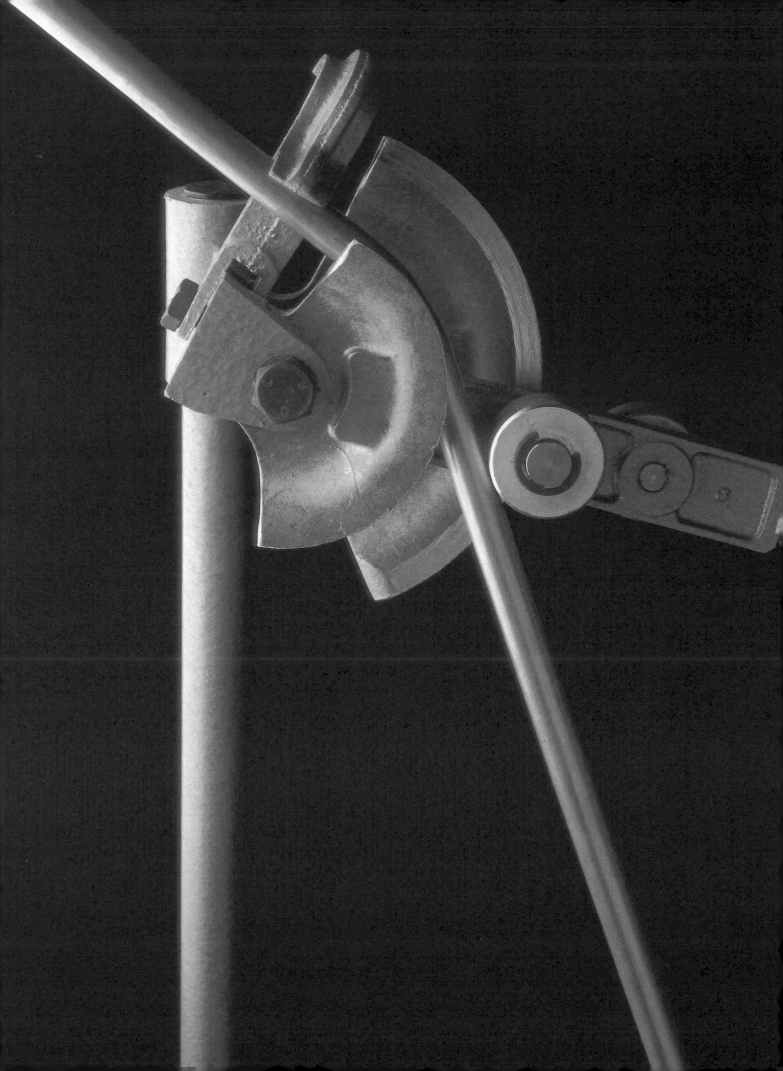

Plumbing techniques

Bending and joining tubes

You can bend most of the light gauge tubing used in domestic plumbing systems quite easily and you will need to do this when running lengths of tube round corners or when installing tubing in awkward situations.

Incidentally, bending tube is always preferable to incorporating angled fittings into the tube run, since any fitting of this sort will tend to restrict the flow of water through the tubes.

Bending tubing

There is no problem about bending copper tube, which is the most commonly used in the domestic system. You can also bend the more expensive stainless steel tube, but do not attempt to do this to chromium-plated tube. If you do, the plating will crack and the tube itself, which is more brittle than other types of metal because of the plating process, may break.

If you are working with 15mm (or ½in) tube, you can bend this over your knee, using a suitable size bending spring. But to ensure more accurate and consistent bends, you should use a bending machine and former, which you can hire for the work as you need them.

Bend radius If you are not using a bending machine with formers and you wish to bend a heavy gauge tube, the radius to which the tube can be bent can be measured from the centre of the bend arc to the axis of the tube. Bend radius depends on the diameter of the tube, its wall thickness and the bending method you employ. If the diameter of the tube is not more than eight times the wall thickness of the tube, the following applies:

● If the tube is bent without internal support, the minimum radius (to the centre line of the tube) should not be less than four times its diameter.

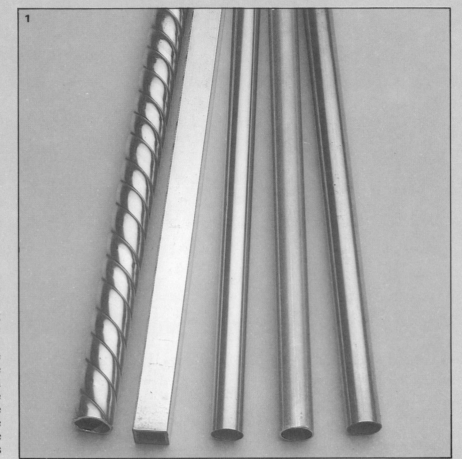

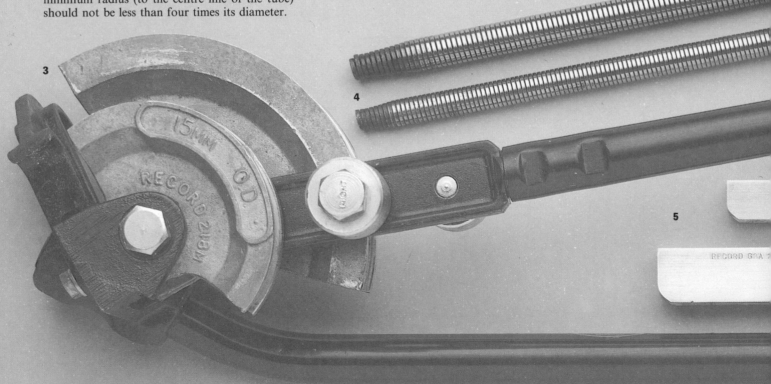

1 Types of tube: (from left) fluted brass, rectangular section, standard brass, aluminium and copper

2a Unless bend radius is at least four times diameter of tube, wrinkling may occur at throat and thinning on heel of tube

2b To determine bend allowance (heating length), you will need to know bend angle and radius

3 Bending machine
4 Bending springs
5 Formers for bending machine
6 Pipe cutter

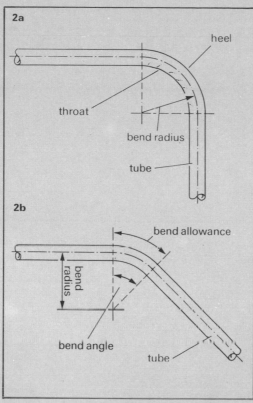

2a

heel

throat

bend radius

tube

2b

bend allowance

bend radius

bend angle

tube

Large radius bends are easier to form, but tight bends will cause some thinning of the metal on the heel (or outside) of the bend; they will also increase resistance to flow.

Cutting tubes
Use a pipe cutter to cut copper tubing; other types of tube may be cut with a fine-tooth hacksaw. After cutting tubing, remove any burr from the inside of the tube with a rat's-tail file and clean the outside of the cut with emery cloth.

Using filler Filler can be used in light gauge tubing to prevent it thinning while being bent. Pack the tube firmly with dry silver sand or resin and plug the ends to prevent losing the filler during bending.

Annealing metal
The copper tube used in domestic plumbing systems is normally sold in a 'half hard' condition, which ensures that it does not sag when clipped in straight, horizontal runs. However, it is still soft enough to be bent as required.

Copper gradually gets harder with age and old tube may therefore not bend that easily. In this case you will need to soften the tube around the section to be bent and to do this you have to use the annealing process.

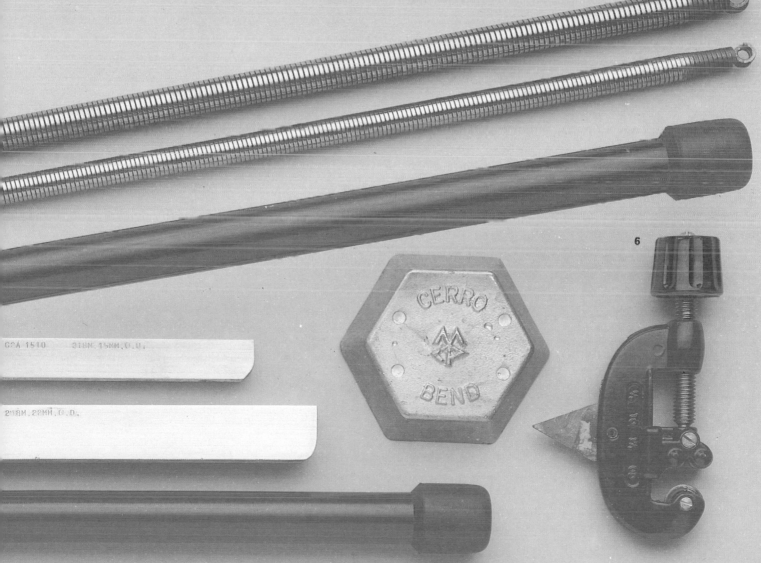

Heat the area around the section of tube to be bent, working an extra 50mm (2in) or so at either end. Use a propane blowtorch and heat the tube carefully and evenly along the length of the bend.

It will help if you have any firebricks handy to place these behind the heated section of tube, since these will reflect back any wasted heat.

Continue heating the tube until it glows an even red colour; then immediately quench the heated section in cold water. The water should be in a suitable, heat-resistant container. Take care when you immerse the tube where the open end points, since hot water may shoot out of it if the other end of the tube is immersed in the water.

If you get any discoloration on the outside of the tube, you can clean this off with wire wool.

Bear in mind that you cannot anneal stainless steel in this way.

Bending methods

Depending on the gauge of tube you are working with and the number of bends you have to make, there are two ways of bending tube – over the knee, with the help of a bending spring to prevent the tube from kinking, or with a bending machine.

Bending over the knee This is suitable where you only have to make a few simple bends in 15mm (or ½in) copper tubing. You can bend 22mm (or ¾in) tube using this method, but you will need more strength and skill to ensure an accurate bend. One point to remember is that copper tube made to BS 2871 may kink if you are using this method to make tight bends.

If you use the knee method, the bend in the tube must be at least 150mm (6in) from the end of the tube to allow you sufficient leverage on the tube.

First insert inside the tube a greased bending spring of the same diameter as the tube you are bending. Sit or kneel with one knee bent at right angles to the body and hold the work so that the centre of the proposed bend is directly over the vertical plane of the knee. It will help if you place a folded duster on your knee underneath the tube.

Make sure the bending spring is positioned centrally through the section to be bent and then pull each end of the tube back towards you evenly to form the bend at the knee. Before you complete the bend, move the tube about 25mm (1in) to either side and then finish the bend. This will ensure that the bend does not have too tight a radius.

To remove the bending spring, twist it clockwise to reduce its diameter so that you can slide it out of the tube. One way to ensure the spring comes out easily is to overbend the tube slightly and then bring it back to the required angle.

If the bend is a long way from the end of the tube, attach a piece of strong cord to the loop at the end of the spring. Then measure the distance from the centre of the proposed bend to the end of the tube and mark this length from the middle of the spring onto the length of cord with a strip of tape. This is to ensure that when you feed the spring into the tube you will position it in the right place.

Having bent the tube, you can twist and pull on the cord to release the spring. If you want greater purchase, tie the cord onto a piece of wood or rod to provide a handle.

If the spring does jam inside the tube, you can try releasing it by lightly tapping the tube around the spring with a wooden mallet. The normal cause of a jammed spring is bending the tube at too tight an angle.

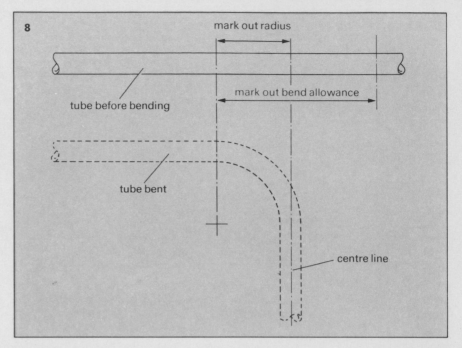

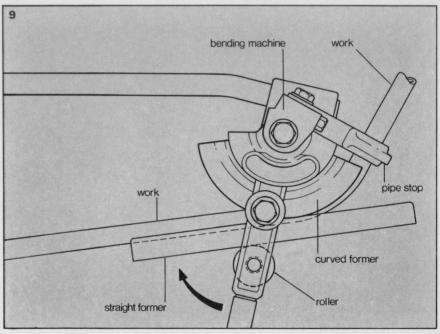

Using a bending machine You can hire a standard bending machine for tubing of 15mm (or ½in) and over. The machine consists of a former mounted on a bar and is held in a vice. A pivoted arm forces a roller over the tube, which is placed in the groove of the former. The machine is suitable for light gauge copper and aluminium tubing and should produce a curve without distorting the tube.

There are different types of machine available, but they mostly use the same techniques. Some are mounted on an integral stand, whereas others are operated freehand. Check first that the correct former has been fitted and that the roller is positioned properly.

Position the tube under the tube stop so that the marked spot for the start of the bend is at the leading edge of the curved former. Fit the straight former in position under the roller and along the section of tube to be bent.

You should still insert a bending spring into the tube; make sure this is in the correct position.

8 Marking out bend allowance
9 Using bending machine

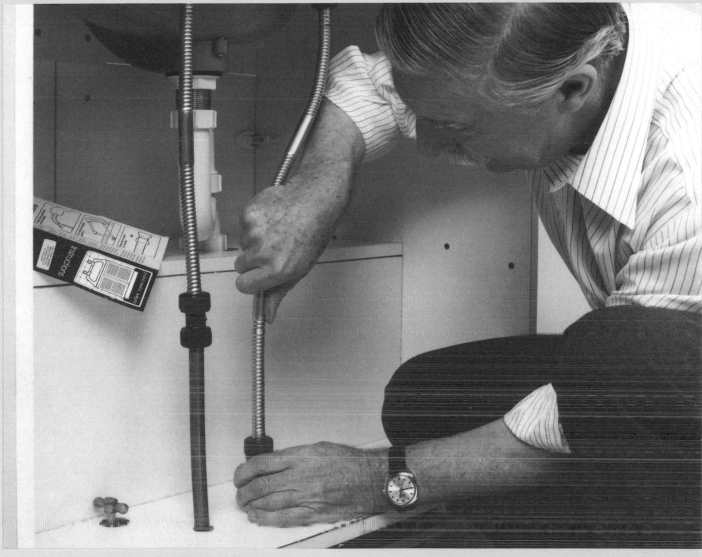

Gently pull down the lever until you have made the bend to the correct angle. Pull the lever down another 2° or so and then remove the tube from the machine. Resting the tube on the floor, bend it back 2° to give you the required angle and to help release the bending spring.

Bend allowance The approximate length of tubing taken up in making a bend will depend upon the required angle of bend. It can be calculated from an approximate formula when you know the required radius and angle of bend; multiply the bend radius by the bend angle and divide by 60 (or more accurately 57.3). The bend allowance should be marked out on the work prior to heating and bending. It is never a good idea to cut pipe to its calculated final length before you make the bend, since errors in bending could leave you with a pipe which is too short. It is easier to trim the straight portion to length once the bending has been completed.

Joining tubing

Metal tubes used in the domestic plumbing system are normally joined using couplings. These can be of either the capillary or compresssion type (see pages 133 to 139). There are also two types of socket makers you can buy, which can be used with copper tube.

The socket makers work on the principle of swelling the end of the tube down the first 25mm (1in) or so of its length so that its internal diameter is slightly larger than the original external diameter. This enables you to insert the end of another length of tube into the shaped end of the first length and make the joint in the same way as for an end-feed fitting by putting flux and solder into the join.

When using these socket makers, fit the mandrel end into the end of the tube to be shaped and hammer the projecting rod to swell the tube. These tools are available in 15mm (or ½in) and 22mm (or ¾in) sizes.

Kopex tubes

These special copper tubes have made the job of connecting up to the system that much easier since they are flexible and not rigid like standard metal tube. They are particularly useful in tight and awkward situations, such as behind wash-basins, baths and sinks, where complicated bends may be needed and the work area is restricted.

Available in 15 and 22mm (or ½ and ¾in) sizes, these short lengths of copper tube have corrugations along most of their length. This means you can bend them easily by hand to the shape you require. At one end you use a union connector to attach the tube to the tail of a tap or valve. At the other end a straight connector is used to make the attachment to the supply pipe.

Installing flexible copper water pipe. Its corrugated construction enables easy hand bending and the plastic push-fit connectors are suitable for hot or cold water supplies.

Working with plastic tubing

Plastic tubing, now available for hot and cold water supplies and drainage, has been welcomed by both amateur and professional plumbers since it is light, easy to handle, long-lasting and cheaper than copper tubing. There are four main types of plastic tubing that can be used in domestic plumbing systems – polyethylene, polypropylene, polybutylene and PVC.

Polyethylene tubing
The advantages of black polyethylene tubing are the ease with which it can be cut and joined, the long lengths obtainable – which eliminate expensive couplings – and its built-in resistance to frost. It is, however, rather clumsy and ugly and does have a tendency to sag, so horizontal lengths need continuous support. It is particularly useful for taking a water supply to a stand-pipe at a distance from the main house supply; when used underground, where appearance is unimportant, it does not need support and its frost-resistance eliminates risk of bursts. This makes it valuable if you want to run a water supply to the bottom of the garden.
Joining polyethylene tubing Non-manipulative (type A) compression joints, such as those used with copper tubing, may be used to join polyethylene tubes. Because the polyethylene is thicker than metal, you will generally need a fitting one size larger than the nominal size of the tube. A metal insert is provided to support the walls of the tube when the cap nut is tightened.

Polypropylene tubing
This type of tubing and its respective fittings have been produced mainly for the DIY market since they are so easy to work with. The polypropylene is coloured white and has a naturally greasy feel to it.

Because polypropylene cannot be solvent-welded, all fittings are provided with ring seals. These have several advantages over solvent-welded fittings. They are much easier to make joints with, they allow for the natural expansion of plastic tubing when subjected to heat, and they can be taken apart quite easily when necessary for maintenance work.

Polybutylene tubing
Available in 15 and 22mm (or $\frac{1}{2}$ and $\frac{3}{4}$in) sizes, this type of tubing is suitable for both hot and cold water supplies. It is flexible and can be bent in a similar way to polyethylene tubing.

The fittings used with this type of tubing are very simple to make. You only have to slide a short

1 Joining polyethylene tubing with a non-manipulative compression joint

2a–e Making a solvent-welded joint on PVC tubing

2a Cut the end of the tube with a hacksaw

2b Remove any burr with a half-round file

2c Roughen the external surface of the tube and the internal surface of the socket with abrasive paper

2d Brush solvent cement evenly over the interior of the socket and over the end of the tube where it will fit into the socket

2e Section through the completed joint

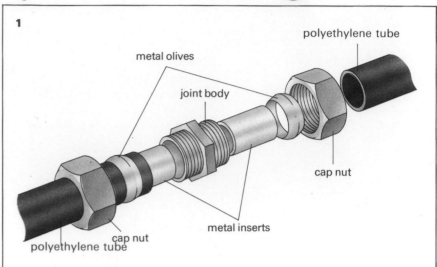

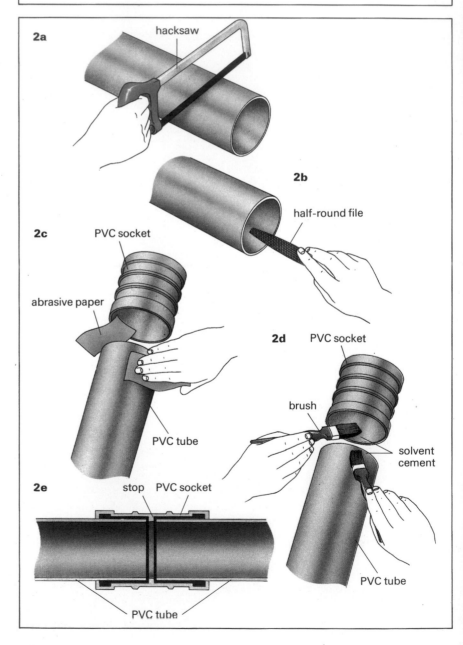

3a–e Making a ring-seal joint on PVC tube
3a Use a Surform to chamfer the cut end of the tube
3b Push the tube into the ring-seal socket as far as the depth stop and mark a line round the tube to indicate this depth
3c Pull out the tube and mark another line 10mm nearer the tube end; when you form the joint, make sure you insert the tube only as far as the final depth line to allow the joint to expand
3d Insert the sealing ring in the cleaned socket and join the tubes together
3e Section through the finished joint

metal liner into the cut end of the tube and then push this end into the plastic fitting. The seal is made by a rubber 'O' ring and the tubing is held in place with a spring grab ring.

PVC tubing

PVC tubing is semi-rigid and therefore not normally bent. You can get a range of fittings for this type of tubing and these are either solvent-welded or compression. Normally coloured grey, PVC tubing is suitable for cold water services.

A modified version – known as muPVC – is becoming more widely available. Coloured white, it is suitable for carrying hot water and is being accepted in some areas by the local water authorities. Large diameter tubing – 36, 42 and 110mm (or $1\frac{1}{4}$, $1\frac{1}{2}$ and 4in) – is used for waste services and has either solvent-welded or ring-seal fittings.

Here we give general instructions for making solvent-welded and ring-seal joints. Manufacturers of PVC tubing and fittings do supply detailed instructions, which vary slightly from one make to another, so check carefully those of the manufacturer who supplied your materials.

Solvent welded joint Cut the tube end squarely with a hacksaw or other fine tooth saw and remove all swarf or burr with a half-round file. Roughen the exterior surface of the tube and the internal surface of the solvent-weld socket with medium glasspaper and wipe with a clean cloth to remove any particles. Don't use steel wool since this will polish the surfaces. Check the length and alignment, then apply a coat of approved spirit cleaner and degreaser to the inside of the socket and to the tube end for at least the distance it will fit into the socket.

Using a spatula or brush, apply solvent cement evenly to the tube end and the interior of the socket. Push the tube end hard into the socket with a slight twisting motion, hold it in position for about 15 seconds and then remove any surplus cement with a clean dry cloth. The joint may be handled after two or three minutes, but it should not be put into use for 24 hours.

Fittings As with compression and soldered capillary fittings used with copper tubing, there is a variety of fittings available for connection to tap and ball-valve tails and other screwed connections.

Warning There are two nominally cold water supply pipes for which uPVC tubing with solvent-welded joints should not be used. These are the supply pipe from the cold water storage cistern to the hot water storage cylinder and the supply pipe to the primary circuit of an indirect hot water system. The water in these two pipes can become very hot at times.

If you wish to use plastic tubing for these and other hot water runs, you must work with muPVC or polybutylene tubing and fittings.

Ring-seal joint One advantage of ring-seal jointing is it allows for the expansion of a waste-pipe resulting from the drainage of warm wastes from sinks, baths and basins. A 4m (or 13ft) length of PVC or polypropylene pipe will expand by over 13mm ($\frac{1}{2}$in) when subjected to an increased heat of 39°C (70°F).

To make a ring-seal joint, cut the tube end square with a fine tooth saw. Chamfer the end with a file. Insert the tube into the ring-seal socket as far as the pipe stop and mark round the tube with a pencil to show the insertion depth. Withdraw the tube and make another pencilled mark 10mm (or $\frac{3}{8}$in) nearer to the tube end than the original one: it is to this mark the tube must finally be inserted to form the joint.

Clean the recess within the ring-seal socket and insert the sealing ring. Lubricate the tube end with a little petroleum jelly and push it firmly home past the joint ring, then withdraw it until the second mark you have made is level with the edge of the socket. This will allow a 10mm (or $\frac{3}{8}$in) space for expansion at each joint.

Bending plastic tubing

Because polyethylene and polybutylene tubing are both flexible, lengths of either can be bent to the desired angle.

If you bend these types of tubing cold, you will have to clip the bent section into position. Try to ensure that the bend is as gradual as possible – preferably not less than 150mm (or 6in) for 15mm (or $\frac{1}{2}$in) tubing.

You can bend the tubing to a tighter angle if it is heated. The usual method is to immerse the section to be bent in boiling water.

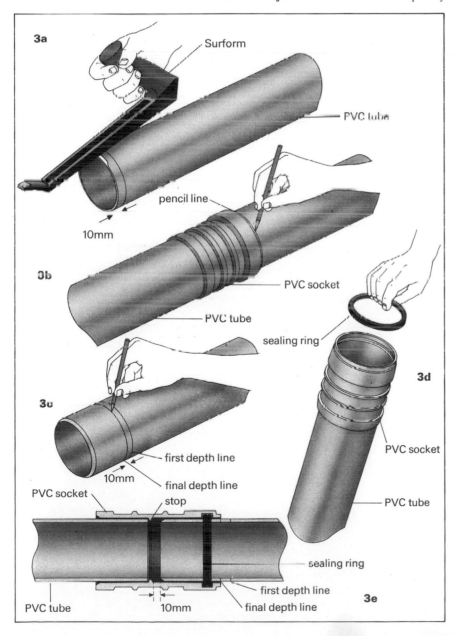

3a Surform
PVC tube
pencil line
10mm
3b
PVC socket
PVC tube
sealing ring
3c
first depth line
10mm
final depth line
PVC socket
stop
3d
PVC socket
PVC tube
sealing ring
PVC tube
first depth line
10mm
final depth line
3e

A discarded galvanized cold water tank can take up valuable storage space in your loft, but removing it does present a few problems. A tank of this kind is heavy and normally too large to pass through an average-sized loft opening, particularly in houses built in Britain before 1950, as the tank was usually placed on the ceiling joists before the loft was finished. The simplest solution is to cut the tank into small sections which will easily pass through the loft opening. For best results use a general purpose saw which has specially hardened teeth and an adjustable handle so the blade can be used at different angles.

Removing an old storage cistern from a loft

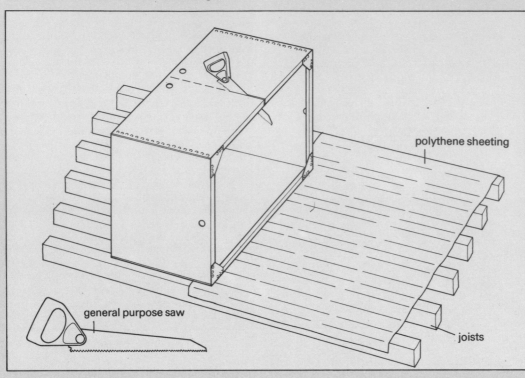

polythene sheeting

general purpose saw

joists

Using a shallow frying pan bale out any remaining water into a bucket and mop up the last drops with a sponge or absorbent cloth. Leave the bottom to dry for a few days, then lay plastic sheeting or heavy brown paper on the floor next to the tank. The sheeting should be slightly larger than the surface area of the tank side or top.

1 Remove the fittings from the tank and turn it on its side so it lies across the joists with the sheeting just under it.

Set the adjustable handle on the saw so the blade is at a shallow angle (**see inset**) and cut across the middle of the tank, working from the open edge

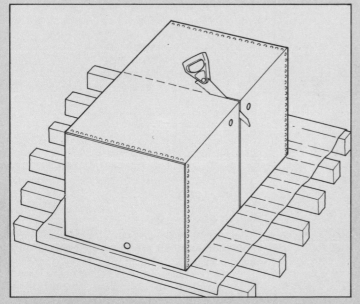

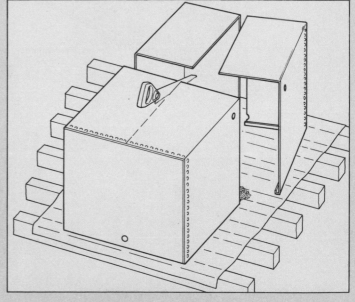

2 Turn the tank over so the top opening is on the sheeting; any sludge and corrosion deposits will fall onto this as you saw across the tank bottom. The underside should be the easiest part to saw through because corrosion is usually worst where the tank has stood on the joists, so the metal will be thinner

3 Then turn the tank onto the cut side and saw through the remaining side. Saw the two halves into quarters in the same way. You can then lower the pieces through the loft opening for disposal, together with the sludge and corrosion deposits wrapped in the sheeting, leaving a clean and useful area where the tank once was

Fitting compression joints

Plumbing jobs will invariably involve fitting together pipes. Compression joints
will link any type of pipe normally found in the home and, apart from their
versatility, they ensure a watertight result if fitted properly.

You will find the compression joints and fittings
now available make extending or replacing your
existing pipework a relatively easy task. There
are two main types: non-manipulative (type A)
and manipulative (type B).

Non-manipulative The type A compression joints
and fittings have many purposes and the range
includes straight couplings, bends, reducing couplings, 'T' junctions to enable branches to be
connected to existing pipe lines, 'cap and lining'

connectors for joining copper tubing to the threaded
tails of taps and ball valves, and fittings with
threaded ends for connecting to screwed iron or
brass sockets.

They are manufactured in metric sizes, the ones
you are most likely to require being 15, 22 and
28mm. Some of them can be fitted without adaptation to the Imperial-sized pipework found in houses
more than two or three years old. For example, 15
and 28mm compression joints can be fitted direct

There is a wide range of
compression joints and
fittings available
1 Straight swivel coupling
(copper to iron)
2 Elbow coupling (copper
to copper)
3 'T' junction
4 Bent swivel coupling
(copper to iron)
5 Wall plate elbow fitting
6 Straight coupling
7 Tank connector
8 Straight coupling (load
to copper)

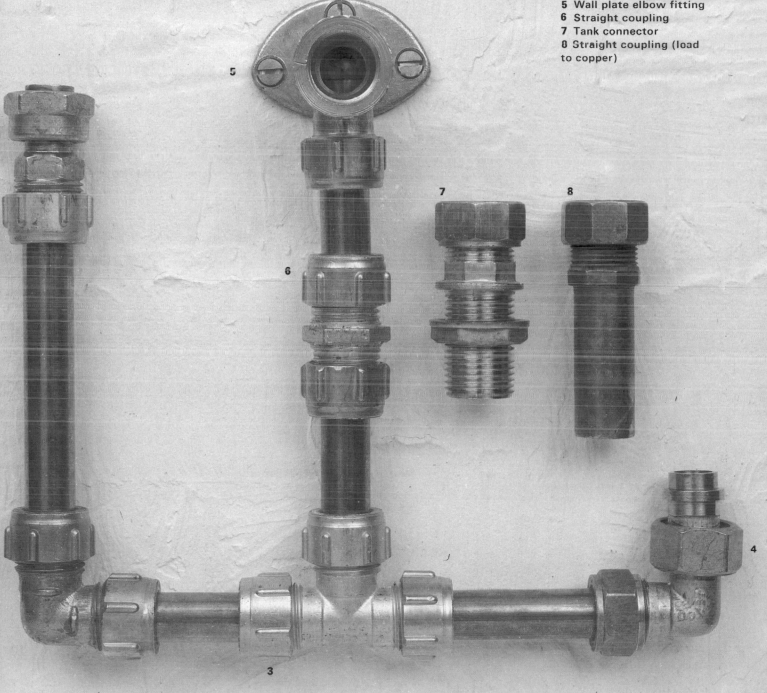

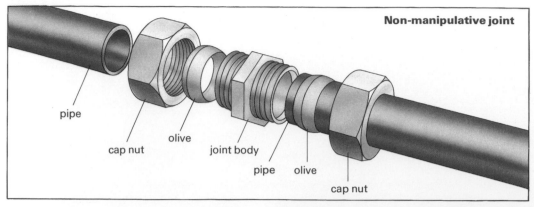

Non-manipulative joint

pipe
cap nut
olive
joint body
pipe
olive
cap nut

Left Components of non-manipulative joint
Below Before fitting joint, smooth down cut tube
Bottom Stages of fixing joint to pipes
Right Components of manipulative joint
Far right Open up pipe with steel drift
Below right Fitting and tightening joint
Bottom right Spring used to support wall of tube while bending

to $\frac{1}{2}$ and 1in tubing respectively, and 12 and 54mm fittings to $\frac{3}{8}$ and 2in tubing. For other fittings you will need an adaptor which you can obtain from your supplier. Adaptors are required to connect a 22mm compression joint to $\frac{3}{4}$in tubing and 35 and 42mm joints to $1\frac{1}{4}$ and $1\frac{1}{2}$in tubing.

Manipulative This type of fitting is less likely to be needed by the householder although water authorities usually insist upon its use for underground pipe work. Manipulative compression joints cannot readily be dismantled nor will they pull apart as a result of ice formation or ground settlement.

Making a non-manipulative compression joint

For work with this type of joint you need only a hacksaw (although for a major project it is probably worth having a wheel tube cutter), file, two open-ended spanners of the appropriate size and joint paste (such as boss white). Before fitting a type A compression joint to a length of copper tubing or pipe, cut the tube end square or square it off with a file after cutting. Remove all internal and external burrs or rough edges with a file or penknife. If you use a tube cutter, this can be fitted with a reamer which will remove internal burrs easily.

Dismantle the joint into its three components: joint body, cap nut and soft copper ring or 'olive'. Slip the cap nut over the end of the tube and follow this with the olive. Smear the outside of the tube and the olive liberally with a joint paste (to give an extra safeguard against leakage) and insert the tube end into the joint body as far as the tube stop. Use your fingers to screw the nut as tight as you can then, holding the joint body with a spanner, give the cap nut a complete turn with another spanner – don't use a wrench here or you may overtighten the nut. One turn should ensure the cap nut compresses the olive against the tube wall to make a watertight joint.

When you have had sufficient practice at making joints you will not need to dismantle the compression joint before fitting it onto the tube end. Simply loosen the cap nut and push the tube end through the cap nut and olive into the joint body as far as the tube stop.

Making a manipulative compression joint

Type B joints do not have an olive. Fitting is begun by slipping the cap nut and joint body over the pipe ends which you then 'manipulate'. This is usually done by hammering an instrument known as a steel drift into the pipe end to open it up. Smear the pipes with a generous amount of joint

Making non-manipulative joint
Filing burr off pipe

pipe   burr   file

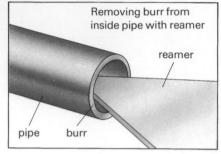

Removing burr from inside pipe with reamer

reamer

pipe   burr

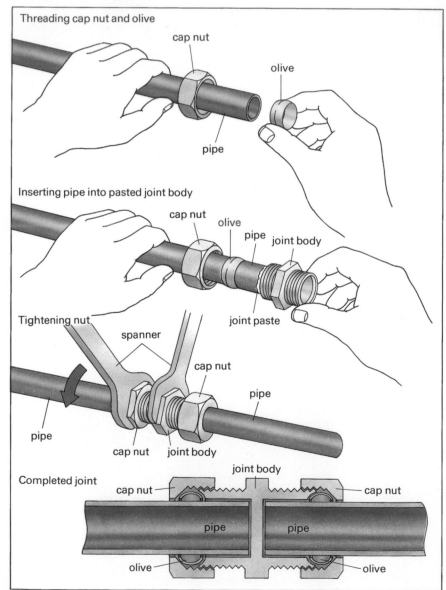

Threading cap nut and olive

cap nut
olive
pipe

Inserting pipe into pasted joint body

cap nut   olive   pipe   joint body

joint paste

Tightening nut

spanner

cap nut
pipe

pipe

cap nut   joint body

Completed joint

joint body
cap nut   cap nut
pipe   pipe
olive   olive

134

Manipulative joint

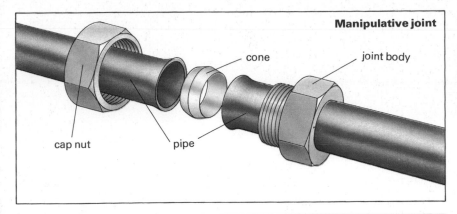

cap nut

cone

joint body

pipe

Screwing cap nut over pasted joint body

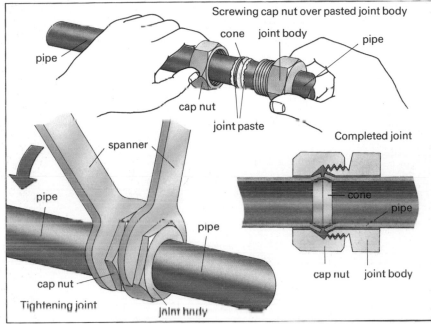

pipe

cone   joint body

pipe

cap nut

joint paste

Completed joint

spanner

pipe

pipe

pipe

cap nut

Tightening joint

joint body

cone

pipe

cap nut   joint body

Making bend in pipe

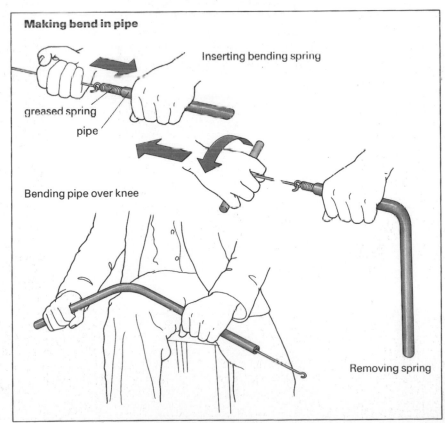

Inserting bending spring

greased spring

pipe

Bending pipe over knee

Removing spring

Making manipulative joint

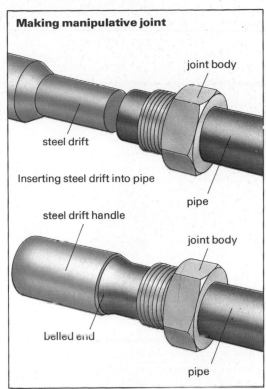

joint body

steel drift

Inserting steel drift into pipe

pipe

steel drift handle

joint body

belled end

pipe

paste, place a cone insert in the belled end of the pipes and tightly screw the cap nut onto the joint body. This secures the pipe ends so they become an integral part of the joint.

Stainless steel tubing

Although light gauge copper tubing is most widely used in modern domestic plumbing systems, you may find some stainless steel tubing. Type A and type B compression joints can be fitted to this material and there is a range of chromium plated fittings for this purpose. The methods for fitting them are the same as for copper tubing but, to prevent the tube end splitting, always cut stainless steel with a hacksaw rather than a tube cutter. You will probably have to use more force when tightening the cap nut to obtain a watertight joint, since stainless steel is a harder material than copper.

Spring bending

There is a variety of bend joints and fittings available but, if you have a major plumbing project in mind, it is worth mastering the technique of spring bending. By this method you can make bends in 15 and 22mm copper tubing and 15mm stainless steel tubing with the aid of a bending spring. This supports the wall of the tube as it is bent and prevents it splitting or the shape of the section distorting.

Grease the spring and insert it in the tube to span the point at which you wish to make the bend. The tube can be bent by hand over your knee. For the best results, overbend slightly at first then bring the tube back to the required angle. To withdraw the spring insert a bar into the loop at the end, twist clockwise to reduce the spring's diameter and pull.

Warning If the tubing kinks at the bend, never attempt to hammer it smooth until the spring has been withdrawn. If you do, you may well find the spring has become locked in the tube and is impossible to remove.

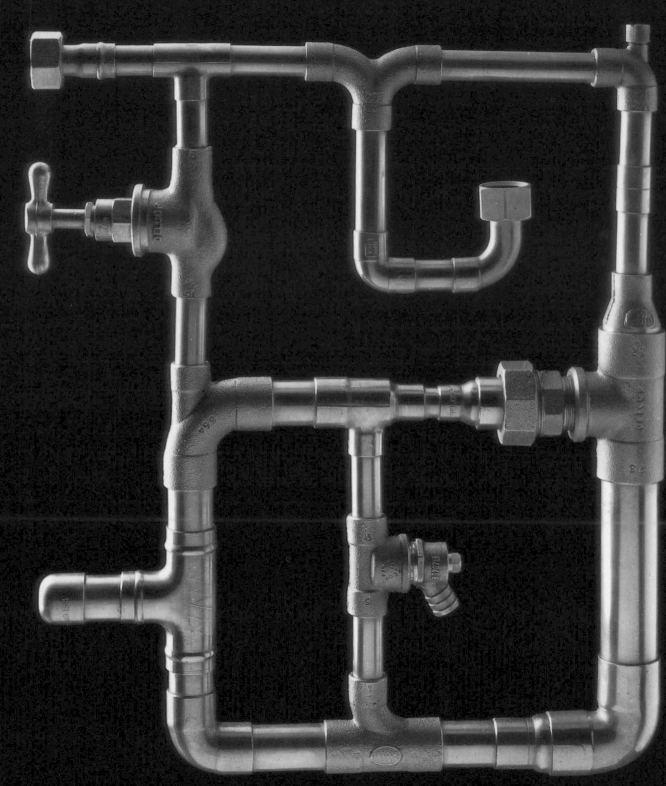

Fitting soldered capillary joints

Soldered capillary joints and fittings are neater, less obtrusive and cheaper than compression joints. Their effectiveness depends on capillary action by which any liquid, including molten solder, flows and fills a confined space between two smooth surfaces. Capillary action can be demonstrated by dipping the end of a small bore transparent tube into a bowl of water. The water rises up the tube to a level above that of the water in the bowl; the smaller the bore of the tube, the higher the water will rise.

To ensure effective capillary action, soldered capillary joints and fittings are manufactured to fit very closely with the lengths of copper tubing for which they are designed.

There are two kinds of capillary joint: integral ring fittings (also known as Yorkshire joints after the name of a well-known make) which incorporate sufficient solder to make the joint, and end-feed fittings, into which solder wire has to be fed.

The equipment you need for making soldered capillary joints is a blow torch (a butane gas cartridge one will do), a hacksaw or tube cutter, a

file, wire wool, a tin of suitable flux (obtainable from the supplier of the joints) and a small sheet of asbestos or pad of glass fibre (to protect flammable surfaces behind the joints being made). If you are using end-feed fittings, solder wire will also be needed for joining up.

Warning When using a blow torch don't forget the fire risk involved. It is all too easy to become so engrossed in making a perfect joint that you do not notice blistering paintwork and smouldering timber. Always use a sheet of asbestos or pad of glass fibre behind every joint as you make it. Take special care when working in confined areas and among the bone dry timbers in the roof space. Plastic materials will be irrevocably damaged if subjected, even briefly, to the extreme heat of a blow torch flame, so be careful when working near an acrylic bath or a plastic WC cistern.

Making a soldered capillary joint
Meticulous cleanliness is the secret of success in making soldered capillary joints. First cut the end of the copper tube square with a hacksaw or tube

Above Soldered capillary joints come in a wide range of shapes and sizes to cope with the plumbing jobs in the home – and include many useful fittings as well. The joints are available either with solder (known as integral ring joints) or without (end-feed), to which you will have to apply your own solder to fit them

cutter and remove any external or internal burr with a file – or with a reamer fitted to the tube cutter. Clean the end of the tube and the bore of the fitting with wire wool or fine abrasive paper and apply chloride based flux to the cleaned surfaces of the tube ends and the fitting. Insert the tube ends into the fitting as far as the tube stop, making sure the pipes align and the ends fit in securely for a watertight joint.

Integral ring fitting If using this type of fitting, you now need only apply sufficient heat to melt the solder, which will then flow to fill the confined space between the tube wall and the inner surface of the fitting. Place a small sheet of asbestos or a pad of glass fibre behind the joint and apply the flame of the blow torch first to the tube either side of the fitting (except in the case of stainless steel tubing – see below) then to the fitting itself. When you see a bright ring of solder all round the mouth of the fitting the joint is completed. Brush off any excess solder while it is still hot, leaving a fillet around the joint.

End-feed fitting Follow the same procedure as for integral ring fitting but, after heating the tube and the fitting, apply solder wire to the mouth of the fitting only. For a 15mm fitting you will need about 13mm ($\frac{1}{2}$in) of solder wire; for a 22mm fitting, 19mm ($\frac{3}{4}$in); for a 28mm fitting, 25mm (1in). Bend the solder wire to mark the appropriate length and feed it into the joint. When the indicated length has been fed in, the joint will be nearing completion. As with an integral ring fitting, the joint is completed when a bright ring of solder appears all round the mouth of the fitting. Brush off excess solder.

Once you have made the joint, leave it undisturbed until the tube and fitting are cool enough to touch. In most circumstances the use of a soldered capillary fitting will involve making more than one joint. There will, for example, be the two ends of a straight coupling, or three ends where a 'T' junction is being inserted in a run of pipe. If possible, make all the joints on one fitting at the same time. If something prevents you doing this, wrap a damp cloth round the joints already made to prevent the solder melting when the next joint is made.

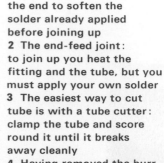

1 The integral ring joint: all you have to do is heat the end to soften the solder already applied before joining up
2 The end-feed joint: to join up you heat the fitting and the tube, but you must apply your own solder
3 The easiest way to cut tube is with a tube cutter: clamp the tube and score round it until it breaks away cleanly
4 Having removed the burr with a file or reamer fitted to the tube cutter, clean the end of the tube and the bore of the fitting with wire wool (or abrasive paper)
5 Before joining up, apply chloride-based flux to the cleaned areas on both the tube and fitting
6 With the integral joint, heat the tube either side of the fitting and then the fitting itself by using a blow torch
7 Make sure you remove any excess solder, while it is still hot, with a brush
8 With an end-feed joint, after heating the tube and fitting, apply solder wire to the mouth of the fitting only. Check the length of wire needed and bend it at the appropriate point. When you have fed that amount into the fitting, you know it is ready to be joined up to the tube

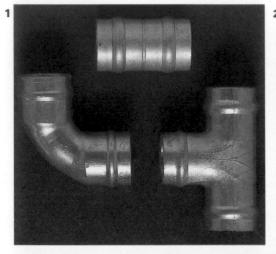

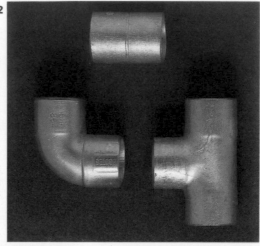

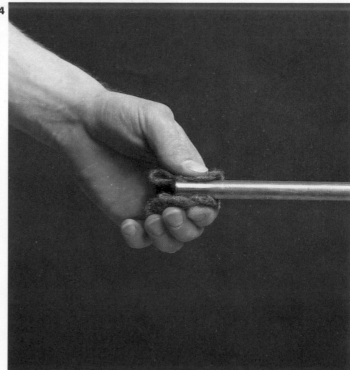

Stainless steel tubing

Soldered capillary joints can be used with thin-walled stainless steel tubing as well as with copper, but here you must use a phosphoric acid based flux – not a chloride based one, since this damages stainless steel. If you have difficulty in obtaining the right flux, don't be tempted to use any other kind: use compression fittings instead of soldered capillary ones. Handle phosphoric acid flux with care or you may burn your fingers: use a small brush to apply it to the tube end and the bore of the fitting. Finally, make sure you direct the flame of the blow torch only at the fitting, not at the tube: besides being a poor conductor of heat, stainless steel marks easily.

Metric fittings

In the case of compression joints and fittings 12, 15, 28 and 54mm metric fittings can be used, without adaptation, with $\frac{3}{8}$, $\frac{1}{2}$, 1 and 2in Imperial-sized tubing respectively. However, this does not apply to soldered capillary fittings, where an exact fit is much more important. If you want to add a metric extension to existing Imperial-sized plumbing by means of soldered capillary fittings, use a specially manufactured adaptor. Where the above sizes are concerned, however, it is simpler to use a compression coupling or 'T' for the actual connection to the Imperial-sized tubing and then, once the first length of metric tubing has been fitted, to carry on using soldered capillary joints.

5

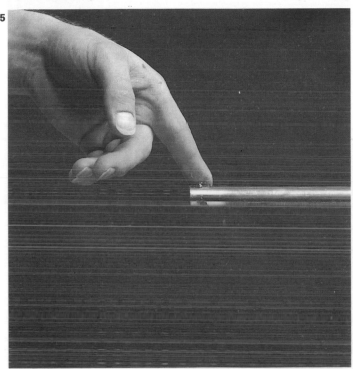

6

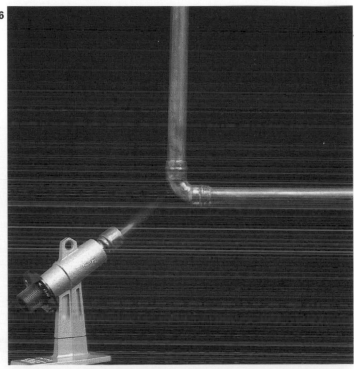

7

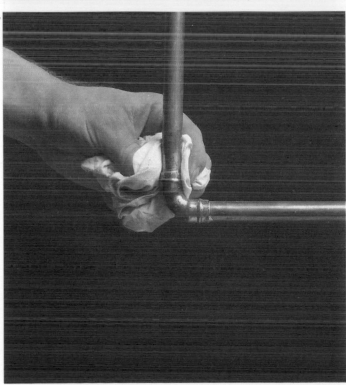

8

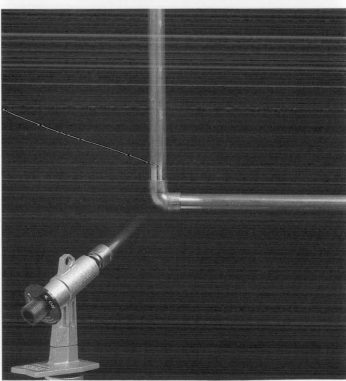

Appendix

Metric conversion charts

Metric prefixes and abbreviations

The metre is used as an example below. The same prefixes apply to litres (l or lit) and grams (g). The abbreviation lit is used for litre when unqualified to avoid confusion with the numeral 1.

millimetre (mm)	0.001	one thousandth metre
centimetre (cm)	0.01	one hundredth metre
decimetre (dm)	0.1	one tenth metre
metre (m)	1	one metre
decametre (dam)	10	ten metres
hectometre (hm)	100	one hundred metres
kilometre (km)	1000	one thousand metres

Imperial measurements are expressed below in yards, feet and inches rather than in decimals for convenience if converting with rulers or measuring tapes which do not include decimal readings.

Feet/metres				Yards/metres				
ft	in		m	yd	ft	in		m
3	3	**1**	0.30	1	0	3	**1**	0.9
6	7	**2**	0.61	2	0	7	**2**	1.8
9	10	**3**	0.91	3	0	10	**3**	2.7
13	1	**4**	1.22	4	1	1	**4**	3.7
16	5	**5**	1.52	5	1	5	**5**	4.6
19	8	**6**	1.83	6	1	8	**6**	5.5
23	0	**7**	2.13	7	2	0	**7**	6.4
26	3	**8**	2.44	8	2	3	**8**	7.3
29	6	**9**	2.74	9	2	6	**9**	8.2
32	10	**10**	3.05	10	2	10	**10**	9.1
65	7	**20**	6.10	21	2	7	**20**	18.3
98	5	**30**	9.14	32	2	5	**30**	27.4
131	3	**40**	12.19	43	2	3	**40**	36.6
164	0	**50**	15.24	54	2	0	**50**	45.7
196	10	**60**	18.29	65	1	10	**60**	54.9
229	8	**70**	21.34	76	1	8	**70**	64.0
262	6	**80**	24.38	87	1	6	**80**	73.2
295	3	**90**	27.43	98	1	3	**90**	82.3
328	1	**100**	30.48	109	1	1	**100**	91.4

Length (linear measure)

Fractions of 1 inch in millimetres

Thirty-seconds, sixteenths, eighths, quarters and one half

in	mm
1/32	0.8
1/16	1.6
3/32	2.4
1/8	3.2
5/32	4.0
3/16	4.8
7/32	5.6
1/4	6.3
9/32	7.1
5/16	7.9
11/32	8.7
3/8	9.5
13/32	10.3
7/16	11.1
15/32	11.9
1/2	12.7
17/32	13.5
9/16	14.3
19/32	15.1
5/8	15.9
21/32	16.7
11/16	17.5
23/32	18.3
3/4	19.0
25/32	19.8
13/16	20.6
27/32	21.4
7/8	22.2
29/32	23.0
15/16	23.8
31/32	24.6
1 inch	25.4

Twelfths, sixths and thirds

in	mm
1/12	2.1
1/6	4.2
1/4	6.3
1/3	8.5
5/12	10.6
1/2	12.7
7/12	14.8
2/3	16.9
3/4	19.0
5/6	21.2
11/12	23.3
1 inch	25.4

Note

Find the Imperial figure you wish to convert in the **heavy** type central column and read off the metric equivalent in the right-hand column and vice versa.

Conversion from inches is only taken up to 40 in the chart below, see next chart for continuation.

Inches/millimetres

in		mm
0.04	**1**	25.4
0.08	**2**	50.8
0.12	**3**	76.2
0.16	**4**	101.6
0.20	**5**	127.0
0.24	**6**	152.4
0.28	**7**	177.8
0.31	**8**	203.2
0.35	**9**	228.6
0.39	**10**	254.0
0.43	**11**	279.4
0.47	**12**	304.8
0.51	**13**	330.2
0.55	**14**	355.6
0.59	**15**	381.0
0.63	**16**	406.4
0.67	**17**	431.8
0.71	**18**	457.2
0.75	**19**	482.6
0.79	**20**	508.0
0.83	**21**	533.4
0.87	**22**	558.8
0.91	**23**	584.2
0.94	**24**	609.6
0.98	**25**	635.0
1.02	**26**	660.4
1.06	**27**	685.8
1.10	**28**	711.2
1.14	**29**	736.6
1.18	**30**	762.0
1.22	**31**	787.4
1.26	**32**	812.8
1.30	**33**	838.2
1.34	**34**	863.6
1.38	**35**	889.0
1.42	**36**	914.4
1.46	**37**	939.8
1.50	**38**	965.2
1.54	**39**	990.6
1.57	**40**	1016.0
1.97	**50**	
2.36	**60**	
2.76	**70**	
3.15	**80**	
3.54	**90**	
3.94	**100**	
7.87	**200**	
11.81	**300**	
15.75	**400**	
19.68	**500**	
23.62	**600**	
27.56	**700**	
31.50	**800**	
35.43	**900**	
39.37	**1000**	

Quick conversion factors – length

Terms are set out in full in the left-hand column except where clarification is necessary.

1 inch (in)	= 25.4mm/2.54cm
1 foot (ft)/12in	= 304.8mm/30.48cm/0.3048m
1 yard (yd)/3ft	= 914.4mm/91.44cm/0.9144m
1 mile (mi)/1760yd	= 1609.344m/1.609km
1 millimetre (mm)	= 0.0394in
1 centimetre (cm)/10mm	= 0.394in
1 metre (m)/100cm	= 39.37in/3.281ft/1.094yd
1 kilometre (km)/1000m	= 1093.6yd/0.6214mi

Quick conversion factors – area

1 square inch (sq in)	= 645.16sq mm/ 6.4516sq cm
1 square foot (sq ft)/144sq in	= 929.03sq cm
1 square yard (sq yd)/9sq ft	= 8361.3sq cm/ 0.8361sq m
1 acre (ac)/4840sq yd	= 4046.9sq m/0.4047ha
1 square mile (sq mi)640ac	= 259ha
1 square centimetre (sq cm)/ 100 square millimetre (sq mm)	= 0.155sq in
1 square metre (sq m)/ 10,000sq cm	= 10.764sq ft/1.196sq yd
1 are (a)/100sq m	= 119.60sq yd/0.0247ac
1 hectare (ha)/100a	= 2.471ac/0.00386sq mi

Quick conversion factors – volume

1 cubic inch (cu in)	= 16.3871cu cm
1 cubic foot (cu ft)/ 1728cu in	= 28.3168cu dm/0.0283cu m
1 cubic yard (cu yd)/ 27cu ft	= 0.7646cu m
1 cubic centimetre (cu cm)/ 1000 cubic millimetres (cu mm)	= 0.0610cu in
1 cubic decimetre (cu dm)/ 1000cu cm	= 61.024cu in/0.0353cu ft
1 cubic metre (cu m)/ 1000cu dm	= 35.3146cu ft/1.308cu yd
1cu cm	= 1 millilitre (ml)
1cu dm	= 1 litre (lit) See **Capacity**

Area (square measure)

As millimetre numbers would be unwieldy for general use, square or cubic inches have been converted to square or cubic centimetres. Conversion from square inches is only taken up to 150 in the first chart below; see next chart for continuation.

Square inches/square centimetres

sq in		sq cm
0.2	1	6.5
0.3	2	12.9
0.5	3	19.4
0.6	4	25.8
0.8	5	32.3
0.9	6	38.7
1.1	7	45.2
1.2	8	51.6
1.4	9	58.1
1.6	10	64.5
3.1	20	129.0
4.7	30	193.5
6.2	40	258.1
7.8	50	322.6
9.3	60	387.1
10.9	70	451.6
12.4	80	516.1
14.0	90	580.6
15.5	100	645.2
17.1	110	709.7
18.6	120	774.2
20.2	130	838.7
21.7	140	903.2
23.3	150	967.7
31.0	200	
46.5	300	
62.0	400	
77.5	500	
93.0	600	
108.5	700	
124.0	800	
139.5	900	
155.0	1000	

Square feet/square metres

sq ft		sq m
10.8	1	0.09
21.5	2	0.19
32.3	3	0.28
43.1	4	0.37
53.8	5	0.46
64.6	6	0.56
75.3	7	0.65
86.1	8	0.74
96.9	9	0.84
107.6	10	0.93
215.3	20	1.86
322.9	30	2.79
430.6	40	3.72
538.2	50	4.65
645.8	60	5.57
753.5	70	6.50
861.1	80	7.43
968.8	90	8.36
1076.4	100	9.29

Square yards/square metres

sq yd		sq m
1.2	1	0.8
2.4	2	1.7
3.6	3	2.5
4.8	4	3.3
6.0	5	4.2
7.2	6	5.0
8.4	7	5.9
9.6	8	6.7
10.8	9	7.5
12.0	10	8.4
23.9	20	16.7
35.9	30	25.1
47.8	40	33.4
59.8	50	41.8
71.8	60	50.2
83.7	70	58.5
95.7	80	66.9
107.6	90	75.3
119.6	100	83.6

Volume (cubic measure)

Cubic inches/cubic centimetres

cu in		cu cm
0.06	1	16.4
0.12	2	32.8
0.18	3	49.2
0.24	4	65.5
0.31	5	81.9
0.37	6	98.3
0.43	7	114.7
0.49	8	131.1
0.55	9	147.5
0.61	10	163.9
1.22	20	327.7
1.83	30	491.6
2.44	40	655.5
3.05	50	819.4
3.66	60	983.2
4.27	70	1147.1/1.15cu dm
4.88	80	1311.0/1.31cu dm
5.49	90	1474.8/1.47cu dm
6.10	100	1638.7/1.64cu dm
12.20	200	3277.4/3.28cu dm
18.31	300	4916.1/4.92cu dm
24.41	400	6554.8/6.55cu dm
30.51	500	8193.5/8.19cu dm
36.61	600	9832.2/9.83cu dm
42.72	700	11470.9/11.47cu dm
48.82	800	13109.7/13.11cu dm
54.92	900	14748.4/14.75cu dm
61.02	1000	16387.1/16.39cu dm
122.05	2000	32774.1/32.77cu dm

Cubic feet/cubic decimetres

cu		cu dm
.04	1	28.3
0.07	2	56.6
0.11	3	85.0
0.14	4	113.3
0.18	5	141.6
0.21	6	169.9
0.25	7	198.2
0.28	8	226.5
0.32	9	254.9
0.35	10	283.2
0.71	20	566.3
1.06	30	849.5
1.41	40	1132.7/1.13cu m
1.77	50	1415.8/1.42cu m
2.12	60	1699.0/1.70cu m
2.47	70	1982.2/1.98cu m
2.83	80	2265.3/2.27cu m
3.18	90	2648.6/2.65cu m
3.53	100	2831.7/2.83cu m

Cubic yards/cubic metres

cu yd		cu m
1.3	1	0.8
2.6	2	1.5
3.9	3	2.3
5.2	4	3.1
6.5	5	3.8
7.8	6	4.6
9.2	7	5.4
10.5	8	6.1
11.8	9	6.9
13.1	10	7.6
26.2	20	15.3
39.2	30	22.9
52.3	40	30.6
65.4	50	38.2
78.5	60	45.9
91.6	70	53.5
104.6	80	61.2
117.7	90	68.8
130.8	100	76.5

Capacity

Fluid ounces/millilitres

fl oz		
0.04	1	28.4
0.07	2	56.8
0.11	3	85.2
0.14	4	113.6
0.18	5	142.1
0.21	6	170.5
0.25	7	198.9
0.28	8	227.3
0.32	9	255.7
0.35	10	284.1
0.70	20	568.2
1.06	30	852.4
1.41	40	1136.5/1.136 lit
1.76	50	1420.6/1.421 lit

Pints/litres

pt		lit
1.8	1	0.6/568ml
3.5	2	1.1
5.3	3	1.7
7.0	4	2.3
8.8	5	2.8
10.6	6	3.4
12.3	7	4.0
14.1	8	4.5
15.8	9	5.1
17.6	10	5.7

Gallons/litres

gal		lit
0.2	1	4.5
0.4	2	9.1
0.7	3	13.6
0.9	4	18.2
1.1	5	22.7
1.3	6	27.3
1.5	7	31.8
1.8	8	36.4
2.0	9	40.9
2.2	10	45.5
4.4	20	90.9
6.6	30	136.4
8.8	40	181.8
11.0	50	227.3
13.2	60	272.8
15.4	70	318.2
17.6	80	363.7
19.8	90	409.1
22.0	100	454.6

Weight

Ounces/grams

oz		g
0.04	1	28.3
0.07	2	56.7
0.11	3	85.0
0.14	4	113.4
0.18	5	141.7
0.21	6	170.1
0.25	7	198.4
0.28	8	226.8
0.32	9	255.1
0.35	10	283.5
0.39	11	311.8
0.42	12	340.2
0.46	13	368.5
0.49	14	396.9
0.53	15	425.2
0.56	16	453.6
0.71	20	567.0
1.06	30	850.5
1.41	40	1134.0
1.76	50	1417.5
2.12	60	1701.0
2.47	70	1984.5
2.82	80	2268.0
3.17	90	2551.5
3.53	100	2835.0

Pounds/kilograms

lb		kg
2.2	1	0.5
4.4	2	0.9
6.6	3	1.4
8.8	4	1.8
11.0	5	2.3
13.2	6	2.7
15.4	7	3.2
17.6	8	3.6
19.8	9	4.1
22.0	10	4.5
44.1	20	9.1
66.1	30	13.6
88.2	40	18.1
110.2	50	22.7
132.3	60	27.2
154.3	70	31.8
176.4	80	36.3
198.4	90	40.8
220.5	100	45.4

Quick conversion factors – capacity

1 fluid ounce (fl oz)	= 28.4ml
1 gill (gi)/5fl oz	= 142.1ml
1 pint (pt)/4gi	= 568.2ml/0.568 lit
1 quart (qt)/2pt	= 1.136 lit
1 gallon (gal)/8pt	= 4.546 lit
1 millilitre (ml)	= 0.035fl oz
1 litre (lit)	= 1.76pt/0.22gal
1ml	= 1 cubic centimetre (cu cm)
1 lit	= 1 cubic decimetre (cu dm) See **Volume**
1 US pint	= 5/6 Imperial pt/473.2ml/0.473 lit
1 US gallon	= 5/6 Imperial gal/3.785 lit

Quick conversion factors – weight

1 ounce (oz)	= 28.35g
1 pound (lb)/16oz	= 453.59g/0.4536kg
1 stone/14lb	= 6.35kg
1 hundredweight (cwt)/ 8 stone/112lb	= 50.80kg
1 ton/20cwt	= 1016.05kg/1.016t
1 gram (g)	= 0.035oz
1 kilogram (kg)/1000g	= 35.274oz/2.2046lb/ 2lb 3.274oz
1 tonne (t)/1000kg	= 2204.6lb/0.9842 ton

Index